D0078367

GLADSTONE'S FOREIGN POLICY

GLADSTONE'S
FOREIGN POLICY

BY

PAUL KNAPLUND

ARCHON BOOKS
1970

Barry University Library

Miami, FL 33161

Published by
FRANK CASS AND COMPANY LIMITED
67 Great Russell Street, London WC1
by arrangement with Harper & Row

Published in the United States in 1970
by Archon Books,
The Shoe String Press, Inc.,
Hamden, Connecticut.

First edition   1935
New impression   1970

SBN 208 00243 X

Printed in Great Britain

DA
563.5
.K55
1970

145401

CONTENTS

———

Preface

DURING and since the war of 1914 great interest has
been shown in topics pertaining to international relations. Enormous quantities of material from the archives
of the great powers have been published, and the memoirs, correspondence, and biographies of diplomatists
and statesmen whose work was principally with foreign
affairs have added greatly to our knowledge of the diplomatic history of the nineteenth century and after. Indeed, the collections of private papers are often more
valuable in clarifying motives for actions and in reveal-
ing the tortuous course of international relations than
the dispatches, reports, minutes, and memoranda that are
found among the papers of the various foreign offices.
In presenting this little book on Gladstone's foreign policy to the reading public, the main purpose of its author
has been to increase the knowledge of the rôle played by
Gladstone, when prime minister, in determining the nature and shaping the character of Britain's foreign policy.
The author hopes also that he may help to deepen the
understanding of Gladstone, the man and the statesman,
and the appreciation of his work and of his age.

Some of the material for this book was collected a
dozen years ago when the author was working on his

monograph, *Gladstone and Britain's Imperial Policy*. In 1923 and in 1926 he examined the Gladstone Papers, then found at St. Deiniol's Library, Hawarden, and in the summer of 1933 he continued his work in this magnificent collection, now deposited in the British Museum. On the last occasion he used the equally valuable papers of Lord Granville at the Public Record Office. The study of Gladstone's foreign policy has been made possible by the great generosity shown by the trustees of his papers in giving the author free access to them. For this he wishes to give expression to his feeling of deep gratitude to the late Lord Gladstone of Hawarden and to his brother, the late Viscount Gladstone. They allowed the examination of private papers without restrictions. In the autumn of 1926 the author enjoyed the privilege of discussing many topics related to the work of Gladstone with his daughter, the late Mrs. Harry Drew, whose deep knowledge of men and affairs of the Victorian era and candid observations concerning them proved very helpful to him. He is greatly indebted to Mr. A. Tilney Bassett who never wearied in aiding the hunt for material, and to the staffs of the manuscript room in the British Museum and at the Public Record Office who have assisted both in searching for and in deciphering difficult passages in documents. The stay in England in 1926 was made possible by a fellowship from the John Simon Guggenheim Memorial Foundation and by aid from the University of Wisconsin; the

university likewise arranged for the visit to London in
the summer of 1933, the copying of documents and typ-
ing of the manuscript, and the necessary leave from
teaching duties to write this book. For all this support
the author wishes to render sincere thanks. His wife
has been his chief assistant and to her he owes the avoidance of many pitfalls.   P. K.

The University of Wisconsin,
  July, 1935.

Introduction

CARLYLE denounced the eighteenth century as lying and bankrupt, an age of cant; similarly writers of our own day often abuse the nineteenth as banal, smug, and hypocritical—forgetting that it is even more risky to indict an age than to indict a nation. The giants of the past have suffered and are suffering the fate of their era. Debunking biographers have enjoyed much popularity of late. Olympians have been pulled off their thrones by authors with facile pens, ample vocabularies, and a willingness to draw upon their imagination to fill gaps in knowledge. They have proved to their own satisfaction and for the encouragement of their readers that many of the mighty dead were frail human beings who owed their elevation to fortuitous circumstances. That truths have been unearthed by the debunkers none can deny; but the pictures drawn by them are apt to be false because of a distorted perspective. The frailties of the great have been magnified, their virtues belittled. Nor is it easy even for the most honest, best trained, and best informed biographer and historian to convey a true image of the past and its leaders. Ideas, like fashions, have their day. Oracles fall from their tripods; the new generation knows them not.

Dethronement has been the fate of many of the great Victorians. To scoff at them has been fashionable; their faith and their earnestness have been derided; puffed up with conceit, the Edwardians and their successors have looked condescendingly at parents and grandparents, their ideas and ideals being regarded as much out of date as their clothes and their furniture. Among the Victorians often disparaged and sneered at is the one who perhaps best represents the age—William Ewart Gladstone. And that the generation that brought about and fought the war of 1914, the generation of the jazz age, and those who hail with delight the pronunciamentos of the latest medicine man of economics have failed to appreciate Gladstone is not surprising. None of the earnest Victorians excelled him in earnestness, in fervor, and in faith. Faith was the very fiber and core of his being—faith in eternal verities, in the perfectibility of man and his institutions, in the ultimate victory of right over might, in the healing qualities of freedom. In religion, in morals, and in statesmanship, he held views discarded and exposed to ridicule by present-day leaders in thought and action. His *Impregnable Rock of the Holy Scriptures* has been blasted; faith has been declared obsolete; our youth has been taught to ask with "Mocking Pilate," "What is truth?" and to beware of inhibitions. He preached peace, tolerance, the brotherhood of nations, and regard for public right—principles now brushed aside and trod under foot. Nazis, Fascists, and

Bolsheviks fill the air with their cries; class is set against class, nation against nation; appeals to force drown appeals to reason; democratic institutions are being thrown into discard; people are hunted down for failure to believe the latest political and economic "ism" or to salute the latest national demigod. Even in finance, the maxims of Gladstone, the greatest financier that ever administered the exchequer of Britain, have long since shared the fate of his collar. For his gospel of prosperity by *thrift*, we have substituted one of prosperity by *spending* and blithely wasted the savings of our grandfathers and mortgaged the earnings of our grandchildren.

Gladstone had a long and full life. Born December 26, 1809, he reached the journey's end May 19, 1898. And he lived actively, filled literally every minute from the day he was a schoolboy at Eton to but a short moment before his death. His interests covered practically every human activity of his crowded age. Art, finance, history, philosophy, religion, science, theology, things theoretical and things practical drew his attention and engaged his mind. He knew many languages, ancient and modern; he traveled often; he met many people; he conducted an enormous correspondence; and he read tens of thousands of books. Few men of his age were more catholic in their reading. From the Bible, Homer, Horace, and Dante to the latest and sometimes trashy French novel, he read, scribbled notes in the margin, and discussed the contents. A fluent talker, a ready debater, and wonderfully successful as a speaker in and outside of parliament, he was also a prolific writer; and hardly a year passed without the publication of one or several of his articles, pamphlets, and books. In the words of Lord Rosebery, there was not one but a hundred Gladstones.

During such a long and active life, Gladstone naturally exposed weak points. Much of what he wrote was fugitive, dealing with controversies such as that with Huxley over the Gadarene swine and that with Manning over the Vatican decrees, controversies which now have scarcely more than an antiquarian interest. That Gladstone's range of knowledge was extraordinary is well established; but he was a child of his age, one in which even leaders of thought succumbed to the temptation to claim omniscience; moreover, political leaders of all ages have always felt compelled to speak with the voice of Jove. Flaws may be found in his theology and in his philosophy; biologists have little to say in favor of his views on evolution;[1] and classicists may not admire his Homeric studies; but even authorities on the uses of the second aorist or of the gerund may be willing to pay tribute to the practical politician who assuaged the pain of defeat of program and party at the polls by reading

[1] Though the common impression that Gladstone failed completely to appreciate the Darwinian theory may be modified somewhat on the strength of evidence supplied by Lord Rendel. See *The Personal Papers of Lord Rendel* (London, 1931), 144, 145.

Homer for the "twenty-fifth or thirtieth time"[2] and the aged, ailing statesman who found solace in translating the Odes of Horace.[3]

The multifarious activities of Gladstone have laid him open to criticism from many quarters. His character and personality have puzzled critics and writers with a bent toward psychological interpretations of motives and action. He used to speak of politicians as the most incomprehensible among human beings, and someone added that he was the most incomprehensible of politicians.[4] He does not fit the patterns created by those who profess to understand the secrets of the soul. The variety of his gifts and the seeming contradictions in his character and actions have supplied analysts with abundant material for speculation. Of mixed Highland and Lowland Scottish ancestry—the mother a devout Evangelical, the father one of the shrewdest business men of his generation—brought up, so to speak, in the counting house and educated at Eton and Oxford, Gladstone had diverse ingredients strangely mixed both in his racial inheritance and in his training for public life. "Oxford on the surface but Liverpool below" was a phrase often applied to him. By being a conservative in his youth and a radical in his old age, he reversed the usual order. A strong Church of England man, who disestablished that

---

[2] John Morley, *The Life of William Ewart Gladstone.* New Edition, three vols. in two. (New York, 1911), III, 353.

[3] *Ibid.,* 510, 512.

[4] Lord Morley, *Recollections* (New York, 1917), I, 321, 322.

church in Ireland and tried to disestablish it in Wales, who removed religious tests for the universities and wished to remove them for the lord lieutenant of Ireland and the lord chancellor of Great Britain,[5] who advocated the admission of Jews and atheists to the house of commons, and who counted agnostics and Roman Catholics among his closest friends, must, many thought, perforce be a hypocrite. A man who held the prime ministership three times after he had passed three score and ten must have had an inordinate love of power; one who was in harmony with his age on so many things must have borrowed his ideas from it; and one who was so ingenious in his explanations must be tricky, neither square nor upright. Thus political opponents, contemporary and later critics, biographers, and historians have wrestled with the problems presented by Gladstone, the man and the statesman, often forgetting that men may grow throughout life, that old men need not be fossilized, that reforms may be urged as means for conserving what is deemed essential, that honest faith and generous tolerance may exist side by side, that consciousness of power and lust for power are not identical, and that simplicity and honesty of character are not incompatible with subtlety of intellect.

No English statesman has gloried more in the name

[5] See his speech on the second reading of "The Religious Disabilities Removal Bill," house of commons, February 4, 1891. *The Speeches of the Right Hon. W. E. Gladstone, 1888-1891.* Ed. by A. W. Hutton and H. J. Cohen (London, 1902), 309-328.

of England than Gladstone did; none has been more eager than he that the British empire should be kept united and strong. Still he has been accused of neglecting to preserve the greatness of England, of attempts to destroy the empire, and of inability to understand the spirit of Greater Britain. This failure to appreciate him is in part due to a difference in the conception of values, of what constitute the essential elements of strength. Gladstone believed in the supremacy of moral power and that the most vital factor in the preservation of the empire was to keep England sound and the people of the empire contented. A follower of Burke, Gladstone obstinately clung to the belief that the offspring of Britain loved freedom and could be kept associated with her only by treating them in the spirit of freedom. He was an idealist in his conception of empire policy, but an idealist who appreciated the *real* nature of intra-imperial relations more fully than the pseudo-realists of his later years. On this, as on a good many other points, the historical development has revealed the soundness of the views of Gladstone. In his conduct of foreign affairs he has generally been considered a dismal failure, especially when his efforts in that field have been compared with those of Bismarck. But the war of 1914, the collapse of empires, the inconclusive peace, and the depression in our own time are the results of the ideals and principles which Bismarck applied and extolled. Bismarck left a legacy of distrust, of haunting fear, of disregard for justice, of a Europe armed to the teeth, of hostile combinations, all of which Gladstone strove to avoid. He fought in vain, and his reputation has suffered thereby. But in this age of uncertainty, distrust, depression, and war scares, it may be well to study how he hoped to lead mankind in the path of justice and peace.

GLADSTONE'S FOREIGN POLICY

Chapter I

VIEWS AND IDEALS

GLADSTONE was born into a war-weary world. The long struggle with France and Napoleon made the peoples of Europe yearn for peace, and the statesmen and sovereigns who met at Vienna tried to satisfy this yearning. A system variously labeled as the confederation of Europe and the concert of Europe was built up, and for a few years after the Congress of Vienna attempts were made to maintain this system by means of periodic congresses. The congresses failed; but both Metternich and his successor as a dominant influence in international affairs, Napoleon III, kept alive the idea of a concert of Europe. Europe had, however, no sooner emerged from the turmoil of the conflict with France than the powerful leavens of nationalism and political democracy began to disturb the internal peace of many states. The middle years of the nineteenth century were years of revolutions, of heroic efforts to right wrongs, of generous thought, and of a new faith in the possibilities of progress.

Britain under the leadership of Castlereagh played a prominent rôle in the overthrow of Napoleon and in the ensuing peace settlement. Following in the footsteps of the younger Pitt, Castlereagh had proclaimed the community of interest of the European nations and had helped to create the alliance of the powers which gave reality to the concert of Europe. But the interests of England and her overseas empire seemed to diverge from those of the continental nations, as those interests were interpreted by Metternich. In particular, Metternich's sponsoring of the doctrine of intervention for the ostensible purpose of preserving peace but in reality for the purpose of throttling nationalism and political liberty aroused apprehension in Britain. Castlereagh and Canning formulated a counter-theory of non-intervention. Britain withdrew from the old continental alliance, but did not repudiate the idea of a European concert. Afterwards Britain occasionally made special engagements for particular and temporary purposes, such as the quadruple alliance of 1834 to deal with the pretenders to the thrones of Spain and Portugal, and the alliance with France, Turkey, and, later, Sardinia, during the Crimean War; but more often English statesmen after 1830 acted only with France in a relation which might properly be described as an *entente*. Single-handed Britain had held her own against a continent led by Napoleon, the greatest military and administrative genius of modern times; her strength had been proved on the sea, on land, and in council; and her institutions, modified in accordance with popular demand, remained safe and unchallenged in an era of disturbances and civil strife. She was not in danger and needed no allies.

After the death of Canning in 1827, Lords Aberdeen and Palmerston became outstanding forces in shaping Britain's foreign policy. The former was an honest Scot, deeply religious, a lover of righteousness and of peace. He strove earnestly to work in harmony with France and he deplored aggressive action by Britain whether in or outside of Europe. Later ages have failed to appreciate the wisdom of Aberdeen; but it made a deep impression on Gladstone who served under him at the colonial office in 1835, was his colleague in the ministry of Sir Robert Peel, 1841-46, and was chancellor of the exchequer in the coalition government of Lord Aberdeen, 1852-55. Lord Palmerston was in most respects the antithesis of Aberdeen. A jaunty man of the world, Palmerston belonged in manners and morals to the regency period and he often shocked Queen Victoria and her husband. He favored peace but was inordinately proud of being English, often contemptuous of foreign statesmen and rulers, and a "bully" who at times rattled the British sword; he was rated high until Bismarck called his bluff. Although Palmerston had little sympathy for democratic movements at home, he favored them abroad; he felt certain that the adoption of British institutions and the British system of government would cure the ills of distracted continental states; and he generally sympathized with nationalistic movements, especially that of Italy. On the last point he and Gladstone saw eye to eye, but otherwise the two statesmen were poles asunder in their basic views on foreign policy; and the brag and bluster of Palmerston strengthened Gladstone's inborn aversion to the methods of what has often been called a strong foreign policy.

The fifty-five years between the fall of the first Napoleon and the overthrow of the third form a period when Britain's trade, industry, and shipping grew at an extraordinarily rapid rate. Britain became the workshop and the banking center of the world. Her own interests demanded that she should adopt free trade, and her own interests likewise prescribed that she should seek to have this policy adopted by other countries. But when the apostles of free trade, Richard Cobden and John Bright, urged a world-wide acceptance of the free trade doctrine, their motives were not narrowly and exclusively nationalistic; they had a vision of a prosperous, contented world in which the sword had been beaten into ploughshares; they believed sincerely that universal free trade would usher in an era of universal peace.[1] In these

[1] Richard Cobden, *Speeches on Questions of Public Policy*. Ed. by John Bright and J. E. Thorold Rogers (London, 1880), 241. John Bright, *The Public Letters of*. Ed. by H. J. Leech (London, 1885), 208, 217.

years the foreign policy of Britain was of course ordinarily shaped by considerations for Britain's real or supposed interests, but it was not devoid of idealism. Support was lent to efforts to overthrow tyrannous governments and to establish free nation states in the belief that such a state system would benefit the people concerned and serve the interests of European peace; and Britain spent millions of dollars on the eradication of the slave trade—a service to humanity for which she received small thanks but many cuffs.

The year 1830 ushered in an epoch of great reforms, and in 1832 Gladstone entered public life. At first he opposed changes and before long Macaulay affixed to Gladstone the famous label, "the rising hope of the stern and unbending Tories." But experience and the influence of Sir Robert Peel helped Gladstone to overcome his youthful fear of change and reform. Before he reached middle age he had become the disciple of Peel in administration, of Canning and Aberdeen in foreign policy, of Cobden in commercial policy, and of Burke in empire policy. In an eloquent passage in 1866 he acknowledged his indebtedness to Burke and to Canning;[2] they had been his mentors as a conservative and they continued to be his guides when he advocated a liberal treatment of overseas Britain and a generous attitude toward liberal movements on the continent of Europe. Gladstone's

[2] House of commons, April 27, 1866. *Hansard*, 3rd series, CLXXXIII, 129; see also Sir Algernon West, *Private Diaries of*. Ed. by Horace G. Hutchinson (London, 1922), 12.

views on foreign policy were affected by the mode and temper of his country and of his age, by the great men of the past and by those whom he considered the wise men of the present, but they also bear the imprint of his own vibrant personality, and he clung to them with remarkable fidelity from youth to extreme old age. He advocated applying the principles of the Sermon on the Mount in dealing with foreign nations—law, justice, and the equal rights of all nations should prevail and be recognized; British statesmen should strive to promote peace, should further the cause of nationality and political liberty, should seek to maintain the concert of Europe; they must avoid land-grabbing and beware of the delusion that peace is promoted by large armaments.

On April 8, 1840, Gladstone launched a bitter attack upon the policy pursued by Lord Palmerston in China. It was denounced on moral grounds. Britain had violated sacred precepts, offended against law and custom, and broken with established tradition by aiding and abetting the trade in opium. In days of old, Gladstone averred, the sight of their flag had raised the spirit of Englishmen "because it has always been associated with the cause of justice, with opposition to oppression, with respect for national rights, with honourable commercial enterprise, but now, under the auspices of the noble Lord [Palmerston], that flag is hoisted to protect an infamous contraband traffic. . . . We, the enlightened and civilized Christians, are pursuing objects at vari-

ance, both with justice and with religion."[3] A similar
verbal lashing was administered to Palmerston at the
time of the second Chinese war, 1857. There was, Gladstone said, no glory for Britain in fighting China. It was
like making war on women and children. Injustice had
been made the basis for the development of the power
of Britain in China. This would never do. Britain should,
in her dealings with the Chinese empire, be guided by
principles of mercy, peace and justice.[4]

Gladstone's wrath was kindled when Lord Palmerston
in the Don Pacifico debate, June, 1850, promulgated
his famous doctrine that Britain should apply the idea
embodied in the phrase *Civis Romanus sum*, so that "a
British subject, in whatever land he may be, shall feel
confident that the watchful eye and the strong arm of
England will protect him against injustice and wrong."
"What then, Sir," said Gladstone in reply, "was a Roman citizen? He was the member of a privileged caste,
he belonged to a conquering race, to a nation that held
all others bound down by the strong arm of power. For
him there was to be an exceptional system of law; for
him principles were to be asserted, and by him rights
were to be enjoyed, that were denied to the rest of the
world. Is such, then, the view of the noble Lord, as to
the relation that is to subsist between England and other
countries? Does he make the claim for us, that we are to

[3] House of commons, April 8, 1840. *Hansard*, 3rd series, LIII, 818-819.
[4] House of commons, March 3, 1857. *Ibid.*, CXLIV, 1802-1807.

be uplifted upon a platform high above the standing-ground of all other nations?" Such action would, in the judgment of Gladstone, tend to foster an "insular temper" and a "self-glorifying tendency." The counter-doctrine, proposed by Gladstone, was to "recognise, and recognise with frankness, the equality of the weak with the strong; the principles of brotherhood among nations, and of their sacred independence." Britain should be guided by the precept "do as we would be done by," she should "pay all the respect to a feeble state, and to the infancy of free institutions, which we should desire and should exact from others towards their maturity and their strength."[5]

Opinions like these were expressed frequently by Gladstone in private letters, in speeches in and outside parliament, and in contributions to periodicals. He often denounced actions of statesmen and rulers, but he was remarkably free from national and racial antipathies. It was a source of grief to him that after eighteen centuries the ideals of Christianity, the ideals of brotherhood and of peace had failed to permeate nations and to mold their relations with one another.[6]

The ancient problem of peace on earth often engaged the mind of Gladstone. He did not favor peace at any price and he rather resented being classed with Aberdeen as a pacifist. Nevertheless, he had a genuine hor-

[5] House of commons, June 27, 1850. *Ibid.*, CXII, 561.
[6] Gladstone to Princess Troubetskoi, August 28, 1892. Copy, letter books, XXIII, 6, the Gladstone Papers, in the British Museum.

ror of bloodshed. With burning eloquence he denounced war as a destroyer of morals, of prosperity, of civilization, and of human happiness. In a speech on October 11, 1853, Gladstone said that war means "that the face of nature is stained with human gore . . . that bread is taken out of the mouth of the people . . . that taxation is increased and industry diminished . . . that burdens unreasonable and untold are entailed on posterity . . . that demoralization is let loose, that families are broken up, that lusts become unbridled in every country to which war is extended."[7] When his friend Tennyson, in *Maud*, rejoiced that, "The long, long canker of peace is over and done," Gladstone remarked: "It may be good frenzy, but we doubt its being good poetry." And Tennyson's assertion that war cured the evil of mammon worship Gladstone flatly denied.[8] As prime minister, he shrank from the blood guiltiness involved in avenging Majuba Hill; only with great reluctance was he persuaded to use force in Egypt; and he could not understand the eagerness to fight the Sudanese who strove to keep their country from the stranger. He was a member of the government that involved Britain in the war in the Crimea, and he defended it afterwards because he thought it had strengthened the concert of Europe. Discussing actions of his second ministry in a letter to John

[7] Quoted by F. W. Hirst, *Gladstone as Financier and Economist* (London, 1931), 156.

[8] W. E. Gladstone, *Gleanings of Past Years: Personal and Literary* (New York, 1886), II, 140, 143-145.

Bright, June 1, 1885, Gladstone admitted that his government had resorted to force, but he contended that in every instance it had been used because honorable obligations had to be fulfilled and because of righteous purposes.[9] He encouraged international peace movements,[10] and in 1894 he retired from public life because he could not abet a race in armaments which he feared would result in an international catastrophe.[11] Throughout life Gladstone was an anti-expansionist. He looked upon Britain as a satiated power and he felt apprehensive because of the burdens imposed by the overgrown and ever growing empire; but he also opposed annexations because he regarded the lust and love of territory as a breeder of war and of hatred among nations.[12] A dog-in-the-manger policy he despised. When Italy in 1881 desired a strip of African coast on the Red Sea, Gladstone observed that Britain could not always oppose territorial acquisitions of other powers on the ground that they endangered the road to India; and a few years later he was willing to let Germany acquire African colonies. Gladstone was second to none in his patriotism and in his pride of country and of empire, but he was also unusually broad-minded in his attitude toward other na-

[9] Copy, letter books, XXII, 45, Gladstone Papers.
[10] Gladstone to Sir Philip Stanhope, October, 1893. Copy, letter books, XXIII, 289.
[11] Gladstone to Lord Acton, February 9, 1894. *Ibid.*, 370.
[12] Speech at Chester, November 12, 1855. Paul Knaplund, *Gladstone and Britain's Imperial Policy* (London, 1927), 193.

tions. The powers of the world should, he thought, grow great in common; and he reflected without envy on the possibility that the United States might surpass Britain in power and in influence and thus become "head servant in the great household of the world."[13] Sentiments so foreign to the theory and practice of statesmen will go far to explain why Gladstone appeared incomprehensible.

Gladstone saw in the great armaments a danger to the peace of the world. This was, indeed, one of the reasons why he opposed Palmerston's efforts to increase the army and navy estimates in the early sixties. Shortly after he had become prime minister in 1868 his foreign secretary, Lord Clarendon, attempted to effect an international agreement to limit armaments. This effort had Gladstone's support and when Prussia blocked it, Gladstone remarked with some asperity that a wet blanket was needed for Bismarck.[14] Writing in the *Edinburgh Review*, October, 1870, Gladstone expressed his conviction that the great standing armies and the prevalence of military ideas carried with them almost a certainty of bringing about war.[15] To charges that Britain in 1870 preached disarmament but clung to her naval supremacy, the prime minister was prepared to answer that despite

[13] W. E. Gladstone, "Kin beyond Sea," in *The North American Review*, September, 1878, CXXVII, 180.

[14] Gladstone to Clarendon, February 16, 1870. Copy, letter books, XII, 150, Gladstone Papers.

[15] *The Edinburgh Review*, American Edition, CXXXII, 299.

Britain's responsibilities for the protection of a wide-spread empire nearly two million pounds had been taken off the estimates and further reductions might take place.[16] However, his zeal for reducing armaments was not shared by the English nation. In the eighties a feeling prevailed that Gladstone neglected the navy,[17] and his opposition to enlarged naval appropriations caused his resignation as prime minister in 1894.

With the men of the Manchester School, Gladstone believed that free trade would promote world unity and thereby lessen the danger of war. He thought that the commercial treaty with France, 1860, had probably averted war; but with the passing years the hope of a general adoption of free trade faded. Nevertheless, and despite rebuffs, Gladstone continued to have faith in the possibilities of international co-operation. He tried vainly to invoke the aid of the concert for the purpose of mitigating the terms of the Treaty of Frankfort, 1871; he saw with regret the failure of the concert on the Turkish question, 1876-77; and he welcomed the Congress of Berlin as a sign of its resurrection. But during his second ministry he found that the concert was an illusion. Most statesmen of his age considered the interests of their country in a narrow sense and would use disturbances in the Balkans, in Armenia, and

[16] Gladstone to Clarendon, April 9, 1870. Copy, letter books, XII, 243, Gladstone Papers.
[17] Frederic Whyte, *The Life of W. T. Stead* (New York, 1926), I, 145-158.

in Egypt simply as pawns in the great game of international politics. Here he had pursued a phantom, and he recognized it to some extent when he spoke of "the old jade concert."[18]

Lord Aberdeen had been a friend of France and had maintained an *entente* with that country. Without being hostile to France, Gladstone showed less warmth in his feeling toward her than had the older statesman. He was pleased with Napoleon III's apparent willingness to reduce armaments, but he deplored the French desire to keep a garrison at Rome; he condemned the French demands for further assurances from the king of Prussia after the candidature of Prince Leopold to the Spanish throne had been withdrawn, regretted the French claims to inviolability of territory, and objected to the terms of the peace imposed by Germany in 1871 not because he was a Francophile but on the grounds that territory was transferred without ascertaining the wishes of the inhabitants and that the treaty would perpetuate mutual hostility and precipitate another war. When he returned to office in 1880, he found an Anglo-French alliance, limited in its operation to Egypt. Neither the alliance nor its object pleased Gladstone; nevertheless, he tried to work with France. This proved impossible, and by 1884-85 he seems to have considered turning to

[18] Gladstone to Granville, October 14, 1880. Copy, Gladstone Papers.

Germany. However, this change of policy was not effected. By the end of the eighties he was convinced that
Britain must avoid all entangling engagements, and he
fully concurred with Rosebery's scrapping, in 1892, of
the Mediterranean agreements concluded by Lord Salisbury. Gladstone then favored a policy of "splendid isolation."

Even before Gladstone had lost his youthful fear of
reform, he appeared as an enemy of the political oppression practiced on the continent of Europe. In cele-
brated letters to Aberdeen, 1851, he emptied an ample
vial of wrath on the government of Naples for its treatment of political prisoners.[19] The cause of Italian freedom and independence was one of the few issues on
which Gladstone and Palmerston could agree. Gladstone sympathized with nationalism and the demands
for political liberty. He looked upon them as means for
the establishment of settled conditions and peace in Europe. Speaking in the house of commons on March 7,
1861, he said that, "The miseries of Italy have been the
danger of Europe. The consolidation of Italy, her restoration to national life . . . will add to the general
peace and welfare of the civilized world a new and
solid guarantee."[20] He similarly favored the unification

[19] *Gleanings*, IV, 1-137.
[20] House of commons, March 7, 1861. *Hansard*, 3rd series, CLXI,
1579.

of Germany and of Roumania.[21] In 1878 he warned
against meddling with the Turkish parliament even
though it might be only a sham affair;[22] he welcomed
the growth of local self-government in the Balkans both
as a solution of the perennial Turkish problem and as a
safeguard against Russian encroachment; and Gladstone
saw in the fact that Jefferson Davis had, as he believed,
created a nation, a strong reason for sympathizing with
our Southern Confederacy. Nor did Gladstone think
that self-determination should be applied only abroad.
He early advocated it for the British colonies and he
demanded it as a preliminary requirement for annexing
new lands.[23] He suggested in January, 1882, that if the
Arabi movement in Egypt was truly national, England
and France should not oppose it, because this would
lead to grief;[24] he had much trouble in making up his
mind about the Mahdist revolt in the Sudan since he
thought the Mahdists rightly strove to be free; he tried
to persuade his countrymen to apply self-determination
to Ireland; and late in life Gladstone expressed to Rosebery his pleasure over having lived in a period of libera-
tion.[25]

[21] House of commons, May 4, 1858, and July 20, 1866. *Ibid.*, CL,
44-66; CLXXXIV, 1247-1250.
[22] *The Nineteenth Century*, March, 1878, III, 603-604.
[23] Knaplund, *Gladstone and Britain's Imperial Policy*, 133.
[24] Gladstone to Granville, January 4, 1882. Original MS., Granville
Papers, Public Record Office; copy, letter books, XIX, 165, Gladstone Papers.
[25] The Marquess of Crewe, *Lord Rosebery* (New York, 1931), 280.

Foreign affairs was not the greatest and most absorbing interest of Gladstone; nevertheless, he interfered decisively at various times in the conduct of the foreign policy of Britain and in international problems. His denunciation of the government of Naples under King "Bomba" aroused both his countrymen and foreign nations to an acute realization of the wrongs inflicted upon the people of Italy; and his philippics against the Turks because of the massacres in Bulgaria and in Armenia not only are classic expressions of moral indignation over wanton and infamous barbarities, they were also efforts to arouse the conscience of mankind, attempts to make nations forget petty jealousies in a common crusade against cruelty and wrong. By settling the *Alabama* question by arbitration, an important precedent was established for peaceful settlement of international disputes. His oft repeated affirmation that Britain had no special interests which ran counter to those of the rest of mankind, his insistence upon the recognition of law, morality, justice, self-determination, the equal right of all nations, have been called "hot-gospelling," the ideas of "a crazy professor";[26] but they fired the imagination of peoples; they embodied rays of hope; they pointed to a goal toward which man has been striving since time immemorial. And events have shown that Gladstone,

[26] J. A. Spender, *Fifty Years of Europe* (New York, 1933), 60; William L. Langer, *European Alliances and Alignments 1871-1890* (New York, 1931), 204.

vhom the Bismarcks, father and son, denounced as an
gnoramus, correctly gauged the effects of the Treaty
)f Frankfort, of the system of alliances which Bismarck
'ounded, of the competition in armaments which he
;ponsored, and of the greed and lust for territory which
Gladstone vainly strove to check.

Chapter II

CHECKS AND BALANCES

Few simplifications have done more mischief than that whereby states are personified. In speaking of England, France, or Germany as persons, we conjure up a vision of a unity, a national will and a national mind which do not exist, and we convey the impression of vices and of virtues that can be attributed only to individuals. The wise dictum of Burke that a nation cannot be indicted is so easily forgotten when we think of nations as individuals. Similarly the habit of identifying the governments of England in the nineteenth century with the prime ministers of the day makes it easy to allot praise or blame; but it also draws a veil over the factors other than the personality, character, and views of the prime minister that have helped to determine actions and policies. The historian must peer behind the scenes if he is to approximate truth in ascertaining and weighing the responsibility for measures. By so doing he finds that the prime ministers of Britain during the last century were less powerful than is commonly supposed. Occasionally they were complete masters and could dictate policies, but these intervals were so rare that they hardly merit consideration. Consequently, before we consider how Gladstone applied his general principles concerning foreign relations and before we can attempt to estimate his own success or failure in this field, we must examine for a moment some of the more important checks and balances that affected the conduct of foreign affairs.

At no time can a prime minister of Britain afford to disregard the force of established traditions, nor can he without a clear mandate from the people dare to risk a violation of engagements concluded by a predecessor. With the gradual democratization of the control of the machinery of the British government, voices were heard clamoring for more popular control over foreign affairs; and Gladstone at various times presented forcible arguments in favor of this demand.[1] No great advances were made in that direction, but it ill-behooved Gladstone as prime minister to disregard the voice of demos. If the electorate as a whole appeared inarticulate concerning international relations, certain well-defined groups were decidedly voluble; humanitarians and missionaries,

[1] House of commons, May 4, 1858; *Hansard*, 3rd series, CL, 45. See also F. R. Flournoy, *Parliament and War* (London, 1927), 117, 122.

traders and capitalists, those representing God, and the spokesmen for mammon often found means to force the hand of the government. As the nineteenth century advanced, the press became more and more a factor in arousing public interest in and shaping public opinion on international issues. Queen Victoria, both during the lifetime of her husband and afterwards, exercised a deep influence on the foreign policy of Britain; the colleagues of the prime minister, and more particularly the one who held the seals of the foreign office, often decided on a course of action in foreign affairs in a sense contrary to the wishes of the premier; not infrequently domestic issues such as a reform of the franchise or the Irish question compelled inaction abroad; and as the British colonies beyond the sea grew in wealth and population they began to exert pressure on the home government in its handling of foreign affairs. Thus in the field of foreign relations there was in operation a complex system of checks and balances, generally hidden from view, during the four terms when Gladstone held the position as prime minister of Britain.

In his later years Gladstone was denounced as a radical. But a close study of his views will disclose that basically he was always conservative, and that he often sponsored changes for the purpose of preserving what he deemed the essential elements in the life and government of England. He revered tradition; and whether in office or in opposition he sought and found precedents for measures advocated or attacked by him. This general observation applies to his foreign policy. Indeed, the foreign policy of Britain suffered few violent changes between 1815 and the close of the century. Only during the second ministry of Disraeli, 1874-80, did foreign affairs become an important party issue; and it is significant that Gladstone attacked the Near Eastern policy of his rival on the ground that he had violated traditions and broken away from the concert of Europe. But when, partly as a result of the criticism of the government's foreign policy, the Liberals rode into office and power in 1880, their leaders took pains to explain that existing obligations would be fulfilled.[2] The Cyprus Convention was not repudiated, and Salisbury's secret engagement with Waddington concerning Egypt was honored to a point where England's own interests suffered. Later, on the eve of the election of 1892, Gladstone pledged himself and party not to alter the course in foreign affairs.[3] However, Lord Salisbury's secret Mediterranean agreements were allowed to lapse, being regarded by Rosebery as personal and therefore not binding.[4] Britain had traditions concerning her relations with practically every country or region in the world; but

[2] Granville to Queen Victoria, September 19, 1880. *The Letters of Queen Victoria.* Ed. by G. E. Buckle, 2nd series (New York, 1928), III, 141, 142.

[3] At Newcastle, October 2, 1891. *Speeches, 1888-1891,* 377-378.

[4] Rosebery to Gladstone, August 27, 1892. Original MS., Gladstone Papers.

certain variations which had occurred in the past created precedents which could be cited for different types of policies.[5]

With the growth of democracy, however, tradition counted for less in the foreign policy of Britain; and with it came the influence of public opinion, a force more potent and more incalculable than the deeds or misdeeds of Pitt, Castlereagh, and Canning. In the fifties, Gladstone demanded parliamentary control over the actions of the government in the Far and Middle East; and he urged that no war should be declared without authorization by parliament.[6] By his pamphlet on the Bulgarian massacres, 1876, by his articles on the Near Eastern policy of Disraeli, and in his Midlothian campaigns Gladstone brought foreign affairs before the bar of public opinion. Thereby he established a precedent and at least the presumption that the mysteries of diplomacy should be revealed to the people. But even in his most violent outbursts against Beaconsfield and all his ways, Gladstone did not go to the length of sponsoring complete parliamentary control over treaty-making; the principle might be sound but he saw serious obstacles to applying it in practice.[7] Treaties of alliance, however,

[5] Thus with reference to Turkey the policies of Pitt and of Canning had not always harmonized.
[6] House of commons, March 6, 1857. *Hansard*, 3rd series, CXLIV, 1947; Flournoy, 117, 122.
[7] Arthur Ponsonby, *Democracy and Diplomacy* (London, 1915), 54-55, 75; *Hansard*, 3rd series, CCLXXVII, 1323-1326.

he put in a separate category, and in private letters he denounced the secret agreements concluded by Salisbury as a departure from tradition and a betrayal of public trust.[8] Queen Victoria noticed, 1880-85, the alarming symptoms of parliamentary control over foreign policy;[9] and Gladstone found that fear of public opinion and of parliamentary displeasure prevented him from handing Cyprus over to Greece, ceding Heligoland to Germany, employing Zebehr in the Sudan, and facilitating the Egyptian financial settlement by a reduction in the interest on Egypt's Suez Canal debt without a corresponding reduction in the interest on Egyptian bonds. In every one of these instances, the general results of the government's foreign policy would have been materially altered if its hands had been free. Moreover, the fissure within the Liberal party over principles in foreign policy which split it wide open at the close of the century was already noticeable in the eighties. Liberal Imperialists like W. E. Forster challenged even Gladstone because of things done or left undone abroad. He had to walk warily lest critics either from the left or from the right within the Liberal ranks join forces with Conservatives and Irish Home Rulers and thus bring down the government. Gladstone's successes on the platform and in parliament caused him to overlook the power

[8] Gladstone to Granville, September 3, 1882. Copy, letter books, XIX, 340, Gladstone Papers.
[9] *Letters of Queen Victoria*, 2nd series, II, 108, 136, 143.

of the press in shaping public opinion at home and in creating impressions abroad.[10] The hostility of the metropolitan papers to the foreign policy of the government of Gladstone proved, indeed, a serious embarrassment in dealing with Germany, France, and Turkey. Bismarck in particular found it difficult to comprehend the relations between the British press and the British government. He was prone to regard attacks on him in *The Times* as inspired and would retaliate by being unpleasant to the representative of Britain in Berlin.

By 1880 the Dominion of Canada was well established, and the self-governing British colonies in Australasia and in South Africa had reached a stage when they were articulate in matters affecting their destiny. Except for a demand to be heard concerning the Panama Canal, Canada made no attempt to influence foreign policy, but both in South Africa and in Australasia the colonists presented claims for annexations that proved annoying and impeded the government's freedom of action in dealing with the colonial aspirations of Germany. The British empire was becoming a league of nations; the outlying portions could not be disregarded, much to the chagrin of Bismarck; and the imperial authorities faced the di-

[10] Granville to Gladstone, October 31, 1880, and January 5, 1882. Original MSS., Gladstone Papers. Gladstone to Granville, November 1, 1880. Copy, letter books, XVIII, 176. See also Stephen Gwynn and Gertrude M. Tuckwell, *The Life of the Rt. Hon. Sir Charles W. Dilke* (London, 1917), I, 316-317; W. D. Bowman, *The Story of "The Times"* (New York, 1931), 283.

lemma of either disappointing the colonies who had powerful supporters at home or offending Bismarck who could create much trouble for Britain in Egypt and elsewhere.

The laws, customs, and conventions of the English constitution are sometimes as puzzling to the people of England as they are to foreigners. Not until the publication of Queen Victoria's letters could students of her era of English history appreciate her position and influence as a sovereign. In a broad sense, the government of England was under the control and supervision of the electorate, acting through the house of commons. The power of the sovereign was limited, but the amount and character of those limitations varied, and in foreign affairs the queen's influence counted for much. In this field the crown held many unabrogated prerogatives; and by virtue of these, and inasmuch as parliament never could supervise diplomacy, and ministers ought not to be left without a check, Queen Victoria quite naturally claimed the right to be consulted and to have her advice heeded in such matters. Furthermore, foreign policy had long been considered one of the peculiar mysteries of kingcraft; the sovereigns in most European countries still exercised wide influence over it, and the sovereigns were knit together by blood and by bonds of common interest. What one sovereign said directly to another often brought results, more especially since they spoke so seldom; realizing this, Gladstone occasionally requested the queen to write private letters to other sovereigns. But Queen Victoria could never be used as a mere tool, and the position of a sleeping partner ran contrary to her conception of her position and her obligations. She had been carefully coached in foreign affairs by her husband; rather early in her reign she informed Lord John Russell and Lord Palmerston that she would insist upon her right to supervise diplomatic correspondence; and the alterations which the dying Prince Consort made in an important dispatch dealing with the Trent affair, December, 1861, are the classic illustration of the power as well as of the beneficent influence of the queen in foreign affairs.[11] The death of Prince Albert deprived her of a wise counselor, and in the seventies she partook rather heavily of Disraeli's heady imperialistic potions. With the advancing years she grew more intolerant of opposition, her interest in the empire became more proprietary in its character, and the spirit of her grandfather, "Farmer George," came to the surface. Although perhaps essentially peaceful, the queen did not shrink from bloodshed, and in the Near Eastern crisis, 1877-78, she at times out-Disraelied Disraeli; indeed, not infrequently she expressed views that lend support to Kipling's thesis about the greater deadliness of the female of the species.[12]

[11] Sir John A. R. Marriott, *Queen Victoria and Her Ministers* (New York, 1934), *passim.*

[12] See Queen Victoria to Beaconsfield, June 7 and 27, July 20, 1877, and January 9, 1878. W. F. Monypenny and G. E. Buckle,

The relations between the queen and Gladstone had been friendly during the lifetime of the Prince Consort, and they were tolerable during Gladstone's first ministry; but after his criticism of the Disraelian foreign policy Queen Victoria detested practically everything Gladstone did and said on that topic. His idealistic views she regarded as verbiage and nonsense or worse; and the foreign secretary, Lord Granville, 1880-85, who had formerly been one of her most trusted counselors, passed under the same heavy cloud of royal distrust and displeasure.[13] Whether dealing with the Near East or with Egypt, the queen's influence did little to smooth the way for the government of Gladstone. Her correspondence with Lord Beaconsfield, 1880, and with Lord and Lady Wolseley, 1884, came perilously near overstepping the bounds of propriety for an English sovereign; and in letters to Lord Rosebery, 1892-1894, she evidently sought to undermine the influence of his chief.[14] Mistakes in the conduct of foreign affairs may legitimately be charged against the Gladstone government of 1880-85; but the hostility of a powerful faction in the press and of the queen made work difficult and contributed to failures.

The Life of Benjamin Disraeli (New York, 1910-20), VI, 143-144, 148-149, 152-154, 217.

[13] Philip Guedalla, *The Queen and Mr. Gladstone.* Two vols. (London, 1933); Gladstone, *After Thirty Years,* 317-355; Marriott, *Queen Victoria and Her Ministers,* 158-164.

[14] *Letters of Queen Victoria,* 2nd series, III, 143, 144, 619, 633; *ibid.,* 3rd series, II, 151-152, 158, 262-263.

In theory the Victorian prime ministers chose their
cabinets and exercised complete control over them. In
practice no prime minister, with the possible exception
of Sir Robert Peel, held the sway over his colleagues attributed to him by popular opinion. This is especially
true in the realm of foreign affairs. Lord John Russell,
Palmerston, and Disraeli often felt themselves thwarted,
either by the foreign secretary alone or by a combination
of recalcitrant ministers. Even during his first ministry,
Gladstone at times did not prevail in deciding issues of
foreign policy; and he had less control over the second
ministry than he had over the first. The years 1880-85
were to all appearances not a happy period in Gladstone's
life. Attacks of influenza laid him low at crucial mo-
ments; the ministry abounded in talent but lacked co-
hesion; the rival factions within it agreed on only one
thing, namely, that Gladstone was indispensable as their
head; but they frequently refused to follow his lead when
he was present, and in his absence they often wrangled
and decided nothing. This state of affairs was the more
serious since Gladstone never claimed the mastery in the
field of foreign relations that he could claim on matters
pertaining to finance, administration, and legislation. Furthermore, during the second ministry Gladstone believed
that the time was near at hand when he would be called
upon to render his final account, and in foreign affairs
he was therefore more than ever apt to defer to the
wishes of colleagues who might have a longer lease on

life and be compelled to face the results of the actions of the government.

In conducting the relations with other countries, much was ordinarily left to be decided by the prime minister and the foreign secretary without consultation with all the other members of the government. These two in a peculiar degree shared the power and had to shoulder the blame for decisions. In 1892 Gladstone informed Lord Rosebery that he considered it a fixed and well-recognized constitutional doctrine that the prime minister shared with the foreign secretary the responsibility for the conduct of foreign affairs and that in his experience the foreign policy of the government had usually been shaped through the co-operation of these two.[15] The relations between him and the occupants of the foreign office are therefore of special importance in a study of the foreign policy of Gladstone.

When Gladstone formed his first ministry, in 1868, Lord Clarendon stood unrivaled in reputation as a diplomatist. He had served abroad and he had held the seals of the foreign office in former governments. He appeared so pre-eminent in this field that Lord Derby had tried to induce him to remain at the foreign office with the change of government in 1866, but Clarendon had declined the offer out of party loyalty.[16] The victory of

[15] Gladstone to Rosebery, September 23 and 25, 1892. Copies MSS., Gladstone Papers.
[16] For a recent appraisal of Lord Clarendon by Professor Harold Temperley see *The Journal of Modern History*, September, 1932, IV, 397-399.

the Liberal party in the election of 1868, and the assumption of the prime ministership by Gladstone made Clarendon's return to office as secretary of state for foreign affairs inevitable, although the queen, on personal grounds, objected to it. Shortly after the government had been formed, Gladstone confessed to Clarendon that he trembled at the prospect of sharing the responsibility for foreign affairs because he felt unfit both in capacity and in knowledge.[17] The available records indicate that the prime minister lived up to this humble statement and that he abstained from meddlesome interference. Clarendon carried on negotiations with France and with Germany with the full approval of Gladstone but without specific guidance or instructions from him. When Clarendon in February, 1870, suggested the desirability of counteracting the irritation caused in the mind of Napoleon III by the loss of the queen's friendship and the attacks in *The Times* by a public commendation of the recent policy of the emperor of the French, Gladstone followed the suggestion and so earned Clarendon's praise.[18]

The death of Clarendon in June, 1870, brought to the foreign office Earl Granville, who held that office for the remainder of the first and throughout the second ministry of Gladstone. Granville had been foreign secretary for a short period in 1852, he was a suave diplomatist of the

[17] Gladstone to Clarendon, January 11, 1869. Copy MS., Gladstone Papers.
[18] Clarendon to Gladstone, February 11 and 16, 1870. Original MSS., Gladstone Papers.

old school who had been an adviser of the queen when Palmerston and Russell held the reins of government, and the queen hailed with delight his promotion from the colonial office to the foreign office. In 1870 he was on terms of intimate friendship with Gladstone also, and so remained until his death twenty-one years later, thereby eventually forfeiting the friendship of the queen. Granville has fared badly at the hands of historians; like Russell and Palmerston before him, Granville was outshone by Bismarck. There is, indeed, some superficial resemblance between Granville and Palmerston; both did much work with a jauntiness that suggested indolence, and both were in the habit of spicing private letters with facetious remarks. Granville was known for his unfailing courtesy and good humor, although Herbert Bismarck complained of being lectured to by Granville, somewhat in the manner of Palmerston.[19] Granville, however, did not enter the foreign office with the prestige of Clarendon; he took up his duties at an unpropitious moment, just as France and Prussia were ready to fly at each other's throats, and he suffered in reputation for his failure to control a whirlwind not of his own making. The course of events compelled Gladstone to give more attention to foreign affairs after the first part of July, 1870; but various suggestions made by him were opposed by Granville, who was sustained by a majority in the cabinet.

When Gladstone and Granville returned to office in

[19] *Die Grosse Politik*, IV, 100.

1880 they were both unpopular with the queen, although
the prime minister looked blacker to her than did the
foreign secretary. Relying upon the strength of past relationship, Granville believed he could regain the queen's
favor for himself and perhaps for his chief,[20] but he failed
completely. Queen Victoria apparently came to dislike
him even more than Gladstone inasmuch as she suspected
him of weakness. Occasionally this suspicion also seems
to have entered the mind of Gladstone, who at times in
letters to Granville suggests a bold note or a firm stand.
On the other hand, Granville had little confidence in the
diplomatic skill of Gladstone and was uneasy every time
the prime minister discussed high politics with the representatives of foreign powers. Shortly after Granville became foreign secretary in 1870 he courteously but firmly
reminded the prime minister of the fact that the conduct
of foreign affairs rested with the one who had charge of
the foreign office. "May I venture to make you a request," he wrote, "which does not come from any jealous
feeling, although probably from one of conscious weakness? I imagine that the Prime Minister has an undoubted
right to communicate directly with our Representatives
abroad, or with Foreign Ministers in London—but I think
it is in his interest as much as in that of the Foreign Sec-

[20] Granville sent Gladstone a copy of his letter to the queen of
September 19, 1880, *Letters of Queen Victoria*, 2nd series, III, 141-
142, and asked him "to keep out of it." Granville to Gladstone, September 19, 1880. Original MS., Gladstone Papers.

retary that he should only appear as the 'Deus ex Machina.'

"Both English and foreign diplomatists like the double communication, particularly when the Prime Minister is not only officially superior, but personally immensely so.

"Bernstorff once boasted to me that he liked going to you. 'I like having two strings to my bow'—They like checking what is said by one, by what is said by the other—& drawing inferences accordingly—they find you overflowing with original & large ideas, every one of which is invaluable for a despatch—they find very few ideas in my conversation, and those of a negative character."[21]

In the later correspondence between Granville and Gladstone there is no hint that the former felt that his chief had overstepped the bounds of propriety in his discussions of foreign affairs; and Gladstone appears to have reported faithfully the private conversations and correspondence which he had on this topic. It is not so clear whether Granville was equally open and frank. He carried on a very large private correspondence with British representatives abroad, and on at least one occasion he assured Goschen, then at Constantinople, that not all of these private letters were shown to the prime minister.[22] But generally speaking, the relations between the two

[21] Original MS., *ibid;* Lord Edmond Fitzmaurice, *Life of Second Earl Granville* (London, 1905), II, 64-65.

[22] Granville to Goschen, October 29, 1880. Copy, the Granville Papers, at the Public Record Office.

Barry University Library

Miami, FL 33161

were characterized by complete harmony and mutual confidence. Not infrequently, Gladstone wrote, as in the case of Egypt, December, 1881, that he would follow Granville's judgment whatever it might be. And it was with unfeigned regret that Gladstone, on account of opposition by the queen, was deprived of Granville's service at the foreign office when he formed his third ministry in February, 1886.[23]

Lord Rosebery was the third earl who served as foreign secretary under Gladstone. A favored and spoiled child of fortune, Rosebery entered public life with glamour around his name and person. Throughout a long life he remained a man of promise. He early acknowledged himself a disciple of Gladstone and acted splendidly the part of host to the crusader in the campaign in Midlothian, 1879. The gifts and services of Rosebery entitled him to an office of some sort when the government of 1880 was formed; but Gladstone, following precedents set by Peel, insisted that the young peer should learn the elements of office-holding in a subordinate position as parliamentary under-secretary.[24] An issue soon arose between them over the need for a Scottish secretaryship, urged with great persistence by Rosebery, always a loyal Scot, and refused by the prime minister. Rosebery finally resigned office in 1883 and went on a world tour, but upon his return he rejoined the government although he

[23] Marriott, *Queen Victoria and Her Ministers*, 174.
[24] Crewe, *Rosebery*, 106.

frankly expressed disapproval of much that the government had done. In the spring of 1885 he visited Germany and performed the difficult feat of pleasing both Bismarck and Gladstone.[25] In February, 1886, he became foreign secretary in the short-lived third ministry of Gladstone; and in 1892, after much persuasion, he returned to this post in the fourth ministry.

Rosebery belonged to the new generation which Gladstone found difficult to understand. No sooner had he taken office in 1886 than he told the German ambassador in London that he was going to address the Germans in the menacing language that they had employed so long.[26] This they understood and apparently liked, and Gladstone soon paid Rosebery high compliments on the way he handled foreign relations.[27] But in the fourth ministry things did not run so smoothly between prime minister and foreign secretary. The Grand Old Man informed his young colleague of the responsibility of the prime minister for the conduct of foreign affairs and told him reminiscently that so far back as Gladstone's memory went the prime minister and the foreign secretary had always presented a united front to the cabinet. But this did not move Rosebery, who urged his views concerning Uganda so stubbornly and with so much skill that both

[25] *Ibid.*, 192-193.
[26] Rosebery to Gladstone, April 27, 1886. Original MS., Gladstone Papers.
[27] Gladstone to Rosebery, April 28, 1886; copy, the Gladstone Papers.

the prime minister and the redoubtable Sir William Vernon Harcourt had to surrender. The Gladstone-Rosebery correspondence about Uganda reveals that the chasm which separated the two men was wider than that of a difference between two generations.[28] They differed in temperament, character, experience, and training. Letters from Lord Rosebery to the queen convey a faint suspicion that at times the attributes of the courtier in him were stronger than the feeling of loyalty to chief and friend. Not only in the case of Uganda but also concerning Egypt, 1892-93, Rosebery presented his ideas with force and self-confidence. By this time the policy represented by Rosebery, liberal imperialism, was waxing; the old-style liberalism of his chief—peace, retrenchment, and reform—was waning in popularity. When Gladstone in 1895-96 urged his countrymen to take steps to save the Armenians from extinction, Rosebery threw up the leadership of the Liberal party in disgust.[29] The cause of humanity failed to move him as it moved Gladstone. It appears, indeed, that Rosebery, the author of brilliant monographs on Pitt and Peel, had in reality little in common with Gladstone, the disciple of both.

When Gladstone first became prime minister the lofty ideals concerning international relations preached so ardently in the middle years of the nineteenth century were gradually being thrown into the discard; a new aggres-

[28] See Chapter IX.
[29] Crewe, *Rosebery*, 428-433.

sive nationalism and a grasping imperialism became the order of the day. Gladstone, however, clung to the ideals of his early manhood, but they became illusions in his old age. The people whom he led, the sovereign whom he served, and the colleagues with whom he worked ceased to believe in his lofty principles concerning foreign policy. They were rejected by the generation which finally rejected him.

Chapter III

THE FIRST MINISTRY, 1868-1874

ON DECEMBER 1, 1868, Gladstone received the queen's request to form a new administration. At that time he conceived his special mission to be the pacification of Ireland, and Ireland and Irish questions loom large in the history of his first ministry, 1868-74. But other domestic issues were not neglected, and this government effected more sweeping reforms in a number of fields than did any other in the long reign of Queen Victoria. When he took over the duties as prime minister no disturbing topic in international relations appeared on the docket except the *Alabama* dispute with the United States. However, this fortunate state of affairs soon changed, and within the next two years the old political arrangement in Europe had been violently upset by the Franco-Prussian War and the establishment of the German empire. These were the most momentous events in foreign relations during the years embraced in the first ministry of Gladstone; but there arose other questions of considerable importance involving Britain's relations with European and non-European powers.

Four months after Gladstone had taken office, he explained in a lengthy letter to the queen's private secretary, General Grey, his views on foreign policy. He expressed as his belief that England would remain faithful "to her great tradition" and would maintain "her interest in the common transactions and the general interests of Europe." "But," he continued significantly, "her credit and her power form a fund which in order that they may be made the most of should be thriftily used." He alluded to the fact that England had shown her strength in the great wars of the early part of the century, but the cost had been heavy. To intervene single-handed in continental affairs entailed great risks and she could not act the part of judge and policeman. On the other hand, she must not convey the impression that she would never fight and never intervene. England "should keep entirely in her own hands the means of estimating her own obligations upon the various states of facts as they arise"; she should not surrender her freedom by previous declarations, nor assume an isolated position, nor unduly encourage the weak to rely upon her protection, but rather restrain the strong from aggression and seek to develop a European opinion as a bulwark against wrong. In this declaration concerning principles of foreign policy, Gladstone adhered closely to his former ideals; and he revealed what seemed to him the important lessons to be drawn from the foreign policy of Palmerston.[1]

Before we discuss the attitude of Gladstone toward the major issues arising from the position of Britain as a European power, we shall survey briefly actions taken and policies pursued elsewhere, some of them on the periphery of the empire. Then, as always in modern British history, dynamic forces on the frontiers involved or threatened to involve the empire in forward movements. The demand for expansion was resisted in the South Pacific and in the Malay Peninsula; nevertheless, measures were adopted which later precipitated the annexation of the Fiji Islands and an increase of British influence in Malaya. In western Africa an exchange of territory was effected with the Dutch, about which the prime minister expressed suspicion lest it mean new annexation; and a war with the Ashanti led to the acquisition of new lands on the Gold Coast. In South Africa the discovery of diamonds in a region outside the British area claimed by both a Griqua chief and the Boer republics precipitated a controversy little noticed at the time but which later proved to be one of the "small beginnings" fraught with mighty consequences. British adventurers were early active at the diggings and, despite opposition by the Boers (especially by the Orange Free State) and by Gladstone, the Diamond Fields became British

---

[1] Morley, *Gladstone*, II, 316-318.

territory in 1872. The Orange Free State demanded that the question of the original ownership of the fields should be decided by arbitration; but the request was refused by the British government. Gladstone in this instance seemed to act contrary to his earlier convictions concerning arbitration, to the practice followed in the dispute with the United States, and to his creed of equal rights for all nations. A study of the documents discloses, however, that in the matter of the claims to the Diamond Fields, Gladstone was misled by the colonial office which assured him that the facts were clear—the Boers had no case.[2]

The Gladstone government inherited a number of disputes with the United States: one dealt with the ownership of San Juan Island south of Vancouver Island, some old ones were connected with fisheries, and a batch of new ones dated from the Civil War in the United States, of which the most serious arose from the exploits of the *Alabama*, a Confederate cruiser built in England during the war. Earlier attempts at settling these disputes had failed, and the temper as well as the demands of the Americans showed a tendency to rise with the passing years. As an easy way out of the difficulty it was suggested, rudely by Senator Charles Sumner of Massachusetts, crudely by the American minister to London,

[2] Knaplund, *Gladstone and Britain's Imperial Policy*, 132-138; see also C. W. de Kiewiet, *British Colonial Policy and the South African Republics* (London, 1929), 284-285.

Reverdy Johnson, and suavely by Hamilton Fish, the American secretary of state, that Britain should cede Canada to the United States; but the government of Gladstone refused to consider this solution. In the autumn of 1870, the European situation seemed threatening, and Gladstone deemed it wise to make haste in reaching a settlement with the Americans. It was agreed to have the various points considered by a joint high commission meeting at Washington, and the British government displayed great eagerness to remove possible obstacles to a peaceable solution. Thus, when the Canadians began to press for compensation from the United States for the damages caused by the Fenian raids, Gladstone chose to have these claims treated as claims against the United Kingdom on the ground that if there had been no Irish question the Fenian raids would never have occurred.[3] By this conciliatory attitude peace was preserved and the points at issue were settled by arbitration, although the awards went against Britain concerning both the ownership of San Juan and the *Alabama* claims. The decision in the latter case aroused in England much hostile criticism against the government, and it contributed materially to the defeat of the Liberals in the election of 1874. But the manner in which the *Alabama* dispute was settled testifies to Gladstone's belief in the efficacy of arbitration; he thereby set a famous precedent for the settlement of disputes between nations.

[3] Knaplund, *Gladstone and Britain's Imperial Policy*, 121-122.

Lord Clarendon had kept in close touch with the European situation before the government was formed. In 1868 he visited the continent and discussed the international situation with Napoleon III; and a few months later he displayed tact and firmness when a minor issue involving railway concessions arose between France and Belgium and rumors began to fly about that war was imminent. Clarendon hinted to the French ambassador, M. de Lavalette, that Britain would intervene if France attacked Belgium.[4] The warning proved effective and Britain's relations with France continued friendly, although Clarendon in the summer of 1869 warned Gladstone that Napoleon III "is now I am sure in a dangerous state capable of a warlike *coup de tête*"; and in the autumn he said: "There is always dirty work behind the scenes at Paris."[5] The situation seemed so threatening that Clarendon made special efforts to pour oil on the troubled waters. He told Napoleon III that Germany desired peace, that the centrifugal spirit was strong in southern Germany, and that no engagement existed between Prussia and Russia. Clarendon said further "that if France was aggressive she wd. do more in a month to cement Germany together than Bismarck wd. achieve in five years & that if Austria joined France agst. Prussia Russia wd. go to the aid of the latter." To this Napoleon

---

[4] Clarendon to Gladstone, April 27, 1869. Original MS., Gladstone Papers.

[5] Clarendon to Gladstone, June 4 and September 24, 1869. Original MSS., Gladstone Papers.

replied that "he had been much pressed to form an offensive & defensive alliance with Austria & Italy, but that he had rejected the project as imprudent & useless —it wd. in the first place irritate Prussia & perhaps drive her into active hostility & 2d such an engagement wd. have no real binding power on Austria & Italy if they did not choose to help him & if it suited them to do so a treaty wd. not be necessary."[6]

At his interview with Napoleon III, September, 1869, Clarendon broached the question of the huge armaments and asserted that they threatened international peace. The emperor agreed but thought no change could be made during the lifetime of the king of Prussia.[7] However, after New Year, 1870, the French showed more interest in the English ideas on disarmament; and, with Gladstone's approval, Clarendon approached Bismarck, who replied that he dared not mention it to the king. The subject was then dropped.[8] But Clarendon continued his efforts to calm the French. When the grand duke of Baden in a public speech indicated a desire for a union with the North German Confederation, Clarendon made inquiries and received assurances from Berlin that the grand duke had not been encouraged by the king of

[6] Clarendon to Gladstone; the letter is dated "Paris Sept. 18/69." Original MS., *ibid.*

[7] *Ibid.*

[8] Clarendon to Gladstone, January 31, February 18, and April 19, 1870. Original MSS., *ibid.* Gladstone to Clarendon, February 7, 16, and 23, and April 9, 1870. Copies, letter books, XII, 140, 150, 165-166, 243, *ibid.;* see also Morley, *Gladstone*, II, 321-322.

Prussia, and means were found to pass this information on to Paris.[9] Clarendon had observed that Napoleon felt keenly the loss of the friendship of Queen Victoria "without, I must say, a just cause," and that Napoleon resented the hostile attitude of *The Times*. In the judgment of Clarendon the emperor had "been a faithful ally to us but English Statesmen cd. not give the good word he wanted to his personal Govt. wh. was unadulterated despotism." Since this government had been changed by 1870 and Napoleon had honestly, Clarendon believed, adopted parliamentary government, "he is entitled to praise for his recent conduct." The foreign secretary suggested therefore that Gladstone should bestow such praise. The prime minister complied, to Clarendon's great satisfaction, and Lord Lyons, the British ambassador in Paris, was instructed to bring Gladstone's statement to the attention of the emperor.[10]

In these matters Gladstone followed the advice given by Clarendon and loyally seconded the efforts of his foreign secretary to insure peace in Europe and to strengthen the Anglo-French friendship. Gladstone was, however, not so much of a Francophile as was Claren-

[9] Clarendon to Gladstone, October 4, 1869. Original MS., Gladstone Papers.

[10] Clarendon to Gladstone, February 11, 1870. Gladstone praised the change of government in France, see *Hansard*, 3rd series. CXCIX, 336; and Clarendon wrote to Gladstone, February 16: "I never read anything more happy & forceful than your allusion to the change of system in France. I have requested Lyons to take care that it is duly brought under the notice of the Emperor tho I am sure he will have found it for himself." Original MSS., Gladstone Papers.

don; and when Italy in the spring of 1870 sought English aid in an effort to persuade Napoleon III to recall
the French troops from Rome, Gladstone, while unwilling to support such an application, would, if asked for
an opinion by France, have made it perfectly clear that
England viewed "the occupation of any part of the
Pontifical territories by French troops . . . with regret,
pain, and disapproval." Personally Gladstone regarded
that occupation as "almost a crime: & the French fear.
to use the power thus given against the madmen of the
Council has been altogether a blunder."[11] Writing to
Clarendon on June 16, 1870, Gladstone said: "It is with
diffidence that I question an opinion of yours but I think
there are reasons quite apart from my own predilections
for abstaining from any endeavour to prevent the Italians
from *asking* us to apply (jointly) to France for the withdrawal of her troops. There is nothing unfair in that
application: the occupation was from the first a gross
outrage: it is so viewed by the people of this country
and by Parlt: & an attempt to stifle any complaints on
the subject would, I think, be held to imply that we regarded it as solved, & would be very difficult to defend
in our seats, or at least in mine."[12]

Ten days after the date of this letter Lord Clarendon
died, and events were then rapidly taking shape which

[11] Gladstone to Clarendon, March 5 and June 15, 1870. Copies,
letter books, XII, 180, 334, *ibid.*
[12] *Ibid.*, 334-335.

made the question of the continuance of the French troops at Rome a matter of small importance. After prolonged backstairs negotiations the throne of Spain was officially offered to Prince Leopold of Hohenzollern-Sigmaringen, a relative of the king of Prussia, and accepted by him. The French government took grave offense at this and remonstrated both at Berlin and at Madrid. The prince then withdrew his acceptance; but when France demanded further assurances from the king of Prussia concerning Prince Leopold and the throne of Spain these were refused. With the will for peace absent at Paris and at Berlin and the passion of the peoples inflamed, a war became inevitable. On July 15, 1870, the government of France decided to throw down the gauntlet, which was eagerly picked up by Prussia. Four days later the Franco-Prussian War broke out.

True to his principle of self-determination, Gladstone had maintained that the choice of a sovereign was a question to be decided by the Spanish people without interference from the outside, nor did he think that the election of Prince Leopold justified the violent language used by the French government, although the secrecy in which the negotiations had been shrouded might cause a certain amount of legitimate resentment. But since the issue of Prince Leopold's candidacy to the throne of Spain endangered the peace of Europe, Gladstone acquiesced in the French request for support in urging him to withdraw. When this was achieved, Gladstone advised

France that the action should be considered "as satisfactory and conclusive." However, the government of France had already decided to go further and to demand assurances from the king of Prussia which he could not or would not give.[13] Two days after Gladstone had urged the French to treat the withdrawal of the candidature of Prince Leopold as the closing of the incident they decided on war. Critics of Gladstone and apologists for Bismarck have united in throwing blame for the Franco-Prussian War on the government of Britain; and they have quoted Bismarck in support of their charges. But neither these charges nor the testimony of Bismarck can be taken seriously. The governments of France and of Prussia wanted war in July, 1870; and both, apparently, felt certain of the outcome. By arrangements with Russia Bismarck had assured himself against danger from this quarter and he had thereby paralyzed Austria. Italy carried little weight; furthermore, she was anxious to acquire Rome. And England with only 20,000 men available for an expeditionary force could do little except by moral pressure, always ineffectual in a crisis. The European concert did not exist, and without support from at least one of the great powers Gladstone could not hope to settle a grave international dispute.

With the dogs of war let loose, a multitude of new

---

[13] Morley, *Gladstone*, II, 325-330; Dora Neill Raymond, *British Policy and Opinion During the Franco-Prussian War* (New York, 1921), 51-66.

questions drew the attention of Gladstone away from his more congenial tasks of domestic and administrative reforms. A cabinet in which John Bright was a prominent member could never err on the point of haste in making preparation for war; and on this point the prime minister was wont to agree with his president of the board of trade. Hence, not until toward the end of July did Gladstone think the state of public opinion warranted effective military preparation for possible eventualities.[14] By this time the publication in *The Times*, July 25, of the so-called Benedetti treaty of 1867, which showed that Napoleon III had been plotting against Belgium, aroused the British government to take action for the safeguarding of that country. On the Belgian question Gladstone held characteristic views. He denied that Britain had a special and separate duty to maintain the neutrality of Belgium and that she had any particular interest apart from those of a general European character in keeping Belgium neutral and independent. If the Belgians of their own free will decided to join France the affair was their own. But since a violation of the neutrality of Belgium by either France or Prussia might lead both to coercion of Belgium and to a dangerous

[14] "Feeling much altered. Those who were strongly opposed to any measures, are now disposed to confide in the Govt. with regard to them. Those who before would have confided in the Govt., & been silent, are now speaking decidedly to augment our force in one shape or other." Gladstone to Granville, July 29, 1870. Copy, letter books, XII, 405. Gladstone Papers.

widening of the conflict, Gladstone set the diplomatic machinery in motion, with the result that bilateral treaties were concluded with France and the North German Confederation whereby Britain pledged herself to enter the war against the one which violated Belgian neutrality —an arrangement that proved effective.[15] At the same time agreements were reached between Britain, Italy, and Austria to maintain neutrality in the war, and not depart therefrom "without an interchange of ideas and an announcement to one another of any change of policy."

In 1870 Denmark was still smarting from the defeat suffered at the hands of Prussia and Austria in 1864; and she had a further grievance against the former because of a non-fulfillment of a provision in the Treaty of Prague which held out a possibility that part of Slesvig might be returned to the Danish monarchy. Consequently, no sooner had the war broken out than it was

[15] See statement in house of commons August 10, 1870. *Hansard*, 3rd series, CCIII, 1786-1789. When the Franco-Prussian War was over, the Belgians suggested a special Anglo-German treaty for the safeguarding of their neutrality. But Gladstone opposed it. "I am not moved by the Belgian Rhetoric," he wrote to Granville December 29, 1871. "We did a very special act under very special circs. and I should be very sorry if this were to become a precedent for every day; as I have no doubt you would also." Original MS., Granville Papers. In a letter to Granville, October 11, 1870, Gladstone denied the existence of special British interests "as connected with the affairs of the European Continent." Copy, letter books, XIII, 98-99. Gladstone Papers. Gladstone's views on Belgian neutrality were severely criticized by J. W. Headlam-Morley in *The Cambridge Historical Journal*, II, 163-164.

rumored that Denmark would attack Prussia. The rumor caused Gladstone some concern. He suggested that Britain should join with Russia in urging France not to bring pressure to bear on Denmark and that it should be pointed out to Prussia that she might remove "the cause of danger on the side of Denmark by making a fair arrangement of the matter as to territory now in difference."[16] Denmark remained neutral, but the territorial question had to await the settlement following the war of 1914.

Sea power played a small rôle in the Franco-Prussian war. France controlled the sea and could therefore obtain arms and other supplies from abroad. Bismarck complained and denounced Britain—most likely for political effect—for her traffic in arms with France. In international law there was no case against Britain, but Gladstone was not happy about the export of arms. On October 9, 1870, he forwarded to Granville a suggestion which had appealed to him although he thought it probably would not hold water; the suggestion was to the effect that the export of arms should be declared "illegal, placing it on the footing of a private wrong, & giving to the Foreign State injuriously affected the power of proving & obtaining remedy in the cts. of the exporting country." The idea caught the fancy of Granville but he agreed with his chief that it was impractical.

[16] Gladstone to Granville, August 2, 1870. Copy, letter books, XIII, 8, Gladstone Papers.

Barely six weeks after the formal outbreak of the war its outcome had been decided by the surrender of a great French army at Sedan, September 2, 1870. Two days afterwards Paris rose, a republic was proclaimed, and a provisional government, the Government of National Defense, took office. The equivocal position of the new French administration added to its difficulties and supplied Bismarck with material for intrigue which he used or was suspected of using from time to time. On September 6, Gladstone agreed with Granville that the instructions to Lord Lyons at Paris concerning the government of France might be communicated to Brunnow, the Russian ambassador in London; and Gladstone suggested that in thus informing Russia of the action of the British government they might "add the expression of a hope that we should walk together in the matter of recognition, neither proceeding upon theory, but each being bound to recognize well-established facts."[17] But in this desire to act with Russia, Gladstone was not actuated by any hostility to the government of France; on the contrary, about the middle of September he was greatly disturbed by the circulation of rumors which seemed "to indicate an intention of high-handed interference with the internal concerns of France"; and "Bismarck's broad hint to the neutral powers to advise the French to convoke the old Legislature" Gladstone characterized as "repugnant to all English ideas." He re-

[17] *Ibid.*, 49-50.

gretted the necessity for postponing the official recognition of the new régime in France, the friction between Paris and the government at Tours, and the delay in convening a national assembly. Although he considered the French government guilty of bringing on the war, Gladstone deprecated suggestions that France should be bled white; and the nature and character of the prospective peace absorbed much of his attention from September, 1870, until February, 1871.

From the opening of hostilities Gladstone was ready to use the influence of England to bring them to a speedy termination. Words and phrases such as "good offices," the services of Britain, advice, mediation, and intervention were often used by him in connection with discussions of the war. But the memory of rash suggestions and utterances in 1862 about the Civil War in the United States made him timorous of action; Britain must not move alone except when requested to do so by both parties.[18] If Russia in particular could be persuaded to join Britain, the situation would be different; but Bismarck had taken such precautionary measures that Rus-

[18] While believing that mediation should not "be offered except with the condition of its being acceptable to both parties" and no advice proffered "except there is reason to believe it will be effective." Gladstone thought that "we have laid down these propositions hitherto as applicable to the sole advice of the British Govt., but have never bound ourselves to decide that Neutral Powers or some combination of them should never offer mediation or advice except under precisely the same limitations." Letter to Granville, October 15, 1870. Original MS., Granville Papers. See also Morley, *Gladstone*, II, 343-345; and Fitzmaurice, *Granville*, II, 53-57.

sia had no desire to intervene in conjunction with Britain or as a member of a combination of neutrals.

When the war broke out it was generally expected that France would win, but the early German victories quickly dispelled this illusion. Then speculation grew rife concerning the nature of the eventual peace. It was rumored that Bismarck would demand Alsace and Lorraine from France; and before long statements from the German headquarters gave substance to the rumors. By the middle of September the question was eagerly discussed by the British press; and the forlorn, roving mission of the French statesman, Thiers, gave impetus to the discussion. Meanwhile the provisional government of France propounded the doctrine of the inviolability of her territory and proclaimed grandiloquently that not a foot of her soil or a stone of her fortresses should be surrendered to the enemy. The inviolability theory made some impression upon Bright, but it left Gladstone unmoved. France of all countries, he said, had the least title to speak about inviolability of territory. Were not her annals filled with records of annexation and had she not less than a dozen years ago acquired Savoy and Nice as the price for aiding Sardinia against Austria? The talk about not ceding any territory he termed extravagant; the idea of punishing France as a disturber of peace he disregarded; nor did he think the cession by France and the acquisition by Germany of Alsace and Lorraine would upset the balance of power in Europe. Gladstone was more concerned with the ethical principle involved in the trafficking in people as if they were chattel, with the effects of such an action on the prospect of settling various disturbing European questions, and, above all, with whether a peace on such terms would promote tranquillity and stability in Europe. The question seemed to him one of tremendous importance; and partly for the purpose of securing a wide discussion of underlying principles and partly in order to arouse general public interest in the problems at stake, Gladstone took the unprecedented step of discussing the war in an article published in *The Edinburgh Review*, October, 1870; and he hoped, with surprising naïveté, that the authorship could be kept secret.

Gladstone worked hard to win support for measures which might have insured a just and lasting peace. On September 25, 1870, he completed a long memorandum on the cession of Alsace-Lorraine. Having elaborated on the topic that Bismarck allegedly wanted the provinces for the purpose of insuring the safety of Germany, Gladstone proceeded by asking: "1. Who it is that makes the demand. 2. What it is that is demanded. 3. Why it is that the demand is made." To (1) Gladstone remarked that the demand had not been fully and freely authorized by the people of Germany. Under (2) he emphasized that the cession involved the fate of more than a million people "who, with their ancestors for several generations, have known France for their country." The issue seemed to Gladstone basic and fundamental. "The transfer," he wrote, "of the allegiance & citizenship, of no small part of the heart and life, of human beings from one Sovereignty to another without any reference to their own consent, has been a great reproach to former transactions in Europe; has led to many wars and disturbances; is hard to reconcile with consideration of equity; and is repulsive to the sense of modern civilisation." In discussing (3), Gladstone admitted "that Germany is entitled to take ample security against France," but was the acquisition of Alsace and Lorraine the best and the only method whereby the safety of Germany could be insured? "It seems to be worth while to consider," he said, "whether the military neutralisation of the territory in question, and the destruction of all its fortresses, would not, without its being withdrawn from French allegiance, obtain the object of giving security to Germany."[19]

As was his wont in such matters, Gladstone submitted the document first to Lord Granville, who replied on September 26: "It seems to be an admirable argument the more so as it is the sort of thing Thiers ought to have said & did not."[20] But Granville objected to suggestions offered by Gladstone. If England insisted on a

[19] Original MS., Granville Papers.

[20] Morley, *Life of Gladstone*, II, 345, mistakenly applies this remark to Gladstone's article in *The Edinburgh Review*. Granville wrote: "I am dying for the proofs [of the article] which have not yet appeared. Your MS. [i.e., the memorandum] however arrived this morning." He then proceeds to argue against the line of action suggested by Gladstone. Copy, Granville Papers.

full and free expression of German feeling on the peace terms, Granville feared German chauvinism would be aroused against the liberals of Germany; he doubted the wisdom of "suggesting any terms of peace unless at the particular moment when both parties wish for a solution"; and he surmised that the plan of neutralizing the provinces would prove unpalatable to the inhabitants of Alsace and Lorraine.[21] Gladstone replied by intimating that Britain might properly sound Austria on the subject of consulting the wishes of the people before they were transferred; he thought representatives of neutral powers might supervise such a plebiscite; and he disavowed any intention of having Britain act alone.[22] "I am much oppressed," he wrote to Granville September 30, "with the idea that this transfer of human beings like chattels should go forward without any voice from collective Europe if it were disposed to speak." On the same day the memorandum of September 25 was discussed in the cabinet,[23] which, Gladstone reported to Bright on October 1, agreed to it in principle but did not think it timely and therefore refused to act. With his customary tenacity Gladstone argued the case in letters to Bright and to the Duke of Argyll, but failed to gain support. To Professor Max Müller Gladstone voiced his doubts whether the annexation of Alsace and Lor-

[21] *Ibid.*
[22] Gladstone to Granville, September 26 and 28, 1870. Copy, letter books, XIII, 73-74, Gladstone Papers.
[23] Morley, *Gladstone*, II, 346; Fitzmaurice, *Granville*, II, 62-64.

raine would enhance the safety of Germany; but the
German professor supported Bismarck. The queen was
interested in the question but not too well pleased with
the crusade of the prime minister. To her he wrote on
October 5 a long argumentative letter in which he asserted that the failure to ascertain the wishes of the people transferred by treaties had been a serious defect and
had caused many disturbances in the past; and that to
do so would insure peace, be in harmony with recent
practice, and have a direct bearing on the Belgian and
the Near Eastern question. He stoutly maintained that
the terms of the prospective peace were of great interest
to and legitimately concerned all of Europe.[24] But again,
he stood alone.

Granville showed more concern over the bombardment of Paris than over the transfer of Alsace and Lorraine. Gladstone approved of attempts to enlist the support of Russia against the bombardment but he was more
alarmed over the effects of a blockade of Paris. A suggestion that Britain should purchase French ironclads,
Gladstone vetoed. It would, he said, be difficult to ascertain their true value; he had heard that the French iron
was bad; he thought it would be deemed an invidious act
and cause discontent in English dockyards and among
contractors; and if a low price were paid, Britain would
be accused of benefiting from the plight of France,
whereas if a high price were paid, Germany would ac-

[24] Guedalla, *The Queen and Mr. Gladstone*, I, 256-257.

cuse Britain of giving aid to the enemy.[25] But these were side issues. Despite failure to gain support for his point of view Gladstone continued to argue the question that a vote of the people should precede the transfer of Alsace and Lorraine to Germany. In a letter to Bright, November 16, Gladstone wrote: "It is now too plain that its [the war's] horrors are prolonged, only on account of the conflicting views of the parties with reference to Al. & Lor. England I think can never contemplate with satisfaction the transference of unwilling populations from one country of Europe to another. That these populations are unwilling seems to be quite clear. The question I think will soon arise whether we can continue altogether silent on this subject. In different modes & degrees, both Russia & Italy appear to have spoken disapprovingly."[26]

Undaunted by the ill success of his first memorandum, Gladstone, toward the end of November, prepared another and more elaborate statement of the problem raised by the proposed cession of Alsace and Lorraine. He first summarized the German arguments in demanding these provinces and then proceeded to demolish them. He elaborated on the point that "the aggrandisement of Germany by consolidation from within her territories, is not a matter of which other countries are entitled to take

[25] Gladstone to Granville, December 10, 1870. Copy, letter books, XIII, 192, Gladstone Papers.
[26] *Ibid.*, 150-151.

any hostile cognisance. But so soon as Germany begins the work of aggrandisement by the annexation of territory taken from a neighbor she steps out of her own bounds & comes upon a ground where every country is entitled to challenge & discuss the title." He argued, further, that "this violent severance & annexation of an unwilling population would be a measure of a nature entirely retrogressive with reference to the public practice of Europe," and he produced evidence for this assertion from the peace settlement at Vienna and subsequent arrangements. In the case of Alsace and Lorraine the violence against right and usage would be extraordinary inasmuch as the people concerned were to become "not only the friends of their enemies, but the enemies of their friends." In conclusion, Gladstone claimed that if Germany exercised prudence and self-command in this case she "would raise herself thereby to a remarkable height of moral dignity, & would acquire a claim to the lasting gratitude of Europe."[27] But none would support him in helping Germany to gain this elevation.

Still, Gladstone refused to admit defeat. He asked Henry Reeve to write something about Alsace and Lorraine: "For it seems by no means impossible that those

[27] See Appendix I. Gladstone argued the points further in a letter to Granville, December 5, 1870. "I frankly own," he wrote, "I can see no plan wholly but I go so far with Mill as to be disposed to think it might not be the worst of all plans, if the fortresses were destroyed with no power to replace them for 20 years. I admit that at this moment we have no opportunity to speak." Copy, letter books, XIII, 181-182, Gladstone Papers.

little provinces may be the central hinge on which for long years to come the history of Europe may vitally depend." And to Granville Gladstone wrote: "I have an apprehension that this violent laceration and transfer is to lead us from bad to worse, and to be the *beginnings* of a new series of European complications." On February 3, 1871, Gladstone suggested that Granville might "inquire from and through Brunnow whether in case the proposed terms of peace when known should seem to be such as [to] menace the future stability of peace in Europe. Russia would be inclined to consider how far in concert with other Powers she might endeavour to exercise a mitigating influence." A conversation which Gladstone had with Brunnow, February 7, seems to have raised a flicker of hope which proved illusory.[28]

In the early part of February rumors circulated concerning the peace which Bismarck would dictate to France. There was talk about surrender of French ships and cession of Pondicherry, and speculations on the size of the indemnity raised the figures to two billion dollars. But none of these points alarmed Gladstone. Unlike the peacemakers at Paris in 1919, Gladstone believed "there is a sort of natural limit to the sum which can be raised within a given time, & to the time which any calculating people would be content to agree upon for the payment." What to him was "heavy and menacing" was

---

[28] Gladstone to Granville, February 3 and 8, 1871. *Ibid.*, 301-302, 307.

"the question of territory; or rather the question of the human beings who inhabit it."[29] A conference on the Black Sea Question was then in session in London, and Gladstone expected that the French representative might make an appeal to the neutrals. To meet such a contingency, he urged Granville to be prepared to act *"at extremely short notice"* and especially to seek the aid of Brunnow "since on the co-operation with Russia depends the possibility of being useful."[30] But the opportunity did not arrive. Not until February 24, 1871, the day when Bismarck presented his peace terms to France, did Gladstone admit defeat. Oppressed with forebodings he wrote on that day to Professor Max Müller: "I am afraid . . . that Germany, crowned with glory & confident in her strength, will start on her new career to encounter the difficulties of the future without the sympathies of Europe: which in my opinion no nation, not even we in our sea girt spot, can afford to lose." If Bismarck had seen these words he would, no doubt, have sneered at "the crazy professor." But forty-eight years later, in the same Hall of Mirrors at Versailles where Bismarck had proclaimed the German empire, the representatives of Germany stood, stripped of allies and of sympathy, to receive the terms of another peace treaty dictated in a spirit of hatred and revenge, the

[29] Letter to Granville, February 3, 1871. *Ibid.*, 301-302.
[30] Letter to Granville, February 18, 1871. *Ibid.*, 321-322.

spirit which Gladstone had condemned and Bismarck had fostered.

Gladstone based his hope of successful intervention for the purpose of mitigating the peace terms upon the possibility of Anglo-Russian co-operation. This was not to be, partly because Russia, with the connivance of Bismarck, seized upon the period of the war as a favorable one for freeing herself of the galling restrictions on her naval strength in the Black Sea imposed by the Treaty of Paris. Apparently her action was not unexpected, but it came at an inconvenient moment. Gladstone had in 1856 opposed this particular provision in the Treaty of Paris.[31] Therefore he could not well object to its abrogation; but he could and did resent the theory advanced by Russia that by her own act "without the consent of the co-signatories to the treaty she could release herself from its obligations." To accept this doctrine would increase the international anarchy which Gladstone deprecated. Consequently he took an active part in the discussions with Russia on the premises for her act and he seconded Granville's effort to convene an international conference to consider this question; but both privately and publicly he deplored the strong language used by Odo Russell in securing Bismarck's support for the conference.[32] However, it met at Lon-

[31] *Hansard*, 3rd series, CXXXVIII, 1058, 1060-1063; CXLII, 97-98.
[32] Fitzmaurice, *Granville*, II, 73-74. "I am much concerned that he [Odo Russell] has won Bismarck by representation about our going to war which really had not the slightest foundation." Gladstone to

don, November, 1870—March, 1871. With reference to
the Russian armaments in the Black Sea the conference
could only recognize a *fait accompli*; but concerning
the nature and character of treaties and the means for
abrogating them, the conference gave international recognition to the views of Gladstone. It was officially
recorded as an "essential principle of the law of nations
that no Power can liberate itself from the engagements
of a treaty, nor modify the stipulations thereof, unless
with the consent of the contracting Powers by means
of an amicable arrangement."[33]

In this episode Gladstone and Granville might claim
to have snatched victory from defeat, and here we may
properly close our discussion of Gladstone's connection
with the foreign policy of his first ministry. He had
throughout adhered closely to principles which he had
formerly proclaimed. Political opponents denounced both
the policy and the principles upon which it rested as
weak and inglorious; and historians supplied with a
plethora of after-the-event wisdom have on the basis of
the conduct of the foreign relations, 1868-74, accused
Gladstone of want of knowledge, of insight, and of
imagination. It is doubtless true that he lacked familiarity
with the murky waters of diplomacy; that his beam

Granville, December 6, 1870. Copy, letter books, XIII, 183-184, Gladstone Papers.

[33] Fitzmaurice, *Granville*, II, 76; Morley, *Gladstone*, II, 352-356.
A lengthy memorandum by Gladstone, dated November 9, and notes,
dated November 25, 1870, are found among the Granville Papers.

compass of Christian ethics was ill suited for navigation therein; and that he showed distrust of his own judgment. But whether it is called insight and imagination or named with the even vaguer term prescience, his vision of the effects of the Treaty of Frankfort proved unhappily to be true; later generations have applauded his actions in the matter of the Geneva arbitration; he won a victory for law at the London Conference; and, though blood flowed in torrents in 1870, he could have repeated the famous boast of Walpole—no English life was lost in war on the continent of Europe. Reasons and excuses for choosing the opposite road, leading to Armageddon, could easily have been found.

Chapter IV

THE RETURN OF THE LIBERALS

THE reform activities of the Gladstone government, 1868-74, antagonized many interests; and the results of its foreign policy, especially the Geneva arbitration award, exposed it to charges of truckling to foreign states and of having sacrificed the prestige of Britain in international affairs. The Conservatives won a resounding victory in the election of 1874, and for six years Disraeli stimulated the imperialistic sentiment of the British people. In so doing he had the support of a compact body of conservative opinion, always distrustful of idealism and what savored of radicalism in foreign policy and ready to respond to catchwords about the glory and interests of Britain and her empire; a considerable section of the press, with *The Times* in the van, strongly seconded the imperialistic exertions of the government; and the queen fell in with the views of her prime minister and even urged him on when he seemed to falter.

66

But the mid-nineteenth-century idealism was still a living force, and, roused by the revivalistic oratory of Gladstone, it brought about a reaction which hurled Disraeli (now Earl of Beaconsfield) from his pinnacle in 1880 and restored his rival to the seat of the mighty. For five crowded years the aged pilot of English liberalism sought unsuccessfully to stem the swelling tide of imperialism. The task was hopeless from the start. After some struggle and a good deal of floundering, the course of England was shaped in conformity with the new views in world politics.

By 1874 a growing number of Englishmen began to grasp the unpleasant truth that in Bismarck Europe had received a master and that in molding the destiny of his own country and that of its neighbors he had for a dozen years flaunted or ignored England. The arbiter of the affairs of Europe in 1815 had sunk to a secondary position.[1] This was galling to national pride, and the old Jew, the "alien patriot," set out to restore England to the position she had occupied under Castlereagh. Disraeli knew little about foreign affairs, he was uncertain as to the course to follow, but he saw his goal clearly. With a detachment mingled with contempt, he viewed the emotions that so often stirred Gladstone and the eternal truths enunciated by him. No English statesman has ex-

[1] Sir Robert Morier complained in 1873 that England now ranked with Holland and Denmark. Mrs. Rosslyn Wemyss, *Memoirs of Sir Robert Morier* (London, 1911), 296.

ceeded or even equaled Disraeli in strength of will and in fertility of mind. If patience was necessary, he had it; if a bold stroke need be struck, he would strike it; if the goal could be reached only by devious routes, he would follow them; but the goal was never out of sight. And thus, although he might have made light of massacres, such as that in Bulgaria, 1876, publicly honored the Treaty of 1856 while breaking it in secret, proclaimed from the housetops that the territorial integrity of Turkey must be maintained, and in the closet secured a Turkish island for Britain and promised Turkish provinces to her friends; in the eyes of adoring multitudes, which included his sovereign, Beaconsfield occupied at the Congress of Berlin in 1878 a position analogous to that held by Castlereagh at Vienna in 1815. Amid fanfares he returned from Berlin bringing "peace with honour." Englishmen proudly though mistakenly believed that their country had again become the umpire of the affairs of mankind.

The Near Eastern policy was the most striking effort of Disraeli to salve the wounded pride and stimulate the self-confidence of his countrymen, but it was not the only field in which his government performed deeds that appealed to British imperialists. During the years 1874-80 islands in the Pacific came under British sovereignty; Britain strengthened her hold on Malaya; amirs of Baluchistan and farmers of the Transvaal yielded allegiance to the British crown; Quetta and Kandahar were seized; Cabul was occupied; British influence was extended over Afghanistan and scientific frontiers were sought for India; the power of the Zulus was broken; England became intrenched in Egypt; and the route to India was allegedly safeguarded by the purchase of Suez Canal shares and the acquisition of Cyprus.

But this splendid medal had a reverse side which for a time remained hidden from view. The concert of Europe of 1815 could not be restored in 1878 because Bismarck had no faith in it. He was moved not by concern for mankind but by concern for the supposed weal of his creation, the German empire. By the Cyprus Convention of 1878 Britain assumed responsibilities for Turkey in Asia, responsibilities for actions of a government over whom Britain could not exercise any effective control; and as a result of this agreement she became entangled with promises to France. As the prime mover in convening the Congress of Berlin, Britain was considered the chief executor of the arrangements made there. Egypt proved to be a hornet's nest from which Britain could not be extricated; she had annexed the Transvaal hastily, and the need for repentance came in due time; and in Afghanistan and in the land of the Zulus events soon transpired that brought mourning to thousands of British homes. In 1878 the British lion roared lustily; two years later he licked his wounds.

Long before this, however, Gladstone had emerged to slay the dragon of imperialism. After the defeat in

1874, Gladstone retired from the leadership of the Liberal party, leaving Lord Hartington, the Whig heir to the duke of Devonshire, as successor on an uneasy throne. But battles with Cardinal Manning over the Vatican decrees and other congenial occupations did not absorb all the abundant energy of the retired premier. Uprisings in the Turkish provinces of Bosnia and Herzegovina brought the perennial Balkan question forward in 1875, and the great statesmen of Europe turned their attention to Turkey and proceeded to demonstrate that the collective acts of men of great intelligence may be both stupid and heartless. The disaffection in other Turkish provinces resulted in disturbances; and in the summer of 1876, the Turkish government began to pacify Bulgaria by means of massacres.[2] The government of Disraeli had from the beginning refused to sanction coercive measures for Turkey; and the prime minister, a section of the press, and members of high society in London made light of the reports of Turkish excesses, seeing in the reports only anti-Turkish propaganda. But the English conscience which had been aroused in days of old by tales of the miseries of Negro slaves and, although to a lesser extent, by evidence of sufferings in mines, factories, and workshops at home, could not be drugged; and when Gladstone in a famous pamphlet,

[2] Harold Temperley, "The Bulgarian and Other Atrocities, 1875-8, in the Light of Historical Criticism," in *Proceedings of the British Academy 1931* (London, 1933), 105-130.

The Bulgarian Horrors and the Question of the East, published September 6, 1876, called the Turk before the bar of humanity, that conscience was aroused as seldom before. The pamphlet has been compared with Burke's letter on the *Regicide Peace*,[3] and it bears considerable resemblance to Gladstone's own letters on the Neapolitan prisoners; but the tract on the Bulgarian massacres proved more effective in stirring the nation than either of the other two broadsides. He mingled fierce denunciations with appeals to the sentiments of religion and mercy; he spoke as a statesman and as a Christian crusader; and in telling phrases he urged that the Turks should be expelled "bag and baggage . . . from the province they have desolated and profaned."[4] By this pamphlet, Gladstone put his hand to the plough; there could be no turning back. He fought the fiercest and the final duel with his old political adversary over fundamental issues in British foreign policy; against Gladstone's appeal to the sense of the brotherhood of man and to sacred obligations, Beaconsfield, after biding his time, pitted appeals to the need for national and imperial self-preservation. When Russia entered the scene as the champion of the Balkan Christians, he opposed her, basing his policy on the principles of Pitt and of the statesmen who had been Gladstone's colleagues during the Crimean War, and on the policy of that war. By 1878

[3] Morley, *Gladstone*, II, 553.
[4] *Ibid.*, 554.

the pendulum had swung to the side of Beaconsfield. A London mob broke the windows in the residence of Gladstone, and Beaconsfield was received with great ovation when he returned from Berlin. Meanwhile Gladstone had taken up the fight both in parliament and in contributions to periodicals. Finally when, in the autumn of 1879, parts of the reverse of the medal containing the records of the government's achievements began to be visible and when its financial policy stood revealed as a failure, Gladstone undertook the most famous political campaign in English history, named after Midlothian, the electoral district near Edinburgh where he chose to stand as a candidate for parliament. But in reality Midlothian was but the sounding board; he was addressing the British nations. As he formerly had called the Turk to account, so he now called Lords Beaconsfield and Salisbury to the bar of British public opinion for their conduct, particularly in regard to foreign policy. Beaconsfield affected indifference and spoke sneeringly of his opponent's "drenching rhetoric";[5] The Times, now edited by Thomas Chenery, charged Gladstone with being in a state of "rhetorical inebriation";[6] the queen soon voiced her displeasure in no uncertain terms;[7]

[5] Gladstone, After Thirty Years, 49; Letters of Disraeli to Lady Chesterfield and Lady Bradford. Ed. by the Marquis of Zetland (New York, 1929), II, 328.

[6] The Times, November 29, 1879, leading article.

[7] Letters of Queen Victoria, 2nd series, III, 73; Guedalla, The Queen and Mr. Gladstone, II, 17.

and conservative society scorned the Gladstonian appeal
to demos. But Gladstone struck a responsive chord in the
hearts of the electorate, and the voters in the election
of 1880 showed a strong preference for the man whom
Beaconsfield had called a "sophistical rhetorician." Lord
Hartington's leadership of the Liberal party had been
shadowy ever since the re-emergence of Gladstone; the
Midlothian campaign had relegated Hartington and his
lieutenants to a distant background; and the result of
the election was rightly adjudged as a vote of confidence
in Gladstone. The queen was furious over the outcome,
but she bowed to the inevitable and asked Gladstone to
become prime minister for the second time.

Discussion of foreign affairs had played a prominent
part in the attacks on the Conservative government and
had contributed materially to its downfall. Like the
ghost in *Hamlet*, problems in foreign relations, old
declarations of ideals and of principles, statements made
in Midlothian, commitments by the previous government, plans and machinations of foreign rulers and statesmen, and, above all, the *Zeitgeist* refused to be laid to
rest or to be conjured away. For five long years embarrassing issues in foreign and in imperial affairs plagued
the aged premier, aroused dissension within the cabinet,
embittered the relations between Gladstone and the
queen, caused him to lose support at home, and left
Britain without a friend among the powers.

Gladstone returned to the political arena not, as so

often asserted, because of love of power but because he believed he saw tasks to be done which he alone, being fully conscious of his power, could accomplish, because he felt that the nation had strayed from and must be brought back to the straight and narrow path, and because he and only he could keep together in a semblance of unity the discordant elements within the Liberal party. As of old, his chief strength as administrator and statesman lay in his grasp of finance and in his skill in framing and carrying great legislative measures. The Irish question continued to cry for solution; an important measure of political reform, the extension of the franchise to agricultural laborers, was overdue; and problems connected with procedure in parliament, the admission of an atheist, Charles Bradlaugh, to the house of commons, and the goadings of a small band of brilliant and impudent young men labeled "the fourth party," absorbed a great share of Gladstone's attention. An entry in his daughter's, Mary Gladstone's, diary for November 15, 1881, shows that even at that time he seriously considered retiring from public life;[8] the desirability of such a step occupied his mind a great deal during the next two or three years, but issues continued to crowd in, colleagues begged him to stay on, and the needs of the party and of the nation seemed to require that he should remain at the helm; and he did. For two lengthy periods

[8] Mary Gladstone, *Her Diaries and Letters.* Ed. by Lucy Masterman (New York, 1930), 234-236.

in 1883 and in 1884, illness prevented him from taking an active part in the deliberations of the cabinet, and his visits to Hawarden were more frequent and more prolonged than formerly. As a result he was often absent when decisions had to be made.

The government, 1880-85, was rich in'talent, in experience, and in administrative ability, but, torn by factional strife, it was ineffective as a governing body. This was especially true in matters concerning foreign and imperial relations. Lord Granville, foreign secretary throughout the period, lacked resourcefulness; and he and Gladstone neither could nor would play the diplomatic game according to the rules laid down by Bismarck and now adopted by the rest of Europe. When Lord Derby, after much courting, entered the cabinet in 1882 as secretary of state for the colonies, a paralyzing factor was admitted. The most aggressive members of the government, Sir William Harcourt and Joseph Chamberlain, were opposed to an active imperialistic policy, and the chief of the other faction, Lord Hartington, lacked energy. As a result prolonged discussions without decision often characterized the meetings of the cabinet.

The relations between the prime minister and the queen added materially to the discomforts of the government and impeded its freedom of action. The queen had taken Gladstone's strictures on Disraeli's foreign policy as a personal affront. She refused to give Gladstone her confidence, was often less than civil to him; and his loyalty to the crown, his unfailing courtesy and sublime patience failed to remove the royal distrust or soften the wrath. Queen Victoria regarded Gladstone as her grandfather had regarded Charles James Fox.[9] Their views on foreign relations clashed on almost every issue. Deficient in sympathy and in imagination, the strong but pedestrian mind of the queen was repelled by the idealism and the humanitarianism of Gladstone. And because she was more earthly, she represented a stronger and more abiding element in the English nation. The queen and Gladstone agreed in distrusting Bismarck, but on most other topics in foreign policy they were poles apart.

The hostility of the press increased the difficulties of the government. In a letter to Gladstone, October 31, 1880, Granville complained bitterly of the attitude of the press. "The Times," he wrote, "which has lost its influence at home is still powerful abroad. . . . The Daily News is supposed to represent you, but it is not handy and its attacks upon Bismarck & Austria do mischief. . . . I do not see the remedy.

"I am a bad hand at it, I am civil to some of the press, but what they want is constant information and briefs. I am always inclined to be reticent, and have no fertility. You of course have no time."[10]

[9] Guedalla, *The Queen and Mr. Gladstone*, II, *passim.*
[10] Original MS., Gladstone Papers.

In his reply, dated the following day, Gladstone confessed himself worse than Granville in handling the press. He used John Morley for this purpose, but not more than six times during the last several months had he let things out. He had shown willingness to answer questions of newspaper men, but they did not ask any; and due to failing eyesight and to pressure of work, he admitted he read the newspapers very inadequately. "No doubt," he wrote, "under the late Govt. there was continuous action."[11] Bismarck, as is now well known, manipulated the press of Germany and could not understand the relations of Gladstone to the press of England. The attacks upon Bismarck to which Granville alluded were regarded as inspired by the British government.

Thus the press helped to deepen the abyss separating Gladstone and Bismarck at a time when good relations between the governments of Britain and of Germany were most needed. Bismarck was conscious of social forces in Germany that were inimical to him and to his system, and haunted by phobias he considered the success of Gladstone in the election of 1880 as a distinct threat to the existing order. Free trade, the English parliamentary system, and the ideas of the English Liberals were anathemas to Bismarck; and to him Gladstone represented all that was objectionable in domestic and foreign policy. The leader of the English Liberals had many interests and wide sympathies; with an intense patriotism

[11] Copy, letter books, XVIII, 176, *ibid.*

he combined love for mankind; to him nationalism and
internationalism were complementary, not conflicting,
ideas; he envisaged a day when the battle flags were
furled and the nations brought to a realization of their
common interests. The less cultured German scoffed at
all this. His German god was not the Balder but the
Thor of Nordic mythology, although in action the Bis-
marckian model often came nearer to that of Loki. The
mid-nineteenth-century cry "above all nations humanity" he looked upon as sheer nonsense. His nationalism
was narrow and belligerent. The Englishman was so
sure of England's strength that he saw no need for ad-
vertising it; the German, conscious of the fact that his
country was exposed to many dangers, felt impelled to
show its strength. Bismarck favored peace based on
fear; Gladstone hoped for peace based not on alliances
but on an appreciation of common needs and a recognition of right and justice; and he perceived correctly
the motives of Bismarck when he wrote to Granville,
September 21, 1884: "As to Bismarck, I incline to the
belief . . . that when he has supported and when he
has opposed he has been governed by one and the same
principle all along"—the principle being, of course, the
promotion of the interests of Germany. Since Bismarck
was known to hate Gladstone,[12] he was suspected of

[12] Granville to Northbrook, August 16, 1884, copy, Granville
Papers. A memorandum by Lord Tenterden, October 30, 1880, contains a summary of a report made by Lord Odo Russell on Bismarck's views on Gladstone and the English Liberals. According to

plotting against the government of Gladstone from the very beginning, and the brusque tone used by Bismarck in the Anglo-German colonial controversies, 1884-85, laid him open to charges of employing the methods of blackmail.

Austria-Hungary had become the ally of Germany before the advent of the Liberals to power in 1880. In earlier days Gladstone had shared the views of Palmerston with reference to the dual monarchy and publicly expressed the hope that Austria would always remain one of the great powers of Europe.[13] Discussing the problems of Austria in *The Edinburgh Review*, October, 1870, Gladstone said that the break-up of Austria-Hungary would be good neither for Europe, nor for the Eastern question, nor for the people of the dual monarchy. The best solution of its problems, as he saw them, would be a federal arrangement. But the Austrian occupation of Bosnia and Herzegovina angered Gladstone; it ran counter to his views of what constituted a sound policy for Austria-Hungary in the Balkans; and in a speech at the Music Hall, Edinburgh, March 17, 1880, Gladstone rashly asserted: "There is not an instance, there is not a spot upon the whole map, where you can lay your finger and say, 'There Austria did good.' "

this report Bismarck feared and distrusted Gladstone as one who encouraged the growth of Socialistic ideas. *Ibid.*

[13] House of commons, July 20, 1866. *Hansard*, 3rd series, CLXXXIV, 1252.

These words came home to roost after he had become
prime minister, and he was compelled to apologize for
them, in return for which he received what then seemed
satisfactory but have since proved to be prevaricating
assurances from the government of Austria-Hungary
concerning its plans for Bosnia and Herzegovina.[14] Although this supposedly closed the incident, it left scars;
and the English government continued to suspect Austria-Hungary of a desire to extend its dominions to
Salonica, which in the judgment of Gladstone would
further complicate the problems of the Balkans. The
statesmen of Austria-Hungary and the Liberal leaders
in England frequently clashed over Near Eastern questions; and since Bismarck often felt compelled to support
the ally of Germany on such occasions, Anglo-Austrian
friction reacted unfavorably upon the relations between
Britain and Germany.

In the controversy over the Near Eastern policy of
Disraeli, Gladstone denied that Russia threatened the in-

[14] W. E. Gladstone, *Political Speeches in Scotland*. Revised ed.
(Edinburgh, 1880), II, 41; Fitzmaurice, *Granville*, II, 200-207. Count
Carolyi, the Austrian ambassador in London, wrote to Gladstone
May 1, 1880: "As to our position towards the Eastern affairs, I can
only express in the most positive manner that we have no desire
whatever to extend or add to the rights we have acquired under the
Treaty of Berlin." Original MS., Gladstone Papers. But in a separate
protocol to the Conventon of Berlin, June 18, 1881, it was stipulated
that "Austria reserves the right to annex these provinces [i.e.,
Bosnia and Herzegovina] at whatever moment she shall deem oppor-
tune." A. F. Pribam, *The Secret Treaties of Austria-Hungary* (Cambridge, 1920), I, 43.

terests of England,[15] and subsequently he expressed a belief that the sympathy of England should be with Russia rather than with Turkey in the war of 1877-78. Because of this, Gladstone was assumed to be a friend of Russia. It would, however, be more correct to ascribe to him an absence of Russophobia rather than positive friendship. With the Russian government and the Russian treatment of subject races he could not sympathize; nor did he favor an extension of Russian influence in the Balkans. All the powers, with the possible exception of France, must, he thought, be carefully watched in the Balkans. His program for the Turkish empire was to develop local autonomy in its provinces, to foster if possible the formation of a Balkan league, and to prevent portions of Turkey from being appropriated by any one of the great powers. As a result there could be little Anglo-Russian co-operation in the Balkans, although Russia showed herself more willing to act with Britain in compelling the Porte to fulfill the engagements agreed upon at Berlin than did the other powers.

In 1870-71 Gladstone had borne a full share of the resentment which Frenchmen entertained toward England for her failure to intervene in the war or to mitigate the peace terms imposed by Germany.[16] After that time the gratitude which some Frenchmen felt because

---

[15] "We need entertain no fear at all that the action of Russia in the present effort will endanger British interests." House of commons, May 7, 1877. *Hansard*, 3rd series, CCXXXIV, 426.

[16] Sir Thomas Barclay, *Thirty Years* (London, 1914), 37.

of the action of England when Bismarck in 1875 was alleged to have plotted to attack France gave way to irritation on account of Disraeli's purchase of the Suez Canal shares. However, in 1879 Lord Salisbury concluded an arrangement with Waddington concerning Egypt which made Britain and France partners, but it was a marriage of convenience fraught with many possibilities of disagreements, and it ended abruptly and stormily. At Berlin, Waddington had extracted certain promises from Salisbury concerning Tunis that proved inconvenient to Lord Granville. Indeed, while on the surface Egypt had brought England and France together and Gladstone was sincerely determined to maintain this *entente*, the two powers soon disagreed on the policy to be pursued in the Balkans, friction developed in Egypt, and clashes occurred over colonial issues. The protectionists in France bitterly resented the old Cobden treaty, and in the negotiations for a new Anglo-French commercial treaty they took occasion to condemn the grasping and selfish policy of England.[17] These factors aided Bismarck in keeping France busy in the colonial field and in preventing her from coming to an understanding with England; and so successful was he that English statesmen suspected, with good reason, that a definite understanding existed between Germany and France.[18] Hence, Gladstone, although a disciple of the

[17] *Ibid.*, 36, 41, 42.
[18] Lyons reported from Paris in September, 1884, that Ferry was controlled by Bismarck (Granville to Gladstone, September 20); and after the fall of Ferry in the spring of 1885, Granville wrote

Francophile Aberdeen, could not follow in the footsteps of his old master and keep together the two western powers.

Gladstone loved Italy. With perfect mastery of her language he combined acquaintance with and deep admiration for her literature and culture. He had aided in no small measure the process of her unification and he took an almost fatherly interest in her welfare. He noted with satisfaction that she acted less badly than the other powers, except Russia, in the Montenegrin boundary question, 1880, and he was more anxious than his colleagues to gratify Italian ambitions for colonies on the Red Sea; but he would not combine with Italy against France in the Tunisian affair, 1881, and he witnessed with dismay that she too was drawn into the orbit of Bismarck and ultimately opposed England in Egypt.

The forces working against a realization of the hope for international relations based on justice, humanity, and reason, which had been raised by Gladstone before his return to office in 1880, proved too strong. The concert of Europe failed completely; a system of alliances took its place; a new era of competition in overseas expansion found the government of Gladstone ill-prepared; and in the Balkans, in Egypt, and in the Sudan, it faced issues which defied solution on the basis of the principles enunciated by Gladstone.

---

to Gladstone, April 2: "Ferry is certainly no loss to us. He arrived at the Quai D'Orsay quite ignorant of Foreign Affairs, & the more he learnt of them, the more subservient he became to Bismarck and the more tricky to us." Original MS., Gladstone Papers.

Chapter V

THE British statesmen of the eighties have been attacked by some critics for their failure to seize lands, especially in Africa, and by others for pursuing a dog-in-the-manger policy. In this decade it became evident that the world at large would not adopt free trade, that Britain would increasingly feel the pressure of foreign commercial and industrial competition, that rivals were seeking to build up colonial empires, and that the *laissez-faire* policy which Britain had pursued with reference to the problems of overseas expansion must be abandoned. At home Britain had capital aplenty; she also had the men and the naval power necessary for taking and holding distant possessions. Overseas, growing British communities in South Africa and in Australasia became conscious of the danger arising from foreign neighbors, they were eager for the promulgation of Monroe doctrines for their respective spheres, and they expected the home government to act on their suggestions for acquiring adjacent territories. With the acquisitive instinct aroused, the colonists could count on powerful allies in England; and they could hold over British statesmen vague threats that a failure to heed colonial wishes might lead to a disruption of the British empire. When questions involving new annexations arose, both Conservative and Liberal governments in Britain had to steer between the Scylla of foreign hostility and the Charybdis of the ill-will of colonial and home opinion. Since the leading colonies possessed self-government, the imperial authorities had but slight control over them; and the colonial office which was intrusted with the duties of keeping them happy was co-ordinated in the government with the foreign office, which must endeavor to maintain friendly relations with foreign countries.

With the opening of the eighties all the powers, except Austria, sought to acquire colonies. France, who had earlier colonized in a desultory fashion, began in earnest to build up a great overseas empire—political expediency and supposed economic needs urged her on. Bismarck had loudly professed indifference to the question of German colonial expansion, but he had to consider political, social, and economic forces within Germany. In the *Kulturkampf* he had come out second best; and the Socialist movement had assumed such proportions by 1881 that he deemed it necessary to take the wind out of the sails of the Socialists by far-reaching social legislation. Before that time he had encouraged the growth of industry by tariff legislation; and when the commercial interests of Bremen and Hamburg, assisted by a small but aggressive element in other parts of Germany, began to clamor for overseas possessions, Bismarck sensed the drift of opinion and decided to assist in securing colonies for the German empire. Russia continued her glacier-like expansion in Asia, which seemed to move toward India. Even Italy, late to be unified and struggling in a morass of internal difficulties, joined in the race for colonies. But nearly everywhere the new colonizing powers were faced with the fact that British traders or missionaries or agents or adventurers had been earlier in the field, and that Britain could claim preemptive rights in innumerable places where she had not seized or colonized the land. It was tempting for the "have-nots" to combine to squeeze the one who had. British statesmen were therefore compelled to watch the rise and fall of opinion at home and in the colonies and to keep a weather-eye on acts and designs of rivals in every quarter of the globe. The questions of the Near East, Egypt, and the Sudan are linked with problems involving distant portions of the British empire and rivalry with nearly all of the great powers in Asia, Africa, and the South Seas.

In the Midlothian campaign, Gladstone had singled out for condemnation the annexation of the Transvaal and the acquisition of Cyprus. These acts were condemned as reprehensible, and he repudiated them.[1] Upon becoming prime minister, evidence was presented that purported to show that the Boers of the Transvaal were reconciled to being British subjects; the obligations of the imperial government to the natives in the Transvaal were emphasized; and hopes were entertained that a federation of white South Africa, favored by Gladstone, could be secured. But this hope vanished; the self-government promised to the Transvaal was delayed; the Boers rose and defeated small British forces; and the Transvaal, or South African Republic, secured its independence, subject to a few restrictions, in 1881. The forward policy pursued by the Conservative government on the Indian frontier was reversed. Britain withdrew from Afghanistan; Kandahar, which the queen ardently desired to keep, was given up; but Quetta and portions of Baluchistan, which had come under British control, 1876-79, were retained. Gladstone in 1880 considered handing Cyprus over to Greece,[2] but this proved inexpedient. The power of the Zulus had been broken in the war of 1879 and Zululand divided among thirteen petty chiefs, nominally independent, before Gladstone

[1] Morley, *Gladstone,* III, 27-28.
[2] In a letter to Granville, December 17, 1880, Gladstone discussed a proposal then under consideration to settle the Greco-Turkish boundary dispute by a transfer of the island of Crete to Greece, and said that if this took place "it seems to me not unworthy of consideration whether Cyprus might not be properly handed over by the Porte and us, in sovereignty not in mere occupation." Copy, letter books, XVIII, 226, Gladstone Papers.

returned to power in 1880; but the arrangement was unsatisfactory, and after various expedients had been tried, including that of restoring the warrior king, Cetywayo, the land of the Zulus passed under direct British control.[3]

By 1885 three or perhaps four factors strongly affected British policy in South Africa. The first was the aggressive attitude of the politicians in the Cape Colony who demanded that the coast of South Africa from the southern boundary of Portuguese West Africa to the southern boundary of Portuguese East Africa should come under the British flag. The second factor was the activities of the South African Republic, whose qualified independence as established by the Pretoria convention of 1881 was somewhat extended by the London convention of 1884. The Transvaal Boers longed for an outlet to the sea, but the Gladstone government followed the traditional British policy of thwarting such efforts by seizing land to the west and to the east of the Boer republics. German activities on the sub-continent of Africa reawakened the old British fear of a combination between the Boer states and some European power and greatly stimulated British interest in that region. A fourth factor destined to shape the attitude of Britain toward South Africa was Cecil Rhodes. This able and forceful man was a host in himself; he had been

[3] R. I. Lovell, *The Struggle for South Africa* (New York, 1934), 107-113.

busy dreaming dreams and formulating plans for British expansion in South Africa for several years before the advent of Gladstone to power in 1880; and the influence of Rhodes grew mightily with each succeeding year.[4]

Gladstone viewed British expansion in South Africa in the light that he had viewed imperial expansion for upwards of thirty years. He decried the widening of frontiers, he wished Britain to have no unwilling subjects, and he was willing to admit other European powers to the African fields of colonization. The uprising in the Transvaal in 1880-81 showed that the Transvaal farmers were not reconciled to the rule of Britain and wished to regain their independence. They defeated small British forces, the most impressive of these victories being that at Majuba Hill, February 27, 1881. Considering the numbers involved, this battle was a mere skirmish, and shortly afterwards Britain had ample military forces in South Africa to overwhelm the rebellious farmers. In Britain a clamor arose for avenging Majuba, but Gladstone and his colleagues had decided to restore the South African Republic—to them Britain's power seemed so obvious that there was no need for demonstrating it by shedding more blood. They gave the Transvaal Boers what they wanted, whereupon the opposition denounced this just act as a weak surrender. In December, 1884, the press and a considerable body

[4] *Ibid.*, 36-126.

of opinion in England and the politicians at the Cape were aroused by German colonizing activities in South Africa. Even the colonial secretary, Lord Derby, felt apprehensive and suggested in letters to Gladstone and Granville that Britain should annex the coast between the Cape Colony and Natal, and from Natal to the southern boundary of Portuguese East Africa so that there would be no gap "in which to plant a German colony."[5] Gladstone asked for and obtained an excellent map of South Africa, studied it closely and wrote to Derby:

"I heartily concur in the expediency of filling up the gap in the coast line to Natal. When this is done we shall, I understand it, have all the coast line of the territory for which we are virtually or directly responsible. Why should we go further?

"Is there any reason to suppose the Germans contemplate any assumption on the East coast of Africa?

"Is it dignified, or is it required by any real interest, to make extensions of British authority without any view of occupying but simply to keep them out? Is it not open to a strong positive objection in regard to the coast now in question between St. Lucia Bay and Delagoa Bay? Namely that it tends powerfully to entail a responsibility for the country lying inland, which we

[5] Derby to Granville, December 28, 1884. Original MS., Granville Papers. Derby to Gladstone, December 27, 1884. Original MS., Gladstone Papers.

think it impolitic to assume and which in the case of Zululand we have publicly and expressly renounced?"[6]

Writing to Granville, Gladstone said:

"I think Derby is quite right in wishing to have a continuous line of coast in South Africa: but as to extending the terminus northwards, and (I presume) assuming the responsibility for Zululand outside the reserve, which we have steadily disclaimed, I see great objection to it, and generally, considering what we have got, I am against entering into a scramble for the remainder."[7]

At this time Britain was also involved in controversies with France concerning Madagascar. The imperialistic section of the government wished that Britain should display her strength by using naval vessels to carry mail between Natal and Madagascar and Mauritius. This did not please Gladstone. "The [postal] contract," he wrote to Childers, December 31, 1884, "as it appears to me is not postal but political & has mainly to do with Naval Service on the Coast of Madagascar.

"Whether some such service ought to be performed by the Navy I will not undertake to say; but it is not I think a legitimate use of public revenue to establish services called Postal where there is nothing (in substance not in name) to carry; the practice is unjust to

[6] Gladstone to Derby, December 30, 1884. Copy, MS., Gladstone Papers.

[7] Gladstone to Granville, December 28, 1884, No. 1. Copy, letter books, XXI, 311, *ibid.*

our Postal System & tends to relax and disorganize the administration of a great revenue, and has also a tendency to hoodwink Parliament."[8]

European interest in Western Africa, strong in the heyday of the slave trade, had languished during the greater part of the nineteenth century; but in the seventies and eighties it flared anew. An opportunity for establishing a protectorate over the Cameroons presented itself in 1881-82, but the colonial secretary, Lord Kimberley, objected on the ground that Britain had enough land. Earlier he had protested against letting Portugal extend "her dead hand over the great Congo Waterway";[9] however, the Anglo-Portuguese treaty of 1884, ultimately scrapped, contemplated some such extension, which aroused much opposition in England as well as in France and Germany.[10] The British government failed to act aggressively in Western Africa, France extended her influence, and Germany obtained portions of the Cameroons and of Togoland. Ultimately a private British company sought to repair the mistakes

[8] Copy, *ibid.*, 313.

[9] Kimberley to Granville, June 8, 1880. Original MS., Granville Papers.

[10] Langer, 300. Later in the year Granville proposed that Britain should renew her effort to gain German consent to an extension of Portuguese territory to the south bank of the Congo if Portugal would promise to make commercial concessions in Mozambique and Angola and agree "not to cede Delagoa Bay to any Power without assent of Britain." Gladstone objected to the proposal, which was, apparently, dropped. Draft telegram, Granville to Petre, at Lisbon, December, 1884, and Gladstone's observations thereon dated December 31, 1884. Granville Papers.

of the government by securing concessions from the native rulers of the Niger basin.[11]

Meanwhile, East African questions loomed on the horizon. Here, as elsewhere, the English had been active in the early part of the nineteenth century, the efforts to uproot the slave trade had caused them to patrol the coast, and a flourishing trade had grown up between Zanzibar and India. In 1823 the port of Mombasa was ceded to Britain, but it was later handed over to the sultan of Zanzibar, whose territories were guaranteed by an Anglo-French treaty of 1862. The authority of this ruler extended, however, only to the island of Zanzibar and a narrow strip of coast on the mainland. The highlands of East Africa were under several petty native chiefs. On August 26, 1881, the sultan of Zanzibar asked the British government to be the guardian for his son and delegated to it the power of selecting the regent during the minority of the son; but the offer was declined because it might infringe upon the Anglo-French treaty of 1862. By this time East Africa and especially the Kilimanjaro district had attracted travelers and explorers. A German, Dr. Fischer, a Frenchman, M. Revoil, and an Englishman, Mr. Joseph Thomson, explored and reported on the peoples, climate, soil, and natural resources of the region. In March, 1884, Harry (later Sir Harry) Johnston set out on a scientific expedition to Kilimanjaro; on his departure, Lord Edmond Fitzmau-

[11] The Royal Niger Company.

rice, parliamentary under-secretary in the foreign office, asked Johnston to send home his impressions of the countries he visited. Complying with this request, Johnston wrote a lengthy letter to Lord Edmond from Chagga, Kilimanjaro, dated July 10, 1884. This letter contains a very favorable account of the country. "Here is a land," Johnston wrote, "eminently suited for European colonization, situated near midway between the equatorial lakes and the coast. Within a few years it must be either English, French or German." He reported that the powerful chief of Chagga, Mandara, was very anxious for British protection, and with some chosen English colonists and the expenditure of not exceeding £5000 Johnston would "make Kilimanjaro as completely English as Ceylon."[12] This letter set the ball rolling. Memoranda on Kilimanjaro, the East African highlands, and Zanzibar were prepared by Clement Hill of the foreign office and Consul Holmwood, who strongly favored the extension of British influence in that region.

On the receipt of the letter from Johnston, Lord Granville instructed the British consul at Zanzibar, Sir John Kirk, to discuss the Kilimanjaro scheme with Johnston, and authorized Kirk to use his "discretion as to the action that might be necessary if, in the meantime, there should appear to be any danger of an attempt on the part of another power to forestall us." The telegram

[12] Printed for the foreign office, January 7, 1885, Granville Papers.

was supplemented by a confidential dispatch from Granville to Kirk, dated October 9, 1884; and on November 27, 1884, Granville telegraphed to Kirk: "Endeavor to obtain from Sultan [of Zanzibar] a spontaneous declaration that he will accept no protectorate from and will cede no sovereign rights or territory to any association or power without consent of England."[13]

Granville, Derby, Kimberley, Dilke, and Chamberlain agreed that the sultan of Zanzibar should be encouraged and aided by England in extending his rule inland to Kilimanjaro, thereby keeping the territory out of the hands of foreign powers and insuring to Britain "a paramount influence and free commercial access." This policy was embodied and explained in a confidential dispatch from Granville to Kirk, dated December 5, 1884.[14] But when the draft of this dispatch came to the attention of Gladstone he wrote "a few wild words" and asked for further information "presuming there must be some strong reasons known to you [i.e., Granville], Derby and Kimberley in favour of the plan; but I did not gather from the papers what they were.

"It seems," he continued, "that wherever there is a dark corner in South African politics there is a German spectre to be tenant of it."[15]

[13] *Ibid.*
[14] *Ibid.*
[15] Gladstone to Granville, December 9, 1884. Copy, letter books, XXI, 291, Gladstone Papers.

In response to a request by Gladstone, Clement Hill prepared a new memorandum in which he traced the origins of the dispatch of which Gladstone complained. Hill further explained that the plan suggested in the dispatch meant the extension of the sultan's authority without fighting; the expense would be slight; other powers would be kept out; and the responsibilities of Britain would not be greatly increased. "There is," wrote Hill, "a very large commercial connection between it [i.e., the east coast of Africa] and India; the local trade is almost entirely in the hands of Indian subjects; we cannot refuse to protect them, and we are pledged irrevocably to the extinction of the slave trade. How, then, will our responsibility be materially increased by the addition of the healthiest, and, perhaps, the most valuable portion of East Africa to the dominions of Zanzibar? If that power should fall to pieces, who must be its successor? Could we admit another occupation like that of Madagascar on our alternative route to India? Is it not better to forestall others by encouraging this very moderate, but most precious extension of territory of the power whose natural, though it may be reluctant, heirs we may hereafter become?"[16]

A new memorandum by Consul Holmwood was enclosed with other papers with Hill's memorandum; and

[16] Memorandum explaining No. 86, Confidential, to Sir J. Kirk, dated December 9, 1884. Papers printed for the foreign office, January 7, 1885. Granville Papers.

Kirk was informed that Britain would now accept the offer of regency during the son's minority which the sultan had made in 1881, if this offer were renewed.[17]

Gladstone's opinion of the policy concocted for East Africa is contained in letters to Granville and Dilke. To the former he wrote, December 12, 1884: "The Kilimanjaro [sic] papers, so far as I can make out their purport, leave me I must confess wholly unsatisfied. . . . The tone of the memorandum prepared by F. O. people or others disquiets me, and in places savours much of annexationism. As for instance when it is laid down that we are to seek 'compensation' on the East Coast of Africa for concurring in measures *equal for all* on the West Coast. Either I am very blind, or you and the other ministers concurring in the Draft despatch must have reasons in your mind outside what are there presented.

"My first sense of want [of] proof of the necessity of doing anything. My second as to the thing to be done. I remember nothing of the telegram stated to have laid it down that we ought on no account to be forestalled by other powers in this Kilimanjaroan district. But I should have thought that the proper direction to work in, if we work at all, was to procure if possible the application on the East Coast of the principles which it is now attempted to apply to the West."[18]

[17] *Ibid.*
[18] Copy, letter books, XXI, 292, Gladstone Papers.

Two days later Gladstone wrote to Dilke: "Terribly have I been puzzled and perplexed on finding a group of the soberest men among us to have concocted a scheme such as that touching the mountain country behind Zanzibar with an unrememberable name. There *must* somewhere or other be reasons for it, which have not come before me. I have asked Granville whether it may not stand over for a while."[19] And over it stood, partly it appears because Kirk had doubts about the soundness of the colonial venture suggested by Johnston and partly because the activities and designs of the Germans were not yet fully known or apprehended.

The demand for a Monroe doctrine for Australasia synchronizes with the development of self-government in the English colonies of the Antipodes. Even in the fifties Australasians were alarmed by the activities of the French in the South Pacific, and in the seventies they insisted on British annexation of Fiji, Samoa, New Guinea, and other islands or group of islands south of the equator.[20] Ultimately Fiji was added to the British possessions, but even the government of Disraeli showed reluctance to gratify the excessive requests for annexations.[21] In the middle of the nineteenth century fear that foreign powers might establish penal colonies in

[19] *Ibid.*, 294-295.
[20] *The Cambridge History of the British Empire*, VII, part 1, 354-360.
[21] Sylvia Masterman, *The Origins of International Rivalry in Samoa* (London, 1934), 101-102.

the South Seas had been a predominant reason for the attempts to keep them away. To this fear was added apprehension for the political security of the colonies. But by the seventies the colonists, especially the sugar planters of Queensland, were suspected of agitating for the acquisition of South Sea islands in order to facilitate the recruitment of native laborers. The imperial government had resisted the Australasian demand for annexations on the grounds that they were unnecessary for the security of the colonies and would add materially to the cost of governing and protecting the empire. However, at the beginning of the eighties the Australasian colonies professed themselves willing to shoulder the burden of the cost of governing the new acquisitions; but by this time English humanitarians, led by the Aborigines Protection Society, had begun to regard the Australian colonists, especially those of northern Queensland, with a suspicion hitherto largely reserved for the Boers of South Africa. Ugly stories of kidnapping of Kanakas had put the Australians in a bad light.[22] Since New Guinea was the largest and most populous of the islands which the Australians wanted Britain to annex, it became the center of the strife between annexationists and anti-annexationists.

Western New Guinea had been occupied or claimed by Holland for a long time; but until the eighties the

---

[22] *British Parliamentary Papers* (hereafter cited as *P. P.*), *1883,* XLVII, c.-3641 and c.-3814.

greater part of the island was regarded by Europeans as a no-man's land, the political rights of the inhabitants being here, as elsewhere, completely disregarded. Traders in the service of the East India Company had claimed New Guinea for England in the eighteenth century, and Lieutenant Yule of the royal navy had apparently reasserted this claim in 1846; however, New Guinea did not become a real issue in British imperial politics until 1873 when Captain Moresby hoisted the Union Jack in the eastern part of the island. This act was disavowed by the imperial authorities, but from then on the Australians did not allow the question of New Guinea to lie dormant for any length of time. Demands for annexation, accounts of the natural resources of the island and other factors that made its possession desirable, reports by British and Australian officials, resolutions by Australian legislatures, and remonstrances by humanitarians found their way in a steadily increasing stream to the colonial office. Rumors of German and projected German activities in or near the islands of the Pacific stimulated the zeal of the annexationists who were greatly irritated by the home government's reluctance to act.[23] Finally, on April 4, 1883, Queensland took possession in the name of the queen of the part of New Guinea and the adjoining islands between 141° and 155° east longitude, and the colonial office was informed that this was done in order to prevent the island from being seized by a for-

[23] P. P., *1884*, LV, c.-3863.

eign power. Although Queensland received support
from her sister colonies in Australasia, her act created
consternation at home. Apart from the foreign complications which it might precipitate, the imperial government had to take cognizance of the new power assumed
by Queensland. Clearly, if the self-governing colonies
could annex lands without previous authorization from
home, the imperial government might often be placed
in an awkward position and perhaps become involved
in wars as a result of their acts and policies. The question had many implications and ramifications; but we
are here concerned primarily with the attitude of Gladstone toward it.

On February 13, 1883, Lord Derby wrote to Gladstone: "The New Guinea question, or rather the question which began with New Guinea, and has now developed into a claim to the possession of (virtually) all
the South Pacific islands within a thousand miles of Australia, is likely to give much trouble. I hear that the
whole colony—or rather the whole body of these colonies—is of one mind: that they cannot understand or
conceive why what they wish should not be done without a moment's delay: and that they will express their
opinions in such a manner as to make an answer necessary.

"How much of this is real; how much mere swagger
and bonnie, of which there is always plenty in a young

country: how much is the reckless bidding against each other of rival politicians: is not yet easy to discover.

"But I do not think we can long resist doing something more than we have done as to New Guinea.

"I cannot altogether avoid the suspicion that there is a wish on the part of Australian politicians to pick a quarrel—or at least to assert their independence of the mother country—else why, when they thought they had got what they wanted about New Guinea, did they immediately set up a new demand, with which they must have known that we could not comply?"[24]

The prime minister also discussed the question of New Guinea with Sir Arthur Gordon, lately high commissioner for the Western Pacific and governor of Fiji and of New Zealand, who was in England in 1883. Sir Arthur, the third son of Gladstone's old friend and former chief, the earl of Aberdeen, was a close personal friend of Gladstone; they held identical views on many issues and especially on that of native policy. On the subject of New Guinea, Sir Arthur Gordon had a good claim to be considered an authority, and on this account as well as by reason of their private relationship his judgment was apt to have great influence on Gladstone. Writing to Gladstone April 20, 1883, Gordon expressed a "most earnest hope that you will not be induced, without very careful consideration, to consent to the suggested appropriation of New Guinea by the Colony of

[24] Original MS., Gladstone Papers.

Queensland." He opposed the extension of British sovereignty to New Guinea, and he was particularly hostile to letting the island become a part of Queensland. Britain had, he felt, enough dark-skinned subjects; the seizure of New Guinea might prevent Britain from protesting effectively against the proceedings of the French, and the people of New Guinea had not expressed a desire to become British subjects. Gordon stated emphatically that in his opinion Queensland was not fit to govern such a large and populous dependency as New Guinea. The colonial oligarchy treated the Australian blackfellows as vermin, a similar treatment would no doubt be accorded the natives in New Guinea who might be subjected to forced labor and ill-used in other ways; and, being warlike, uprisings would surely follow. The annexation by Queensland would increase the cost of imperial administration and impose new obligations on the imperial government. As a secondary but yet important consideration in viewing the problem at hand Gordon pointed to "the grave impropriety of allowing a colonial government to force the hand of the imperial government with regard to a matter of imperial policy."[25]

Among the material touching on the issue of New Guinea which reached Gladstone in the spring of 1883 is found the copy of a letter which T. B. Potter, M. P., wrote to Derby, May 18, 1883. On the strength of in-

[25] Original MS., *ibid.*

formation which Potter had received from his son who had been in the South Pacific, he urged the annexation of New Guinea but *not* to Queensland. He deemed it necessary to forestall possible action by the French, and he believed that the Australian federation which he saw coming would insist upon keeping the South Pacific out of the hands of foreign powers. If Britain now seized the opportunity to annex the island, future difficulties might be avoided.[26]

Gladstone's own opinion was expressed in a letter to Derby of May 19, 1883. With the cabinet in mind, he wrote: "We shall, I suppose, soon have the New Guinea case regularly before us. I hope we may find ourselves in a condition utterly to quash this annexation effected by Queensland on her sole authority, for I suppose her to be untrustworthy as well as unauthorized. If the Australian colonies would combine into some kind of political union, we should at all events have much better means of approaching the question. They would present to us some substantial responsibility for whatever they might undertake. I am sorry to find, only a recent discovery with us, that we have already made annexations of some of the circumadjacent islands."[27]

The annexation of New Guinea by Queensland was promptly quashed, but this did not settle the issue. The Australian colonies continued to urge that New Guinea

[26] *Ibid.*
[27] Copy, letter books, XX, 232, *ibid.*

should be annexed by them or by Britain; and the attempt at organizing a federal council for Australia promised to bring the colonies into some form of political union. In the autumn of 1883, Edward Hamilton, Gladstone's private secretary, sent material concerning New Guinea to Sir Arthur Gordon and suggested that Gordon might write to Gladstone on the subject. He complied in a long letter, dated October 8, 1883. Herein Gordon expressed doubt as to whether the Australian demand for New Guinea reflected "the genuine feeling of the working and thinking part of the community." In so far as the desire to acquire the island was genuine, it was, he thought, due to a real but unreasonable fear that a foreign power might seize and establish a penal station in New Guinea "and to a strong *jingo* feeling, in which a vague sentiment that it is a fine thing to extend Australian dominion is combined with great ignorance of actual facts." He believed, however, that the real promoters of the scheme for annexing New Guinea were the sugar growers of Queensland and merchants engaged in the island trade. "These," he wrote, "are both very powerful interests, which every colonial politician will seek to conciliate and propitiate, if he can do so without offense to other sections of the community." Gordon asserted that the objections raised to the separate action by Queensland would not be removed in case a federated Australia secured New Guinea. The interests he had mentioned would still be powerful in politics and the natives would have no influence and receive no consideration. Furthermore, the control of New Guinea would doubtless pass into the hands of the few white men who settled there. "They may be no worse," Gordon said, "than other men, but they should not be exposed to temptations which few men could resist. The same principles which forbid our handing over the government of the millions of India to the small English community there equally forbid our delivering over the millions of the Pacific to a handful of men whose interests are too often strongly antagonistic to those of the people over whom they would exercise absolute control." The situation in Fiji offered an instructive analogy to what would probably happen in New Guinea if annexed by Australia. The white settlers in Fiji openly urged a union with New Zealand for the reason "that native interests would in that event not be considered as they now are." Both the whites in Fiji and the politicians of New Zealand who wished to secure Fiji considered only the interests of the European, to the disregard of those of the native ninety-eight per cent of the population. On the other hand, Gordon pointed out that Australia's trade with the islands in the South Pacific had increased greatly during the last twenty years; that Europeans had obtained much land in these islands; and that white settlements had been founded. He was strongly opposed to annexation; nevertheless, "I am bound to admit that some more efficient steps than have yet been taken for the control of British subjects in the Pacific and also for their protection, appear to be inevitable." He believed, however, that for the present the machinery provided for the high commissioner for the Western Pacific would suffice for New Guinea.[28]

In a long letter to Gladstone of December 7, 1883, Lord Derby referred to resolutions passed by the Australian intercolonial conference, and proceeded: "What can be said in favor of the Monroe Doctrine laid down for the whole South Pacific? A distance of more than 5,000 miles. Australia cannot be secure if any other power is allowed to establish itself between the Australian coast and South America! This is mere raving, and one can scarcely suppose it to be seriously intended, though it is hard to fix the limits of colonial self-esteem.

"So again the proposal that France shall be asked to cede or sell New Caledonia (for that is what it comes to) shows either an amount of ignorance or of assurance which it is not easy to understand.

"The notion that other powers or other nationalities may have rights which an Australian is bound to respect does not seem to have entered the colonial mind."

Derby saw as an essential difference between the Australian claims and the American Monroe Doctrine the fact that the Americans were ready "to fight for their pretensions: the colonists expect us to do the fighting for them." He was inclined to suspect that the leaders

[28] Original MS., Gladstone Papers.

at the Australian conference desired to pick a quarrel with the mother country "by asking our sanction to demands which it is impossible that we should endorse." But despite Derby's strong feeling on the subject of the Australian claims, he had come "to the conclusion that as regards New Guinea we cannot hold out against the demand for a protectorate. I do not contemplate more than a claim formally put forward to the coast of the island so far as it is not in the hands of the Dutch; this would be enough to put an end to the fear (real or affected) of occupation by any foreign power; and the High Commissioner's court, extended and strengthened, would do the rest so far as is necessary at present."

Derby saw no danger of foreign interference, but Britain could not allow a foreign power to seize part of New Guinea: "The Australians would threaten secession if we did, and everybody would be against us. We do not therefore really add to our responsibilities by formally recognizing what is the actual state of the matter. There will be trouble enough later, for it has scarcely dawned on the colonial mind that the natives will desire to keep their lands, and that we shall support them in their rights; but that is not a question for the moment."[29]

Gladstone replied: "With the whole of the condemnatory part of your letter on the Resolutions of the Australian Convention, I need hardly say that I am in abso-

[29] Original MS., *ibid.*

lute sympathy. This is a little qualified when I come
to the affirmative, and to the New Guinea protectorate.

"Is it usual to constitute such a relation without either
the concurrence of the protected state or people or else
the intervention, as in the case of the Ionian Islands, of
a higher authority? This is by the bye.

"I feel many scruples about this protectorate, but I
should pay due deference to your opinion and generally
to those who have a longer lease of politics before them
than I have.

"Apart, however, from the broader considerations, I
should rather doubt the policy of raising the question
of a protectorate in New Guinea as part of an answer
to the preposterous proposals of the Convention. They
have supplied the best possible ground for a negative
answer, and may it not be argued that it would be best
to leave them to raise if they think proper the un-
answered question, treating their scheme for the present
as one.

"Were we to suggest a protectorate as an alternative
they would begin to hook on more to it, and our position would be a false one. So at least it appears to me
at first sight."[30]

Reports from the British ambassador at Berlin in 1883
were so reassuring concerning the attitude of the German government toward the various German colonization projects that Granville informed the colonial office

[30] Copy, letter books, XXI, 18, *ibid.*

in May that he was certain no foreign government had designs on New Guinea.[31] Lord Ampthill had, however, neglected to obtain definite statements from Bismarck himself, and in the following year New Guinea caused the British government much worry. The German chancellor pushed with great energy the German demands for colonies, and before the year was over he hinted broadly that a portion of New Guinea would be part of the price for his support of the British financial proposals concerning Egypt.

Meanwhile, the question of what to do with New Guinea had been earnestly discussed by the cabinet. A majority seems to have agreed with the view expressed by Sir Arthur Gordon in his letter to Gladstone of October 8, 1883, that steps should be taken; but the nature of them gave rise to lengthy debates. After a cabinet meeting on July 5, 1884, Gladstone noted: "New Guinea—Much discussion and scruples of Chancellor, Harcourt, W. E. G. Subject postponed."[32] Derby and, apparently, Childers, whose former residence in Australia had given him an insight into the temperament of the Australian colonists, favored action. When Derby

[31] Special weight was attached to an assurance given by Count Hatzfeldt in April, 1883; and on April 8, 1884, Ampthill reported that a new colonization society had been formed in Berlin, but that there was no reason to suppose that the government of Germany was inclined to support this organization. Public Record Office, F. O. 64:1144. This volume contains a mass of valuable manuscript material; much of it is, however, in print.

[32] Notes taken at the meetings of the cabinet, original MS., Gladstone Papers.

introduced the subject of New Guinea at a meeting of the cabinet, August 6, 1884, a prolonged discussion took place as to whether it should be annexation or protectorate. The chancellor, Lord Selborne, urged the latter course, with definite recognition of the native titles to the land. This was agreed to on the basis of memoranda prepared by Sir Robert Herbert of the colonial office. Native rights should be recognized and respected and the "Native chiefs communicated with where practicable."[33] Two days later Count Münster, the German ambassador in London, informed Lord Granville that the German government had decided to protect German trading interests in the South Seas and that Germany had fixed her attention on the north coast of New Guinea as a field for colonization. Granville replied evasively that England entertained no jealousy of German colonization, that New Guinea had been a subject for communications between the home and the colonial governments, but that no final action had been taken.[34] On the following day Northbrook reported to the cabinet on Münster's conference with Granville, and it was proposed to limit the British protectorate to the southern coast of New Guinea, "with wide meaning of the phrase." The north coast was to be left alone. The colonial office was to make careful inquiries concerning

[33] *Ibid.*; see also Derby to Queen Victoria, August 6, 1884. *Letters of Queen Victoria*, 2nd series, III, 524-525.
[34] Granville to Ampthill, August 9, 1884. Public Record Office MS., F. O. 64:1144.

boundaries and "Terms of commnct. to Münster arranged."[35] Thus the subject of New Guinea had entered the field of high politics, with results that will be discussed later; at present we shall confine our discussion to some of the matters that came directly to the attention of Gladstone and his attitude toward them.

On September 1, 1884, Granville reported to Gladstone that he, Northbrook, and Lyons were "strongly of opinion that the colonial office should not immediately issue a proclamation as to the British limits of New Guinea without further communication with Germany unless we are prepared to quarrel with Bismarck,"[36] and later Granville wrote that Derby had agreed to delay the proclamation of the protectorate; that Germany had complained that the extension of the British protectorate to the northeast coast of New Guinea "comes unexpectedly"; that it had been suggested to leave the delimitation of areas in the hands of a commission; and that "The colonial office and Childers are very strong that we must not irritate the Australians in

[35] "Sat. Aug. 9. 84. 4 P. M. at H. of C. . . . 2. New Guinea. Proposal to limit Protectorate to the S. Coast of N. Guinea with wide meaning of the phrase: Leave N. Coast alone. From Dutch line on the W. including S. E. Peninsula (Munster's Commct. with Granville reported by Northbrook). C. O. to inquire boundary carefully. Terms of commnct to Münster arranged." Cabinet notes, original MS., Gladstone Papers.

[36] Original MS., Gladstone Papers. In a letter of August 29 from the colonial office to the foreign office, it had been strongly urged that Britain should proclaim a protectorate over the greater part of New Guinea. Public Record Office MS., F. O. 64:1144.

this matter and the matter does not brook delay."[37] On
October 4 Granville complained of the slowness of the
colonial office and on October 6 the cabinet decided
"that the declaration of a protectorate extending along
the whole of the southern coast including the islands
contiguous to it shall be made forthwith.

"This is to be done without prejudice to any territorial question beyond this limit. This decision to be
communicated to the German government simultaneously with its execution."[38]

When Bismarck in conversations with Robert Meade
explained that Germany could and would make good
her claims to a part of New Guinea and to adjacent
islands, Derby was much disturbed. "I fear," he wrote
to Gladstone, December 23, 1884, "they [the Aus-
tralians] will have many sympathisers at home. I should
not be surprised at very violent resolutions being passed.
But I think our case is clear. We could not have kept
out the Germans, nor had we any right to do it."[39]

Gladstone was reluctant to extend British rule to
New Guinea and was never in favor of a dog-in-the-
manger attitude toward Germany. "I did not antici-
pate," he said December 31, 1884, "any good from
Meade's interview and as far as I can judge from the
Memn. it has not wrought good. My recollection of our

---

[37] Granville to Gladstone, September 30, 1884. Fitzmaurice, *Gran-ville*, II, 371-372.
[38] Memorandum by Lord Derby, copy, Granville Papers.
[39] Original MS., Gladstone Papers.

proceeding about New Guinea was that we took a part of the coast into protection, without prejudice to any question touching the remaining (unoccupied) part. If this be so—but Meade ought to know better than I— it was without prejudice for the Germans as for us."[40] Granville in reply to another letter from Gladstone, February 1, 1885, wrote: "I quite agree that we should be easy with Bismarck about New Guinea, and that we should avoid the word concession or the appearance of being bullied. But these objects are not easy to combine."[41]

In January, 1885, the question of the Dutch portion of New Guinea was brought unexpectedly before the government by a telegram from Sir H. B. Loch, the governor of Victoria, in which he suggested that Britain should buy the Dutch part of the island. He would secretly ascertain whether the Australian colonies were willing to make contributions for this purpose. Among

[40] Copy, letter books, XXI, 314, Gladstone Papers.

[41] Original MS., *ibid.* On January 29, 1885, Gladstone had written to Granville: "I for my part, and I think you, do not mean to be bullied by them [i.e., the foreign powers], but I am not so sure that all our colleagues are altogether likeminded. I see my way clearly to this that German colonisation will strengthen our hold upon our colonies: and will make it very difficult for them to maintain the domineering tone to which their public organs are so much inclined.

"I suppose B[ismarck] ought to learn from us that whatever be his understandings elsewhere & his present intention towards us, we shall endeavour in every question to be guided by permanent & not fugitive considerations & to treat every German claim which may concern us in an equitable spirit." Copy, letter books, XXI, 340-341, *ibid.*

the benefits which Loch expected from such a purchase
was that it would neutralize the hostile feeling engen-
dered in Australia by the German occupation of New
Guinea. Derby doubted that the Dutch would sell their
portion of New Guinea and he also feared that in case
they would, Germany would demand a share.[42] However, he passed the suggestion on to Gladstone, where
it met with stern opposition. In a long letter to Granville of January 13, 1885, Gladstone analyzed the proposal made by Loch: there was, he thought, no real support behind it; an offer to Holland would be disparaging
to that country inasmuch as Britain could never consider making such an overture to a first-class power;
and to open negotiations with the Dutch would further
complicate the current negotiations with Germany. A
copy of this letter was sent to Derby, and Gladstone
suggested in a second letter to Granville that in fairness
to Derby "the letter should go to the queen who I think
ascribed to him all recalcitration."[43] Derby, writing to
Gladstone, January 15, wanted to make it clear and, ap-

[42] Loch's telegram was received at the colonial office at 2 p. m. on
January 7. It was forwarded to Gladstone three days later. MSS.,
Granville Papers.

[43] Copy, letter books, XXI, 321-324, Gladstone Papers. In a second
letter of January 13, Gladstone said: "Exercise your discretion as to
sending this to H[er] M[ajesty]. It is outspoken. . . . Is then Loch
a Jingo? I can hardly suppose Jingoism to flow into him from Lytton
through those two most pleasing sisters. . . . I am afraid you are at
present bearing the unpopularity in certain quarters of all our re-
calcitrancy, while my iniquities in that respect are greater still than
yours." *Ibid.,* 324.

parently, known that he alone was not responsible for what had been done or left undone in colonial matters. He was not averse to sounding the Dutch about New Guinea and at least obtaining assurances that if they sold, Britain should have the opportunity to buy. To allow Dutch New Guinea to pass into German hands would enrage the Australians and probably create demand for separation.[44]

Due in part to the reluctance shown by the government to extend the British sphere of influence overseas, capitalists and others interested in colonial expansion and in the exploitation of tropical lands began to organize chartered companies not unlike those that existed in the early days of European colonization. Ultimately chartered companies were at work seeking concessions from native chiefs, obtaining leases of land, developing trade, and searching for minerals in Africa, east, west, and south, and in Borneo. The organization of the most famous of these companies, the British South Africa Company, founded by Cecil Rhodes, took place after the Liberals had lost power; the other three were either organized or in a state of being organized before June, 1885. But only the North Borneo Company seriously disturbed the peace of mind of members of the government and of the house of commons. The proposed regulations for the company were circulated within the cabinet in October, 1880; Bright, Chamberlain, Childers,

[44] Original MS., Gladstone Papers.

and Harcourt viewed the company with misgivings; Kimberley and Selborne favored it as a means for forestalling action by other powers; but Forster, Gladstone, Hartington, and Northbrook did not object. Although Gladstone later felt qualms about the company,[45] he defended it in the house of commons in March, 1882. Gladstone admitted that in his judgment Britain's imperial responsibilities were "sufficient to exhaust the ambition or strength of any minister or of any parliament," yet he deemed it futile to attempt to check rigorously "that tendency—that, perhaps, irrepressible tendency—of British enterprize to carry our commerce and the range and area of our settlements beyond the limits of our sovereignty in those countries where civilization does not exist."[46]

It was the misfortune of the second Gladstone government that as a result of this expansionistic tendency Britain became involved in disputes with all the powers which had the same inclination. As the power with the widest ramification of interests and possessions on all continents, Britain faced controversies relating to distant lands and out-of-the-way places with the United States,

[45] Written opinions on the North Borneo Chartered Co. are found among the Granville Papers. Granville wrote to Gladstone about it on December 16, 1881, and January 15, 1882; original MSS., Gladstone Papers. On January 20, 1882, Gladstone told Granville that he could not remember the previous action of the cabinet on the charter of this company and that he feared that it might involve the government in serious responsibilities.

[46] *Hansard*, 3rd series, CCLXVII, 1190-1191.

with Russia, with Italy, with France, and especially with
Germany; and these controversies interlocked in many
ways. Thus, when James G. Blaine, the American secretary of state, in 1881 raised the question of a possible re-
vision of the Clayton-Bulwer Treaty which recognized
the equality of interest of Britain and the United States in
a possible trans-isthmian canal at Panama, Canada claimed
to be heard; actions concerning the Suez Canal were
cited as supplying precedent; Britain sought to act as the
guardian of the interests of the European powers; and
the Panama question influenced Gladstone's views on
that of the Suez Canal. The prime minister of Canada,
Sir John A. Macdonald, scathingly denounced Blaine
and the government of the United States, and suggested
that Lord Granville should give a hint to the government of the United States "that England as a commercial country, and Canada as no inconsiderable portion
of the American Continent had interests in the [trans-
isthmian] canal equal to those of the United States."[47]
Gladstone felt that the claims put forward by Blaine
were extravagant, "and they would not have a shadow
of excuse but for the proceedings of the late government as to the Suez Canal."[48] He was happy to find, in

[47] Macdonald to Lord Lorne, governor-general of Canada, April 28,
1881. Copy, Granville Papers.

[48] Gladstone to Granville, December 23, 1881. In concluding this
letter Gladstone wrote: "For my own part I incline to hope that
we shall endeavour to act as the representatives not merely of
British interest but of all Europe in this important matter." Copy,
letter books, XIX, 152, Gladstone Papers. Granville in reply com-

January, 1882, that Gambetta agreed with the British ideas concerning Panama. "Our safety," Gladstone wrote, "will be in acting as charged with the interests of the world *minus* America." When later in the year the Suez Canal question was pressing, Gladstone counseled caution: "We should consider what precedents we may set up for the United States on the Isthmus of Panama, and possibly for Russia on the Bosphorus."[49]

The Gladstone government in 1880 inherited controversies with Russia in the regions bordering on India; the Afghan situation was uncertain; and, farther west, the old issue of the possession of Herat was apt to cause difficulties at any moment. It was decided to evacuate Kandahar and leave both this stronghold and Herat in the hands of the Afghans and to abstain from any interference in Afghanistan. However, to the north and northwest of Afghanistan lay the country of the Turkomans, divided into several khanates, which offered a tempting field for Russian expansion. One faction in the cabinet wished to resist Russian encroachment in this territory, while another regarded such an encroachment

---

plained of the disgraceful conduct of Blaine: "He does everything to keep up a sordid state of relations with us." Original MS., *ibid*. Gladstone's comments on the draft of a dispatch by Granville, dealing with the Panama Canal question, are dated December 25, 1881. Herein he warned against making forecasts concerning what might happen in the case of a war and suggested a reference to the Monroe Doctrine; "but if you make it, the terms will of course be such as not to constitute any new pledge of adhesion on our part to that doctrine." Copy, letter books, XIX, 155, *ibid*.

[49] Copies, letter books, XIX, 162; XX, 13, *ibid*.

with indifference and even welcomed it. Lord Northbrook, a former viceroy of India, urged in a memorandum of June 9, 1882, that Britain should not oppose the
Russian occupation of Merv. The advance of Russia
meant, Northbrook asserted, the extirpation of slavery
and the slave trade which had been carried on on a
larger scale along the Persian-Turkoman frontier than
in East Africa; he claimed that the Persians in the district of Merv welcomed the Russians, and that Afghanistan had never seriously objected to the incorporation of
the Turkoman khanates in the Russian empire. Furthermore, he recommended a treaty with Russia defining
her frontiers in the Middle East, and that the strength
of Afghanistan should be maintained, if necessary
through an alliance with England. But in his judgment,
"The best defence against possible Russian aggression
on India is to govern India well, husband her resources,
and make her people contented with our rule."[50] With
the last proposition all could agree, although on the
question of Russian advances toward Afghanistan opin-

[50] Printed for the use of the cabinet, June 9, 1882, Granville
Papers. In a letter to Lord Ripon, then viceroy of India, November
24, 1881, Gladstone expressed the opinon that India did not add to
the actual strength of the empire but to its responsibilities. "We
have," he wrote, "undertaken a most arduous but a most noble duty.
We are pledged to India, I may say to mankind for its performance;
and we have no choice but to apply ourselves to the accomplishment of the work, the redemption of the pledge, with every faculty
we possess." They should always keep in mind, he said, that India
"is to be governed for her own benefit not for England's." Copy,
letter books, XIX, 116-117, Gladstone Papers.

ions differed. The issue was brought to a head sharply when the Russians defeated an Afghan force at Penjdeh in March, 1885; Herat seemed threatened; Gladstone delivered a warlike speech in the house of commons, and asked for and received a vote of credit for warlike measures. The Russian government then agreed to arbitrate points in dispute.[51]

In 1881 Italy modestly sought to obtain a port, Assab Bay, on the Red Sea. Granville opposed it; but Gladstone doubted whether Britain always should prevent other powers from acquiring territory on the road to India.[52] Three years later the Italians looked longingly at Massowah, a place which later formed the starting point in building up her colony of Eritrea. Massowah normally formed part of the Sudan. Baring strongly recommended handing Massowah over to Italy in exchange for Italian support for Britain in Egypt, Gladstone was inclined to be accommodating, but other members of the government were reluctant to gratify the desires of Italy.

At the Congress of Berlin, Waddington, the representative of France, had apparently been encouraged by Salisbury and Beaconsfield to seize Tunis, and in March, 1881, the French found a pretext for occupying the country. Granville was greatly incensed, fearing that by this action Malta would be rendered valueless as a Brit-

[51] Langer, 309-314.
[52] Fitzmaurice, *Granville*, II, 235.

ish naval station, and he contemplated some restrain-
ing action in conjunction with Italy. There were, however, the awkward commitments of Lord Salisbury; and
Bright wrote pointedly, "I hope we shall not make the
stir about Tunis which was made about Algiers 50 years
ago. . . . Have we not enough on our hands?" Gladstone gave Granville a free hand concerning Tunis, but
added significantly, "*I am averse to combination.*" Under these circumstances the foreign secretary decided
"to do nothing to irritate the French unnecessarily."[53]

[53] On April 26, 1881, Granville telegraphed to Gladstone from
Walmer Castle: "Italian govr. state that French fleet have orders to
go to Galetta and ask what we are prepared to do in concert with
them. I have asked Lord Lyons whether it is true. In the meantime
I should glad (sic) to have your opinion." Gladstone replied immediately, "I recommend to act freely on your judgment & information *as to sending force* . . . unless you think otherwise *I am averse
to combination.*" Copy, MS., Gladstone Papers. The question whether
to print an extract of a dispatch from Lyons to Salisbury, July 19,
1878, which contained a report of a conversation which Lyons had
had with Waddington on July 18, 1878, caused an exchange of
letters with Lord Salisbury and led to statements by members of the
cabinet. Salisbury objected to the publication of the extract (letter
to Granville, May 14, 1881) on the ground that several statements
stood uncontradicted and that it was only a fragment since the
whole could not be printed. Waddington had made "wild proposals
for an alliance against Germany for the defence of Holland & Belgium: & threats that unless such an alliance is accepted France will
side with Russia." Salisbury had ignored these proposals. "But if,"
he wrote, "you suppress this most delicate portion of the conversation, you suppress my justification for not replying to his [Wad-
dington's] very inaccurate recollections of what passed at Berlin."
Bright thought that "In the interest of the public & to show evil
effects of seizure of Cyprus they [i.e., the Tunis documents] might
be printed. Will, however, abide by Granville's decision." Forster
agreed with Bright. Harcourt said that Salisbury's objections seemed
valid; to this Carlingford, Childers, Northbrook, and Selborne agreed.

Britain and France were still partners in Egypt, and friction over Tunis might complicate matters elsewhere. Acting on encouragement from Berlin, the French pursued an aggressive colonial policy, 1883-85. They had long had designs on Madagascar, where the British, of course, also had commercial and other interests. When it became clear that France harbored hostile intentions the government of Madagascar sent delegates to London, and Britain tendered "good offices." But this offer was declined; the north coast of the island was seized in April, 1883, and British subjects were treated with scant courtesy. The government of Gladstone, however, acted as meekly in Madagascar as that of Peel had acted under somewhat similar circumstances in Tahiti forty years earlier. Although the conquest of Madagascar was delayed ten years, the island was by 1884 earmarked for France.[54] The vigorous French colonial policy in the Far East resulted in a war with China, 1884-85. On the eve of the outbreak of hostilities some discussion took

Chamberlain, Dodson, and Kimberley regretted that the whole story could not be told. Gladstone was at Windsor Castle and lacked time to examine the documents; he believed, however, it would be difficult to suppress them. But Granville decided that public interest did not require their publication. Original MSS., Granville Papers. For further material see Fitzmaurice, *Granville*, II, 234-236, and *Letters of Queen Victoria*, 2nd series, III, 209, 223. The topic has been treated exhaustively by Professor William L. Langer, "The European Powers and the French Occupation of Tunis," in *The American Historical Review*, October, 1925, and January, 1926, XXXI, 55-78, 251-265.

[54] Frederick L. Schuman, *War and Diplomacy in the French Republic* (New York, 1931), 107-114, 117-120.

place as to whether Britain and Germany should invite France and China to submit their dispute to arbitration, but both Gladstone and Granville doubted the wisdom of such a move and the matter was dropped.[55]

Except for the Penjdeh incident in Anglo-Russian relations, the controversies between Britain and the other colonizing powers were small beer compared with those aroused by the entry of Germany into the race for overseas possessions. Not that the colonies coveted by Germany, except the one in East Africa, were particularly valuable; the light soil of Namaqualand and Damaraland in South Africa and the climate and resources of Northeastern New Guinea offered few attractions to citizens of an empire like the British which had "picked the eyes" of so many trans-oceanic lands. Not unnaturally it irritated the Germans that even the crumbs were considered too good for them. Some of the reasons for the ill will aroused by the colonizing activities of the Germans may be deduced from the preceding pages. Rightly or wrongly, British colonies objected to foreign neighbors, and since 1870 there had grown up in England a strong sentiment in favor of the colonies; influential members of the Liberal party such as W. E. Forster and Lord Rosebery were prime movers in organizing the Imperial Federation League in 1884. English

[55] Granville to Gladstone, September 9 and 13, 1884, and note by Gladstone dated September 16, 1884. Original MSS., Gladstone Papers.

pride and English cupidity had been aroused by Disraeli; thoughtful men had a vague presentiment that the spacious, easy-going days in imperial policy belonged to the past, that an era of rivalry and cut-throat competition was dawning, and that Britain ought to prepare for it. We have also seen that the English governmental machinery was of a type that made it impossible to shift gear at a moment's notice. A recent writer apparently shares Herbert Bismarck's disgust with Granville for suggesting that Derby and Kimberley should be present at discussions dealing with Anglo-German colonial claims.[56] Yet this demand was perfectly natural. Questions concerning colonial expansion must be handled jointly by the two departments of which Granville and Derby were the heads, and Kimberley with six years' experience in the colonial office carried much weight in cabinet discussions of such matters. Members of an English cabinet could not be treated by the prime minister as Bismarck treated his nominal colleagues, nor could Gladstone lead his sovereign in the manner the German chancellor led his. The English press was free; and the English prime minister, acting on a mandate from the electors, was restricted by forces which Bismarck either consciously manipulated or largely ignored. Granville and Gladstone have been severely censured for their failure to grasp the fact that Bismarck was in earnest when he pressed for colonial concessions; the charge,

[56] Lovell, *The Struggle for South Africa*, 95.

however, loses a good deal of its force if analyzed historically. When Lord Ampthill in April, 1883, mentioned colonization to Count Hatzfeldt, the German foreign secretary, he laughed it off and assured Ampthill that Bismarck had no interest in it. In August, 1884, Granville asked the British embassy in Berlin for information concerning Bismarck's views on colonization, and the reply called attention to the earlier dispatches from Lord Ampthill.[57] It is easy now to see that Bismarck had altered his course; but British statesmen who possessed fully as much insight and wisdom as their latter-day critics felt certain all along that Bismarck only blustered for electioneering purposes.

Gladstone throughout was willing to make concessions to Germany. He believed that both Germans and Italians had a right to shares in African and other lands now, alas, seized with so much avidity by the powers of Europe. Nor did he fear that by refusing the inordinate demands of the colonies for contiguous territory, Britain ran the risk of disrupting her empire. "We have to remember," he wrote to Lord Derby December 21, 1884, "Chatham's conquest of Canada, so infinitely lauded, which killed dead as mutton our best security for keeping the British Provinces."[58] Granville, likewise, early recommended concessions to Germany; but other members of the government were definitely opposed or

[57] Public Record Office MS., F. O. 64:1144.
[58] Knaplund, *Gladstone and Britain's Imperial Policy*, 155.

believed with Lord Selborne that nothing would be gained in Egypt or elsewhere by yielding to Bismarck. Moreover, in the autumn of 1884 the fate of the reform bill hung in the balance. When Bismarck won his alleged victory on the colonial issue in the early spring of 1885, the bill was safe—by yielding earlier the government might have wrecked a great measure.

In the summer of 1884 Bismarck sounded the British government on a possible cession of Heligoland to Germany, but the domestic political situation was critical and the opposition could cite a long list of surrenders made by the government in Africa and in Asia. Granville believed the cession of Heligoland to be a price worth paying for a satisfactory financial settlement in Egypt, Derby thought Britain might cede it for a fair consideration, but Gladstone and Granville agreed that such an act would be very unpopular and Derby averred that Bismarck was taking the wrong road to get the island; "we cannot be bullied out of it."[59]

That last clause touches another vital reason why Britain and Germany could not agree on colonial issues.

[59] Derby to Granville, August 20, 1884. Original MS., Granville Papers. The question was discussed by Granville in a letter to Northbrook, August 16, 1884, copy, *ibid.*, and in a letter to Gladstone, December 28, 1884. Original MS., Gladstone Papers. In a memorandum of that date Granville wrote, that with the Egyptian financial question and the colonial disputes in other parts of the world satisfactorily settled, "We should be prepared to enter into a friendly conversation of the suggested plan respecting Heligoland, and of the necessary conditions which should attach to it." Granville had apparently informed Count Münster of this. *Ibid.*

British statesmen objected to what they called the bully-
ing methods of the chancellor of Germany, and in addition they believed he was always attempting to stir up
bad blood among the powers. The latter point is so well
known that it is unnecessary to elaborate upon it.
Rightly or wrongly, Bismarck failed to inspire his con-
temporaries with confidence. Dufferin reported from St.
Petersburg that Bismarck was plotting; Goschen at Constantinople, 1880-81, suspected Bismarck of double dealing; and in the Dulcigno affair Bismarck urged Britain
to send her fleet to Constantinople, while counseling
with Austria and Russia as to the best method of thwarting such a move. It was commonly believed that he
aimed at making the Anglo-French *entente* impossible
by egging each on to measures that would offend the
other. He was looked upon as the Loki, the mischief
maker, in international affairs. Gladstone suspected Bismarck of being a liar, considered him impudent, and
believed that his own conciliatory attitude toward German colonization would really not please Bismarck, "as
he probably likes something to strike at." "There appears to be an element in him [i.e., Bismarck]," wrote
Gladstone to Granville December 28, 1884, "which I
do not wish to characterize." The method used by Bismarck in dealing with Britain, sometimes through the
ambassador, Count Münster, and sometimes through his
own son, Herbert, sent on special missions, also aroused
suspicion. Granville trusted too much in the Anglophile

Münster; Herbert Bismarck held a different language, although the latter's own accounts of his interviews with British statesmen ought perhaps be handled with a good deal of circumspection—he was anxious to convince the grim father that he was a chip off the old block. Early in December, 1884, Gladstone was willing to "give Bismarck every satisfaction about his colonial matters." When Lord Derby later in the month complained of the German annexations in South Africa and in New Guinea Gladstone declared that their manners had been objectionable. "But as to the things done, in themselves, I do not know whether we have reasons to complain."

In December, 1884, the reform bill had weathered the severest storms and was nearing harbor; but the frail craft of Egyptian finance was now in the midst of angry seas. For years Egypt had been at the mercy of the powers which regarded her simply as a pawn. Outside of England, no European statesman cared a brass farthing for what happened to the Egyptians. The kourbash might be applied to the back of the fellaheen until it was mere pulp; it mattered not if but the bondholders could cash their coupons. The English had not been guiltless; still they had shown some signs of a more humane spirit. New financial proposals for Egypt were being considered by the powers in the winter of 1885. Britain submitted a plan which required the sanction of the other powers. Bismarck held the key to the situation. Bluntly his son informed Gladstone that German support depended on whether Britain would make concessions to Germany in the colonial fields. The threat was obvious—in relations between man and man the method would have been called blackmail. Bismarck was already familiar with the views of Gladstone, but he wanted to have a public triumph. He got it, and drew thereby a new draft on the future.

Chapter VI

PROBLEMS OF THE NEAR EAST

THE Near Eastern question entered a critical stage in 1876 when the Bulgarian massacres aroused the dormant conscience of Christendom. The chancelleries of Europe, moderately active with Turkish problems since the Bosnia-Herzegovinian disturbances of the preceding year, now began to buzz, and the statesmen of the great powers redoubled their efforts to keep watch of their neighbors' activities. In Britain the government, and more particularly the prime minister, had for about a year utilized the Near Eastern complications as a means for recapturing British international prestige; and Disraeli had shown rather decided pro-Turkish tendencies. The reports of the massacres in Bulgaria proved embarrassing; he sought to minimize their extent, speaking of them as "a coffee house babble"; and the queen, now heart and soul in favor of whatever program her prime minister might prepare, was annoyed with the

excitement caused by the accounts of the slaughter of
some thousands of Bulgarians.[1] But when Gladstone read
the reports from Bulgaria, a fire began to smolder within
him; this he kept under control until the proper psychological moment, and then it burst forth in the *Bulgarian Horrors and the Question of the East*. The queen,
the prime minister, and high society were shocked and
offended. The negative answer to the ancient query,
"Am I my brother's keeper?" was good enough for
them. The contrary creed now sponsored by Gladstone
was not novel, being at least as old as Christianity; but
compared with that of Cain it was an innovation. And
since it was now propounded by a man who was both
a politician and a Christian, a political brand and ban
was fastened unto it. Nevertheless, the British nations
responded strongly to the trumpet call of Gladstone;
"Let justice be done" seemed to be their motto; but, of
course, what could be expected from sentimental historians like Freeman, nonconformist preachers such as
Spurgeon, and the horde of common folk who had never
understood the occult mysteries of high politics!

The attacks levied by Gladstone against the Turcophile policy of the government, his scathing denunciation of the Turks—"the one great anti-human specimen
of humanity"—his demand that they should be removed
from Bulgaria—"the province they have devastated and
profaned"—created the impression that he wished to de-

[1] Buckle, *Disraeli*, VI, 45, 64.

stroy the Turkish empire. Nothing can be more errone-
ous. Gladstone desired the destruction of the barbarous
governmental system of the Ottoman empire; he urged
autonomy for the various nationalities within that empire; but he hoped that it could be preserved. Many
speculations may be offered as to why he did not advocate the destruction of Turkey—fear of the bloodshed
it would precipitate or of the financial losses to investors
in Turkish securities, Britain being directly involved as
a guarantor of a Turkish loan of 1855, or other reasons,
political, economic and humanitarian—but in analyzing
the opinions of Gladstone it may not be amiss to recall
that he had been a member of the government which
fought the Crimean War and of that which aided in
transforming the district of the Lebanon from a turbu-
lent to a peaceful unit within the dominions of the
sultan. Still, the opinion existed in 1880 that Gladstone
was the enemy of Turkey and that he wished to hasten
its expected dissolution. It was commonly believed then,
and this belief has been promulgated by more recent
writers of biographies and histories, that Anglo-Turkish
relations were friendly before the advent of Gladstone
in April, 1880, and that his government ended promising
efforts to reform the government of Asiatic Turkey.[2]

Legends die hard, and most of them can only be
scotched; but it is necessary for a correct understanding

[2] Lady Gwendolen Cecil, *Life of Robert Marquis of Salisbury*
(London, 1921-1932), I, 315, 324-326; Buckle, *Disraeli*, VI, 366-367

of the Anglo-Turkish relations after April, 1880, to reveal their actual state while Salisbury was at the foreign office and Sir A. H. Layard served as the British ambassador to Turkey. In their private correspondence, Salisbury and Layard denounced the sultan as weak, deceitful, and hypocritical; Salisbury had little faith in the possibility of reforming Turkey; and both he and Layard constantly suspected the Turkish government of secret intrigues with Russia. The ink was scarcely dry on the signatures of the Treaty of Berlin when Salisbury wrote on a memorandum by Lord Tenterden that he hoped a rickety government could be set up south of the Balkans, "But it is a mere respite. There is no vitality left in them [i.e., the Turks]."[3] Later Salisbury suspected that plots hostile to Britain were being hatched at Paris and St. Petersburg, and he expressed fear lest "between the Sultan's loss of independence (which *has* happened) & his entire loss of empire (which will happen) the Sultan should during the period of his last agony, which may be a long one, fall under the domi-

[3] Note by Salisbury on a memorandum by Tenterden, December 29, 1878. In this memorandum Tenterden called attention to the possibility that Austria and Russia might effect an arrangement whereby the former would receive Salonica and the latter Constantinople. Salisbury wrote: "I am quite sensible of the danger. I think you foreshorten the prospect & treat as immediate a peril which is some years off. Till the events of last year are a little forgotten I doubt Andrassy carrying either of his Parliaments with him in a forward policy. The conquest of the Albanians will be a very serious matter: & he has even less money than the Russians." The Tenterden Papers, the Public Record Office, F. O. 363:5.

nant influence of Russia."[4] On July 10, 1879, Salisbury wrote: "It seems evident that our relations with Turkey are in a critical state. The Sultan thinks English friendship involves reforms in Europe and Asia and promises no countervailing advantage in money. The Russian alliance promises a long repose from any exertion, philanthropic or other. And as to defence, the Sultan probably thinks with justice that our defence of him will be measured by our own necessities, & not by any claim to favour he can establish."[5]

Two months before Salisbury left the foreign office, he told Layard: "I do not think that a renewal of your good relations of [sic] the Sultan will now effect any permanent good. I fear his character is too full of duplicity—his weakness too confirmed—& his Empire too far decayed. But it will keep matters quiet for a little longer—till the hour is come. It would be of no little advantage to defer the fall of Turkey till our railway has been made to Kandahar. It would be a great success to defer it till the revolution in Russia has taken place. We have everything to gain by postponing the catastrophe."[6] After eighteen months of fruitless effort to

[4] Salisbury to Layard, January, 1880. Layard Papers, British Museum, Add. MSS. 39139.

[5] *Ibid.*; see also Cecil, *Salisbury*, II, 315-324.

[6] Salisbury to Layard, February 19, 1880. Brit. Mus., Add. MSS. 39139. On April 22 Salisbury wrote to Layard: "From the time when I was sent to Constantinople till now, I have tried to induce the Sultan to take the only course by which his Empire could be preserved . . . but my impression is that the Sultan's day of grace is

get Turkey to observe the Treaty of Berlin, Salisbury observed that the time was past when the powers could influence "the Porte by diplomatic thunderstorms."

Layard admitted frankly that the Salisbury-Schouval-off agreement of 1878 destroyed the commanding position Britain had acquired at Constantinople,[7] and it seems evident that this position had not been regained by April, 1880. Writing to Salisbury, January 7, 1880, Layard complained of the "exceedingly unpleasant and delicate" position of the foreign representatives at Constantinople, and that "months have passed without my being able to settle scarcely one question of importance in which our interests are concerned." In language only a shade less violent than that used by Gladstone, Layard described the sultan as "an absolute Sovereign whose weak and suspicious nature and constitutional timidity amounting to actual mental derangement render him liable to the influence of those who may for the time be about him. He may at any moment, if he has not already done so, enter upon a policy hostile to the interests of England, and at the same time likely to bring about, at no distant period, events which may lead to the downfall of this Empire."[8]

---

past & that in every Court of Europe this Empire is looked upon as doomed. For the sake of the Turks I regret this little: but the bloodshed which will probably accompany their fall is not pleasant to contemplate." *Ibid.*

[7] Lord Newton, *Lord Lyons* (London, 1913), II, 160.

[8] Brit. Mus., Add. MSS., 39129, f. 12. This letter contains an interesting account of the results of the recent changes in the Turkish

There was no legacy of Turkish good will for and confidence in England bequeathed by the Disraeli government for that of Gladstone to squander; but the Liberals fell heir to sundry other bequests connected with Turkey which embarrassed them not a little. By the Cyprus convention Britain assumed responsibility for the protection of and for reforms in Asiatic Turkey. The burden was sufficiently onerous to make Cyprus expensive for Britain; but other complications traceable to the Cyprus convention increased the liabilities connected therewith. Since Britain had secured Cyprus France demanded an equivalent and Salisbury made commitments concerning Tunis that aroused suspicion in Italy. Furthermore, with an eye on Tunis, France shrank from stirring up ill will against herself among the Mohammedans and for this reason she refused to co-operate whole-heartedly with Britain in Turkey and in Egypt. Layard and, after him, Goschen complained of the lukewarmness and of the contrariness of their French colleagues, Fournier and Tissot, at Constantinople. Nor was the loss of French support offset by assistance from the northern powers. Russia, of course, had plenty of bones to pick with Britain; Austria wanted to check both Russia and the rising tide of nationalism in the Balkans and

---

government whereby the sultan had acquired absolute power over foreign affairs. In a letter to Sir William White, then at Bucharest, December, 1879, Layard had complained bitterly of the growth of the anti-foreign influence at Constantinople. H. S. Edwards, *Sir William White* (London, 1902), 198.

showed a disposition to deal tenderly with Turkey; and Germany took little interest in the Near East and generally refused to separate herself from her new ally, Austria. Hence, the concert of Europe had ceased to be effective in handling Near Eastern problems after the Congress of Berlin. Numerous engagements imposed upon Turkey at Berlin remained unfulfilled when Gladstone returned to office, and the new government devoted itself energetically to the task of compelling the Turk to observe the Treaty of Berlin.

The British ambassador at Constantinople, Sir A. H. Layard, had acquired the reputation, undeserved as the records show, of being a strong Turcophile. He was therefore in bad odor with the numerous anti-Turk Liberals who cried hotly for his recall. Granville hesitated. Layard was an old friend, the queen stoutly opposed his dismissal, and to remove him would expose the government to a charge of introducing the spoils system. Nevertheless, after two months' hesitation the government granted Layard "leave of absence" and sent G. J. Goschen, a member of Gladstone's first government, as temporary ambassador to Constantinople.[9] Before he went out, Gladstone sent him to Lord Stratford de Redcliffe, of Crimean War fame, to learn if possible the secret of how to impose one's will upon the Porte.[10]

[9] Fitzmaurice, *Granville*, II, 199-200.
[10] "Mr. Goschen is going to Constantinople as Ambassador Extraordinary, & I cannot in such a case forget the only living man who had the secret of imposing his will upon the Porte, or fail to wish

What Goschen learned is not revealed in the documents, but at Constantinople he soon acquired much influence. Count Hatzfeldt, the German ambassador, was then the *doyen* of the diplomatic corps. At the meetings of the ambassadors he generally gave the impression of being scrupulously fair; but time and again Goschen complained of Hatzfeldt's secretiveness, and doubtless on orders from Berlin the German ambassador shrank from taking the lead in discussions. There was on the whole no more harmony among the ambassadors at Constantinople than between the governments which they represented. Tissot, the French ambassador, and Corti, the representative of Italy, were occasionally not on speaking terms, and the relations between Hatzfeldt and Tissot were often strained. This lack of a united front had encouraged and continued to encourage the Porte to evade its obligations.

Greek and Montenegrin boundary disputes had hung fire since the Congress of Berlin. The Turks had been compelled to promise certain rectifications which, being agreed to under duress, they quite naturally strove to evade.[11] Gladstone took a special interest in the Mon-

---

that, if it is communicable, he shd. have the opportunity of learning it, either from yr. lips or in yr. language." Gladstone to Lord Stratford de Redcliffe, May 6, 1880. Copy, letter books, XVIII, 8-9, Gladstone Papers.

[11] Salisbury wrote to Lyons, June 6, 1879, that to avoid divisions at the Congress of Berlin they had gone further "than we thought quite wise" in the matter of the Greek boundary. *Lord Lyons*, II, 183. Shortly afterwards Salisbury suggested that Layard should

tenegrin boundary issue. He greatly admired the people of the Black Mountains, and for the sultan he felt immeasurable contempt. Gladstone was determined that this lying, fraudulent, bloodstained, and wholly despicable tyrant should be compelled to honor his treaty obligations.[12] This proved, however, a formidable task. The queen objected to the use of *real* pressure on the sultan, and the powers cared little for the Balkan boundary squabbles. Nevertheless, the British government succeeded in bringing them before a special conference of ambassadors at Berlin in June, 1880; some changes were made in the arrangements of 1878; the Porte accepted them, but proceeded to postpone putting them into effect. In the case of Montenegro, the struggle centered around the town of Dulcigno which had been promised to the Montenegrins but which was seized by Albanian irregulars, probably at the instigation of the Turkish government which refused to turn them out. Britain proposed and the powers agreed to a naval demonstration off the Albanian coast; but the admirals, except the British, had secret orders not to use force. The Turks,

---

"efface" himself on the Greek questions. Letter to Layard, July 10, 1879. Brit. Mus., Add. MSS., 39139.

[12] Writing to Granville, September 13, 1880, Gladstone spoke of the "Protean shiftings and shufflings of the Sultan, his bottomless fraud, and his immeasurable lying." And to the Duke of Argyll, October 26, 1880, Gladstone wrote that the sultan was not only a liar but he "might compete with Satan for the honour of being the Father of it, and stand a fair chance of winning." Copies, letter books, XVIII, 112, 166, Gladstone Papers.

perceiving this, proceeded to ignore the naval demon-stration. Since the anchorages were poor and the coast stormy it was generally believed that the naval vessels would have to be recalled when autumn advanced.

On September 21, 1880, the powers signed a self-denying ordinance pledging themselves not to seek ter-ritorial or commercial gains from the pending boundary disputes.[13] Two days afterwards the Ottoman govern-ment demanded further promises from the powers be-fore it would surrender Dulcigno. Among them were pledges to abstain from naval demonstrations and from demanding new territorial rectifications.[14] Gladstone considered the new demands insolent, and neither Brit-ain nor any of the other powers would comply with them. On October 4, 1880, the Porte refused to sur-render Dulcigno unconditionally, and the same evening Britain proposed to the powers that the ships assembled in the Adriatic should proceed to Smyrna, blockade the port, and seize the customs.[15] Russia and Italy ap-proved, but Austria refused outright. Bismarck at first instructed Hatzfeldt to advise the Turks to yield, but later informed him not to seek an audience to present this advice; France excused herself on the ground that no action could be taken in Turkey except by the con-cert, and since Austria's action had broken the concert

[13] *P. P., 1881*, C. cd. 2752, p. 2.
[14] *Ibid.*, cd. 2758, pp. 32-33.
[15] *Ibid.*, p. 85.

France could not agree to co-operate with Britain. The British government suggested three alternatives: first, material aid to Montenegro; secondly, demonstration at Smyrna by all the powers; thirdly, that Britain, Russia, and Italy should proceed at Smyrna as suggested in Granville's note of October 4, acting as the mandatories for the concert of Europe in a fashion analogous to that followed by Britain and France in the Lebanon affair of 1860. To all of these Austria replied in the negative.[16]

The Smyrna proposal emanated from Gladstone. Goschen suggested, September 28, sending the fleet to Constantinople; Granville inquired from Northbrook how long it would take the fleet to reach Constantinople —the reply was "four days." Lord Odo Russell reported from Berlin that Bismarck regarded the Smyrna action as an ineffective half-measure and asked why Britain did not send the fleet to the Turkish capital. Similar advice came from Lyons at Paris and Plunkett at St. Petersburg. And Granville wrote to Gladstone October 9: "I am rather inclined to the rash or timid extremes—Smyrna en trois would certainly not make the Turk yield." But Gladstone studied carefully the question of forcing the Straits against Turkish opposition and concluded that the risks were too great; on the other hand an examination of the trade at Smyrna convinced him that if the

[16] Gladstone to Argyll, October 14, 1880. Copy, letter books, XVIII, 147, Gladstone Papers. Goschen, writing to Granville, October 12, gave an account of the proceedings of Bismarck and Hatzfeldt. Original MS., Granville Papers.

powers occupied this gateway to Asia Minor the Turks would yield. On October 9 the Turkish government learned of the British proposal concerning Smyrna, but not of the Austrian rejection; and on the same evening the sultan conveyed to Goschen a definite intimation that Dulcigno would be surrendered. However, the formal note to this effect was not delivered until October 12, its delivery being finally accomplished perhaps as a result of a Havas telegram which reached Constantinople on the preceding day, to the effect that Austria, France, and Germany agreed with Britain. Goschen telegraphed to Granville in the evening of October 12: "Note has come at last. Smyrna has done it, that's clear."[17] And Lyons wrote three days later from Paris: "I attribute the giving in about Dulcigno entirely to your Smyrna proposal." His biographer holds a different view, but it is tinged with the bias of party.[18]

Gladstone would have proceeded with the Smyrna proposal supported by Russia and Italy without a mandate from the other powers. He thought that Austria behaved shabbily though in a straightforward fashion, and he did not know that Bismarck in August, 1880, had

---

[17] *Ibid.*

[18] Lyons to Granville, October 15, 1880, original MS., Granville Papers; *Lord Lyons*, II, 232. By comparing the dates it seems certain that Goschen's statement of October 12, 1880, must be given greater weight than his later version of what caused the sultan to yield. Goschen was informed in the evening of October 9 that Dulcigno would be surrendered; this happened nearly two days before the Havas telegram reached Constantinople.

concerted with Russia on the best means to frustrate a possible British attempt to force the Straits; but his distrust of Bismarck was so deep-seated that when Odo Russell's report of Bismarck's suggestion that Britain should send her fleet to Constantinople came to the attention of Gladstone, he wrote: "I do not receive a statement of B's opinion without misgiving, and I am sensible of great risks in the measure he irresponsibly recommends."[19]

At the Congress of Berlin, Greece had been promised a slice of Turkish territory, but no effort was made to delimit the area. The question dragged on until the conference at Berlin stipulated that some portions of Epirus and Thessaly should be transferred to Greece. France had shown a decided interest in the Greek boundary question both in 1878 and in 1880; but Gladstone thought that the conference had been rather liberal with the Greeks and suggested on June 19, 1880, that a good price might be paid to Turkey for part of the territory she was to lose. Later he discovered that the king of the Greeks was willing to offer the sultan money for Janina. Gladstone believed that money should be paid not for Janina but for the southern slopes of the Olympus, awarded to Greece by the conference although hardly

[19] Gladstone to Granville, October 9, 1880. Original MS., Granville Papers. For discussion as to possible action by Austria, Germany, and Russia in case the British fleet entered the Dardanelles see memorandum by Hohenlohe, August 4, 1880. *Die Grosse Politik,* III, 147.

intended to be so awarded under the provisions of the
Treaty of Berlin.[20] Until the middle of October, 1880,
the interest in the Montenegrin dispute overshadowed
that in the Greek. With the Dulcigno trouble out of
the way, the powers were free to turn their attention to
Greece. Gladstone considered her case weaker, and on
October 15 he suggested to Granville that they might
let France take the lead. "If it makes her bones ache so
much the better." Sir Charles Dilke tried unsuccessfully
to elicit a statement from Gambetta, then the most powerful man in France, on the Greek question. "But the
wily Genoese," Granville told Gladstone, October 17,
1880, "seems to have had the best of it, as to not letting
out a word as to what is to be done at present with the
Greek question or any other—he objects to finance [ap-
parently money payment] which would have been a
good stop gap." Gladstone still hoped that France would
resume the initiative in the Greek question; if she refused, he was willing to await developments.[21] Meanwhile he, at Goschen's suggestion, paid high tribute
to the good qualities of the Turks in his speech at the
Guildhall, November 9, 1880.[22]

[20] Gladstone to Granville, August 11, 1880. Original MS., Granville Papers.

[21] MSS., copies and originals, Gladstone Papers.

[22] Goschen to Granville, October 7, 1880, deciphered telegram,
Granville Papers. For Gladstone's speech at the Guildhall see *The
Times*, November 10, 1880. Goschen thought that Gladstone "over-
did the civil act" in this speech about which the Turkish press said
very little. Goschen to Granville, November 19, 1880. Original MS.,
Granville Papers.

When France refused to take Greece under her wing, Goschen proposed, and was supported therein by the home government, that the Greeks and the Turks should negotiate directly; but this, too, failed to bring results. Before the close of 1880, rumors began to circulate about a possible Austro-Russian understanding concerning the Balkans, and the year 1881 had hardly opened before diplomatists suspected that the League of the Three Emperors had been renewed.[23] France was now ready to proceed in Tunis; Britain knew this and realized she could not act effectively in the question of the Greek boundary. The only hope of solving this puzzle lay in getting Bismarck to assume the lead; France was courting his friendship, and Austria was not likely to oppose him. Consequently, during Goschen's sojourn home, December, 1880, to January, 1881, it was agreed that he should return to Constantinople via Berlin and Vienna. His interview with Bismarck proved a great

[23] Calice, the Austrian ambassador to Constantinople, told Goschen in October, 1880, that "if he were Austrian Foreign Minister, he should be inclined to square Russia and settle the Eastern Question that way." Goschen to Granville, October 5, 1880. Original MS., Granville Papers. "Looking . . . ahead I fear there may be some risk of a reconstitution of the alliance between the three Emperors, and of squaring the questions to arise in the Balkan Peninsula." Gladstone to Argyll, October 14, 1880. Copy, letter books, XVIII, 147, Gladstone Papers. Goschen wrote from Vienna, February 8, 1881, that he had tried to find out whether there was any foundation for Granville's idea that a new league of the three emperors was about to be formed, but Goschen did not think it existed, although Bismarck had spoken very cordially of Russia. Original MS., Granville Papers.

success. Upon receiving the report of it from Goschen, Granville rejoiced at having Bismarck "harnessed . . . to the omnibus with a premium upon his power to pull it at the hill."[24] However, there were still many chances for "a slip 'twixt the cup and the lip," as events proved. In February Bismarck had agreed to take the initiative in effecting a settlement of the Turco-Greek boundary disputes; his views were conveyed to Hatzfeldt; but to the amazement of Goschen, the German ambassador acted for weeks as if he had had no positive instruction, showed great deference to the wishes of Austria, who was pro-Turk, and left the impression that Bismarck was double-crossing Goschen by sending Hatzfeldt secret instructions at variance with the opinions expressed at their interview.[25] During the winter of 1881, several means were suggested for breaking the deadlock over the Greek frontier question. Bismarck proposed handing Crete over to Greece as an equivalent for Thessaly. Russia approved, but neither Gladstone

[24] Granville to Goschen, February 10, 1881. Copy, Granville Papers.
[25] "Ambassadors speak as if *real* pressure on Turkey through threat of war is out of the question. . . . Hatzfeldt secretive though he has strong instructions from Bismarck," February 21, 1881. Hatzfeldt is queer, does not push Bismarck's plan at all, watches Calice and never dissents from him, March 1, 1881. Bismarck has behaved in an extraordinary manner; Hatzfeldt claims he has no instructions, March 5, 1881. Hatzfeldt will not lead—says Germany not interested, has apparently been "pulled up" by his chief. Tissot, the French ambassador, has also been "pulled up"—probably Bismarck is back of this, March 11, 1881. Letters, Goschen to Granville, original MSS., Granville Papers. In a long letter of March 17, Goschen gives a clear picture of the confusion that existed at Constantinople. *Ibid.*

nor Granville was enthusiastic, and when both the sultan and the king of Greece opposed it, the matter was dropped.[26] Another possible solution was the transfer of Cyprus by Turkey and Britain to Greece. Gladstone had considered such a step in 1880, but when Goschen mentioned it, February 25, 1881, the situation had changed. The British government had decided to evacuate Kandahar and to restore the South African Republic. Granville said that Goschen had argued well in favor of ceding Cyprus, "but it does not smile to me at present. I do not think it an unwise proposal, but one must pay some attention to public opinion." The foreign secretary evidently felt that the news of further surrenders would seriously weaken the position of the government, but Goschen renewed the suggestion in a telegram of March 25, 1881. The message ran: "By way of reminder only. Cyprus and my letter of twenty-fifth ult. Let me simply add that if Cyprus were thrown in with present Turkish proposal the programs of compensation for Epirus would be carried out; the present difficulties would vanish; England would acquire an immensely strong position for pressing Greece; total offered would be more valuable than the Berlin award. Peace ought to be certain; Europe grateful; Turkey convinced of in-

[26] The sultan seems to have favored it for a while, thinking that by ceding Crete all Greek claims would be satisfied; but when he found that this was not the case he objected to the cession of Crete. Bismarck and Russia favored the Cretan plan while Austria would rather see Greece expand on the mainland.

disputable disinterestedness and England relieved in a
most honourable way of a convention which Mr. Gladstone called an act of madness. My taint of Jingoism is
a guarantee to you that this suggestion does not come
from [one] who is usually addicted to giving up."[27] But
the ambassador's eloquence failed to move the prime
minister and the foreign secretary. Britain had lost prestige by the South African settlement, and a surrender
of Cyprus at this moment would be a risky undertaking.
Granville therefore replied to the proposal of Goschen:
"I have betrayed your confidential views to Gladstone.
They tempt us much, but we do not see our way."[28]
It took further negotiations, with pressure applied to
both parties, to patch up the Turco-Greek boundary
issue.

At the Congress of Berlin Bulgaria had been confined
to narrow limits north of the Balkans. However, the
Bulgarians in the newly constituted autonomous province of Eastern Roumelia, south of the mountains, desired union with their kinsmen to the north. The issue
touched the question of self-determination which Gladstone had favored for so long; it touched also an international arrangement; and it interested both Austria and
Russia. Because of threatening complications, Gladstone
in 1880 supported Granville's efforts to suppress the
movement for a union of the two Bulgarias. He feared

[27] Deciphered telegram, Granville Papers.
[28] Copy, *ibid.*

that it might lead to a demand "for reconstituting the Bulgaria of San Stefano" and precipitate a collision between Austria and Russia. But if Turkey on her own accord or perhaps as a result of cash payments would consent to the union, Gladstone would not oppose it. On the question of the position of the minorities in the newly emancipated provinces, Gladstone agreed with the queen and sent a stern warning to the Bulgarians to desist from persecutions.[29] But the two were in complete disagreement concerning the policies and personality of Prince Alexander of Battenberg. To the queen he was "dear Sandro," whatever he did in Bulgaria was right, and his difficulties she attributed to the evil machinations of Russia. Gladstone shared Goschen's low opinion of the prince's ability and statesmanship. Goschen wrote in June, 1881, that the violent acts of Prince Alexander could not be defended and he attributed them to the prince's weakness in accepting bad foreign advice.[30] Gladstone was more outspoken in his condemnation. When Prince Alexander tinkered with the constitution of Bulgaria in an effort to strengthen his own position, Gladstone wrote, "The idiot, for such he seems practically to be, does not see that he can only fight the Russians (apart from violence, and from foreign support) by a frankly popular policy"; and he suggested

[29] Gladstone to Granville, May 22, June 10, and July 12, 1880. Copies, letter books, XVIII, 20, 39, 68, Gladstone Papers.
[30] Goschen to Granville, June 11 and 21, 1881; original MSS., Granville Papers.

that Lord Dufferin, then British ambassador at Constantinople, might devote some of his attention to the
larger aspects of the Bulgarian question. "If we could,"
Gladstone observed, "make that whipper-snapper of a
prince see that he ought, like the kings of Greece and
Roumania, to make himself strong by keeping faith and
trusting his people, I cannot help thinking that we might
do something by friendly influence to diminish his
troubles on the Russian side."[31] When two years later
the union of the two Bulgarias was accomplished, Gladstone described it cautiously as "in itself good," although
the news made him uneasy.[32] The terms of this union
were not definitely arranged until 1886 during Gladstone's short-lived third ministry at a time when the
British government made an effort to leave the Balkan
and other international questions severely alone.

Britain had no special treaty obligation concerning
Bulgaria—it was different with Asiatic Turkey. By the
Cyprus convention Salisbury assumed responsibility for
the defense and in a measure for reforms in this portion

[31] Gladstone to Granville, October 12 and 13, 1883. Copies, letter
books, XX, 342, 344-345, Gladstone Papers. At the same time Gladstone suggested that the Russian government should be made aware
of the British "feeling on behalf of Bulgarian *law & liberty*, within
the limits of the Treaty [of Berlin] against *any* be they who may,
Princes or States, who tamper with it." Gladstone to Granville,
September 22, 1883. *Ibid.*, 320.

[32] "International law touches the question . . . the foolish ambition
which may get the upper hand in Austria, & the sharp feud of Slav
& Hellene also cause misgivings." Gladstone to Granville, September
22, 1885. Copies, letter books, XXII, 85, *ibid.*

of the Turkish empire. He secured the appointment of
military consuls but soon discovered that the reforms
entailed a severe burden on Britain and, if carried out
conscientiously, they were almost certain to drive Turkey into the arms of Russia. The military consuls were
withdrawn in 1882; and although Gladstone's interest
in improving the position of the Asiatic subjects of the
sultan, and that of the Armenians in particular, was perhaps keener than that of Lord Salisbury, he believed
that the surest way of achieving the desired object was
to make it a concern of the European concert. That this
was no mere subterfuge, a device for escaping onerous
obligations, is clear from the persistency with which
Gladstone urged the cause of Armenian reform. While
the boundary questions held the center of the stage,
those dealing with reforms in Armenia lay dormant;
but no sooner were the boundary disputes more or less
settled than Gladstone turned his attention to that country. In a conversation with Lord Dufferin who succeeded Goschen as ambassador to Constantinople in the
summer of 1881, Gladstone suggested that Dufferin
should try to secure the appointment of an able and
trustworthy governor of Armenia with sufficient power
and "reasonable independence." "I also hinted," Gladstone wrote to Granville, "as a means of procuring this,
at the small value we set upon our nominal, sole, and
illegal title (referably to the Treaty of Paris) to interfere between the Sultan and his Asiatic subjects gen-

erally."[33] Dufferin followed the instructions and brought the Armenian problem before an early meeting of the conference of the ambassadors to Turkey; but with the exception of the Russian his colleagues "rather went out of their way to let me know what a bore they thought it."[34] Bismarck, whose friendship the sultan eagerly sought at this time, cared nothing about improving the lot of the Armenians, and single-handed Britain was powerless. Nevertheless, Gladstone did not let the matter rest. In April, 1882, he expressed surprise at Dufferin's failure to mention Armenia to the sultan. "That consummate rogue," Gladstone remarked, "is pretending alarms which he does not feel, in order to prevent us from pressing reforms which cause his corrupt and narrow mind real alarm. These reforms we had virtually for the present narrowed to the point of Armenia. We may not have the power of making him do what he ought, but we have the power of making him feel uneasy and insecure while he does not do it, and ought this power to be, as Dufferin's letter implies, virtually renounced."[35] Shortly afterwards Britain was deeply involved in Egypt; and Turkey, as well as the other powers, could increase her difficulties there. By a curious twist of fate the sultan was in 1883 in a strong position.

[33] Letter books, XVIII, 353, *ibid*.

[34] Dufferin to Granville, August 9, 1881. Original MS., Granville Papers.

[35] Gladstone to Granville, April 13, 1882. Copy, letter books, XIX, 242, Gladstone Papers.

Granville thought that: "The Central Powers are toadying Turkey, Italy is anxious to use her as a counterpoise to France, while France and Russia may at any time try to use her as a catspaw against ourselves."[36] Under these circumstances it is not surprising to find Granville writing to Dufferin: "Gladstone is rather keener about the possibility of doing something in Armenia at present than I am."[37] This "keenness" was revealed in letters from Gladstone to Granville of September 22, October 13, and October 15, 1883. On September 22 Gladstone wrote: "Reports from Armenia: Has not the time come when Dufferin should follow up his former representation with a strong statement as to the serious nature of the policy pursued there, and the impossibility of our doing anything, after the engagements of '78 have been so dealt with, to defend or maintain such a state of things?" The 13th of October he said that the matter of Armenian reforms "appears to burn. I wait with anxiety Dufferin's Report, and I hope he will recommend some intelligible representation to that arch-liar and arch-cheat called the Sultan, one of the greatest calamities, in himself, with which Turkey has been visited." On October 15, he read Dufferin's account of an interview with the sultan and expressed unwillingness to dispute against the ambassador's "superior knowledge." "What I am anxious and very anx-

---

[36] Granville to Dufferin, April 27, 1883. Copy, Granville Papers.
[37] October 11, 1883. *Ibid.*

ious for," Gladstone wrote on that date, "is this, that when the crisis comes, as come it will, we, or the British Government of the day, may be able, unequivocally able, to show the world that it is freed from all obligations to assist the Sultan in maintaining his vile and shameful rule over Armenia." This seemed indisputable to Gladstone, but he professed himself unable to suggest the form for achieving it. He was surprised at finding that Dufferin apparently hoped the sultan would launch reforms on his own initiative. "I am not aware," wrote Gladstone, "that he has ever done a good act towards any of them [i.e., the Armenians], except under compulsion or the immediate fear of it, and I am afraid it is too late for him to mend."[38] Toward the end of the year Armenia again worried Gladstone. "The Armenians' case," he wrote to Granville, December 28, 1883, "is really deplorable." Should Britain not try to enlist the support of Russia and Italy for efforts in their behalf? "May it not be a duty to put ourselves in a position to show that we have exhausted *every* means of friendly action; and this seems to be the only one remaining, as direct sole application has failed, and the three other Powers are hopeless."[39] But nothing was achieved. The Armenians were left to their tragic fate.

Although reforms in Armenia seemed to Gladstone most pressing, he was fully aware of the need for

[38] Copies, Gladstone Papers.
[39] Copy, letter books, XXI, 42-43, *ibid*.

changes in the government of the European provinces
of Turkey. Britain's primary object concerning Turkey
was, he said in 1880, the introduction of reforms, not
any extension of her own power. And the bases for such
reforms were in his judgment the establishment of local
liberty and the appointment of right-minded and efficient governors who enjoyed sufficient independence
not to be "a mere leaf to be blown off at a breath from
Constantinople."[40] Viewing the Balkan problems in their
larger aspects, Gladstone held the same opinion concerning them that he held concerning Belgium, namely, that
Britain had no interest in them apart and different from
those of most of the other countries. The problems
should be approached with an eye to promoting the
happiness of the Balkan peoples, not for the purpose of
strengthening one or the other of the great powers.
With reference to the Balkan question he wrote September 7, 1883: "I think that *all* the Great Powers, unless it be France, are subject to temptation, and therefore to be watched rather than confided in. During the
spring of 1880 I was *falsely* accused by some among
the Jingoes of trying to promote a union of the Balkan
States *inter se*. But the thing appears to me excellent,
and by far the best barrier against all aggression. I should
like to see Roumans and Hellenes join in it. Bulgarians
as vassal states have no right to do the like: but Turkey

[40] Gladstone to Rosebery, July 7, 1886. Copy, letter books, XXII,
217, *ibid.*

would do wisely (if this Sultan could do anything wise) to sell the rights, and the Bulgarians to buy it (in their two divisions) even at a smart price. France might in such a matter take the same view with us."[41]

Lord Dufferin strongly suspected that Germany sought to increase her influence in Turkey; and on September 20, 1881, he wrote: "Can it be that Bismarck's project for a colonizing railway to Bagdad with the view of preventing the emigration of his Germans to America is being revived?" But these rumors did not seriously disturb Gladstone except inasmuch as Bismarck might through Constantinople cause difficulties in Egypt. The two powers that needed watching were, he thought, Austria and Russia. The former was accused of harboring a desire to reach the Ægean, and the Russian designs on Constantinople were of long standing. With reference to possible Austrian projects, Gladstone wrote on September 1, 1883: "Austria has been ostentatiously taught to turn her eye eastward, by friends and pretended friends in the West, and I fear that Bismarck only waits his opportunity to egg her onwards in that direction, taking compensation in his own neighbourhood. It is, I am convinced, a mad policy for her. She has difficulty enough with the Slavs she has who differ in race only—to rule Slavs of another religion will be a yet more hazardous experiment, unless she could become a real Slav Power, and I do not see that this is

[41] Gladstone to Granville. Copy, letter books, XX, 313, *ibid.*

possible."[42] A month later he observed: "I regard the effectual transformation of Austria into a Slav Power as impossible, and the efforts as most unwise and formidable for herself"; and in another letter to Granville Gladstone compared the position of Austria and Russia in the Balkans. "In my view," he said, "the cases of the two are extremely different in almost every point. The Russian *people* have strong sympathies with the Balkan populations. There is no Austrian people of which this can be said, though a fraction has sympathies and another fraction, the Magyar, antipathies. Russia as a state, again, can work among these populations with far greater force, having a hold upon them by the past and the future, such as Austria has not. This may of course tempt Russia more strongly in proportion. Again Russia has much greater motive for disturbing Turkey: while Austria seems to have a notion, probably a very false one, that she can strengthen herself by extension eastwards. Unfortunately it has long been her besetting sin to make light of the sympathies of the populations. On the whole, any fear I have of Austria is in the main fear that Bismarck may think fit to propel her. But for the present I do not believe that either Austria or Russia can desire a crisis."[43]

In 1875, General Schweinitz, a friend and possible mouthpiece of Bismarck, expressed to Sir Robert Morier

---

[42] Gladstone to Granville. *Ibid.*, 308.
[43] Gladstone to Granville, October 3 and 7, 1883, *ibid.*, 334, 337.

his surprise at Britain's efforts to keep Russia out of Constantinople because if she possessed that city all Europe would have to combine to keep her in check.[44] Gladstone did not go so far as to wish to have Russia established at Constantinople; but he strongly repudiated the theory that it was in a special sense the duty of England to keep her out. In a letter to Rosebery of July 4, 1886, Gladstone complained that "we have, with what I think incredible and inexcusable folly, allowed ourselves to be catspaw of the other Powers in relation to the Black Sea and the Straits. On the merits of the case, I cannot conceive anything more absurd. If there is anywhere a strong interest in opposing Russia's free use of the Straits, it is an interest of Austria, or of Italy, or of the free states of the Danube."[45]

In discussing questions concerning the Turkish empire Gladstone repeatedly referred to the Treaty of Paris by which the powers guaranteed the integrity of that empire and recognized its problems as a concern of them all. Gladstone wished to keep Austria and Russia out of the Balkans; he based his hope for reform in Turkey upon the development of local autonomy and the appointment of honest and efficient governors; he was much disturbed by the situation in Armenia; but he believed that only by concerted action by the great powers could the lot of the Armenians be ameliorated.

[44] Wemyss, *Memoirs of Morier*, 361.
[45] Copy, letter books, XXII, 214, Gladstone Papers.

However, efforts to obtain such action failed. He denied that Britain should act the part of a policeman in Turkey, and after Britain had entered Egypt such a rôle was, indeed, out of the question. There was need for a European concert to deal with the issues, old and new, presented by the Ottoman empire, but the concert was a mere phantom. To the cries from the Balkans and from Armenia the powers were content to reply with Cain, "Am I my brother's keeper?"

Chapter VII

EGYPT, 1880-1885

EGYPT supplied Gladstone's second ministry with a multitude of baffling problems. The international status of the country was perplexing; its internal affairs were chaotic; foreign powers, especially Britain and France, had interfered repeatedly in the government and financial administration of Egypt since 1875; and the two western powers exercised in 1880 a joint, ill-defined hegemony in the land of the Pharaohs. Egypt formed a part of the Turkish empire, a regular tribute was paid to Turkey, and the sultan might at the instigation of or when permitted by the powers interfere in Egyptian affairs. Ordinarily, however, the viceroy or khedive of Egypt enjoyed immunity from interference by the sultan. But since the country belonged to the Ottoman empire its government was restricted by the so-called "Capitulations" whereby foreigners residing in Egypt enjoyed many privileges and immunities, the most important being the right to be tried in the consular courts and freedom from taxation. International treaties binding on the Turkish empire, such as the Treaty of Paris, applied also to Egypt; and under their provisions excuses might be found for the powers to act jointly or severally in Egypt as their real or alleged interests seemed to dictate. In addition to the consular courts functioning in Egypt there were also mixed tribunals which could render judgments against the government, apart from the regular native courts. The country had long suffered from chronic misrule; and the unwise borrowing and spending of the Khedive Ismail, powerfully aided by the leech-like activities of international bankers, European and Levantine contractors, and a host of other carrion hunters, had reduced the country to bankruptcy. A series of investigations by financial experts working singly or in partnership or as members of international commissions had resulted in the creation of an international debt commission and the regulation of Egyptian finances by an international agreement known as the Law of Liquidation, completed shortly after the Liberals assumed office in Britain in 1880. During the years immediately preceding 1880, representatives of Britain and of France had acted as controllers of finance and had had seats in an Egyptian ministry; an experiment in responsible government had been tried and had failed; the Khedive Ismail had been deposed and his son Tewfik Pasha appointed as successor by the sultan at the request of the powers; taxes had been collected with the utmost severity in efforts to pay the interest on foreign bonds; and Britain and France had agreed (September 19, 1879): "That the two governments should make it clearly understood to the Khedive that they would not tolerate the establishment in Egypt of political influence on the part of any other European Power in competition with that of England and France; and that they were prepared to take action to any extent that might be found necessary to give effect to their views in this respect."[1]

The Gladstone government, therefore, found Britain joined with France in Egypt by a secret pact which was in effect a treaty of alliance; but the arrangements offered a wide scope for backstairs intrigue by representatives of the two powers, or of the other powers, or of Turkey, or of Egypt. Indeed, the whole set-up in Egypt invited underhand dealings by the controllers, among the members of the debt commission, between the controllers and the debt commission, or the ministry of finance, or the consuls general. Moreover, the administration of the state property and revenue-producing services such as the public lands (divided into two groups, the Daira and the Domains), the customs, the railways, and the port of Alexandria was divided into so many separate units, the majority of which had an

---

[1] Salisbury to Malet, September 19, 1879. Copy, Granville Papers; see also *P. P., 1884*, LXXXVIII, c.-3967, p. 1.

Englishman, a Frenchman, and an Egyptian in joint control, that a maximum of friction and overhead expense was incurred. Add to this a swarm of foreign officeholders, some of whom enjoyed large salaries, battened on a poverty-stricken country where the peasants, the fellaheens, went hungry and almost naked and the native officeholders, including the officers of the army, were woefully underpaid or not paid at all. Indeed, the results achieved in Egypt by the joint efforts of the greatest statesmen and some of the most skillful financiers of Europe were such that in their extravagant madness they could hardly have been excelled if produced by a select committee chosen from the padded chambers of Bedlam.

Egypt was to the Liberal government of 1880-85 a upas tree with many branches. But for our purpose we shall single out those of the dual control, the nationalist movement, the establishment of single control by Britain, and the financial problem—the last supplying, indeed, a lusty crop of offshoots. The emphasis will, of course, be laid on the attitude of Gladstone toward these problems and his share, or lack of it, in policies followed and measures adopted. In the fifties Gladstone had foreseen the importance of the Suez Canal for the British empire; but when his rival, Disraeli, purchased nine-twentieths of the shares in the Suez Canal Company in 1875, Gladstone criticized severely the stock-jobbing activities of the government. And this act, which later proved finan-

cially so profitable, often put the English government of
the eighties in an embarrassing position as minority stock-
holder in a private French-controlled company. At one
time Gladstone as prime minister considered further government purchase of Suez Canal shares, drawing a characteristic distinction between the initiation and the com-
pletion of an act or policy.[2] But nothing came of this,
and the Suez Canal negotiations of the period will not
be discussed here. One point dealing with the Suez Canal,
however, needs to be mentioned at the outset. The dividends on the shares which Disraeli bought in November, 1875, had been hypothecated for loans, and Britain
could not, therefore, collect on them until 1894. Meanwhile, Egypt paid to Britain interest at the rate of five
per cent per annum, amounting to £192,000, on the
sum paid for these shares, and the British government
thus became one of the creditors of Egypt. This point
is of special interest in connection with Egyptian finance,
but there is no indication that Gladstone was influenced
in his attitude toward Egypt by considerations based on
the creditor-debtor relation between Britain and that
country.

In 1877 Gladstone had predicted that "our first site

[2] "In regard to this very vague intimation [to purchase shares]
about the Suez Canal, I agree with you that to continue and complete is not the same thing as to begin, but on the other hand I do
not think more can be said than that there is no call absolutely
to close the door and prevent ourselves from knowing what is really
offered or intended." Gladstone to Granville, September 27, 1882.
Copy, letter books, XX, 13, Gladstone Papers.

in Egypt, be it by larceny or be it by emption, will be
the almost certain egg of a North African empire."[3] He
did not desire such an empire for Britain, and he worked
hard to prevent its founding; but forces beyond his control proved too strong, and little more than two years
after Gladstone had become prime minister British soldiers occupied both Cairo and Alexandria. The first steps
in this direction had been taken by Disraeli and Salisbury. Gladstone found Britain exercising with France
a control over Egypt which kept the other powers out.
The Law of Liquidation went into effect in the summer
of 1880, and for about six months everything seemed to
go smoothly. But discontent smoldered under the surface; seeds had been planted for a nationalist, an Egypt
for the Egyptians, movement; and the revenues allocated for the service of the debt left insufficient sums
for the internal administration and for the army. The
army was unpaid and thousands of officers were dis-
charged. The Egyptians saw foreigners by the hundreds
enjoying lucrative appointments; and the officers of the
army, although poorly trained and educated judging by
European standards, fully comprehended the existence
of both personal and national grievances, and being soldiers they knew of means for bettering their position.
In this respect a precedent had been set early in 1878
when Ismail Pasha had dismissed a ministry and effected
a restoration of his own power at the request and with

[3] *Gleanings,* IV, 357-358.

the support of mutinous soldiers. What had been done once might be repeated; and in January, 1881, military disturbances broke out in Egypt and for the rest of the year the country suffered from unrest, friction, and political and military plots. It will thus be seen that the appearance of a serious Egyptian problem coincided with the squabbles concerning the Greco-Turkish frontier, the revolt in the Transvaal, the British withdrawal from Kandahar, the French occupation of Tunis, and the renewal of the League of the Three Emperors.

In September, 1881, the Egyptian situation began to pass beyond the control of the local government. The khedive failed to keep the army in check, and the country threatened to lapse into a state of anarchy injurious to the foreign interests so deeply intrenched therein. Turkey, as the suzerain power, had the right to interfere when needed, but this might prove a case of one devil ejected and seven worse ones installed. Nevertheless, C. Rivers Wilson, one of the several Englishmen who spoke authoritatively although disharmoniously about the Egyptian situation, believed that a Turkish general might restore order in the army and thereby help to quiet the country.[4] By this time Gladstone had

"Rivers Wilson says a Turkish general carrying orders to the regiments to be disbanded would be obeyed: but can we take his word?" Granville to Gladstone, September 11, 1881. Gladstone jotted on the deciphered telegram: "I answer. The point is one in which I should agree if our friend of whom I always speak agrees but not otherwise." Original MSS., Gladstone Papers. It has not been possible to identify the "friend" of whom Gladstone speaks.

been reconciled to and placed a good deal of faith in the possibilities afforded by the Anglo-French control. In a letter to Granville of September 12, 1881, Gladstone wrote: "The French seem to attach importance to our steady union and co-operation in Egypt. This seems to me the main matter, so far as the affairs of that country are concerned." He considered, however, the possibility of Turkish intervention, and his views were summarized, on September 13, as follows:

> "1. Steady concert with France. 2. Turkish General to go if need be. 3. Turkish troops, in preference to any others. 4. No British or French force, unless ships be needed for *bona fide* protection of subjects. 5. Apart from all this, I long for information on the merits of the quarrel; as on these I suppose may depend the ulterior question of reducing or disbanding the army."[5]

A lull in the Egyptian storm caused Gladstone to urge circumspection in the matter of a Turkish mission to Egypt; he hoped the person chosen "will be sent without any ostentation of authority." Turkish envoys went, were well received; but their mission did not materially affect the situation in Egypt, where the prime minister, Cherif Pasha, sought assistance from a Chamber of Notables summoned for that purpose. In November

[5] Original MSS., Granville Papers. To the letter of September 13, Granville replied: "I agree in all your 5 points." Original MS., Gladstone Papers.

Gambetta became head of a new French government wherein he also held the post as foreign secretary. He favored friendly relations with Britain and joint forward action in Egypt. But when the army colonels in Egypt showed signs of great activity in December, 1881, Granville had grown suspicious of France. He foresaw the need for sending troops to restore order in Egypt and was anxious not to be anticipated by the French. "We certainly ought not," Granville told Gladstone on December 15, "to be the first to break with France. They will propose joint occupation which is very awkward. I am not sure that it would not be better, hateful as it is, to insist upon Turkish Occupation, under strict conditions." Gladstone replied: "I prefer as heretofore the Turkish to joint occupation but will follow your opinion whatever it may be."[6]

Meanwhile the Egyptian Chamber of Notables began to claim the position and power of a national parliament with control over the budget. But a large portion of the revenues and expenditures were regulated by an international agreement, the Law of Liquidation, which might be entirely upset if the Notables obtained the desired power, and this upset might prove harmful to the interests of the bondholders for whom the powers acted as unofficial agents. Gambetta then took the lead and suggested a joint Anglo-French note for the purpose of

[6] Note on back of Granville's letter. Original MS., Gladstone Papers.

curbing the Notables and maintaining the existing system, using as a pretext that the prerogatives of the
khedive must be preserved. Granville received the French
dispatch on January 2, 1882, and forwarded it immediately to Gladstone with a covering letter in which he
said: "I incline to agree with Gambetta's draft."[7] Gladstone expressed his willingness to follow Granville in
agreeing to the proposed joint note; but he felt uneasy
and apprehensive about Egypt and the policy the government was asked to sanction. Granville had suggested
that the language held in Egypt by Malet, the British
agent, should be approved. Gladstone did not demur.
"Yet," he wrote to Granville, January 4, 1882, "I think
words might be added conveying to Malet an assurance
of our reliance on him not to commit this country to a
total or permanent exclusion of the Chambers for handling the Budget.

"I suppose," he continued, "we are entitled to hold
the present position so far as it is necessary to guarantee
the pecuniary interests on behalf of which we have in
this somewhat exceptional case been acting in Turkey.

"But I should regard with utmost apprehension a
conflict between the 'Controul' [Britain and France]
and any sentiment truly national, with a persuasion that
one way or other we should come to grief in it.

"I am not by any means pained, but I am much surprised at this rapid development of a national sentiment

[7] Original MS., *Ibid.*

and party in Egypt. The very idea of such a sentiment
and the Egyptian people seemed quite incompatible.
How it has come up I do not know: most of all is the
case strange if the standing army be the nest that has
reared it. There however it seems to be, and to claim
the respect due to it as a fact, and due also to the capa-
bilities that may be latent in it for the future. 'Egypt
for the Egyptians' is the sentiment to which I should
wish to give scope and could it prevail it would I think
be the best, the only good solution for the 'Egyptian
question.' "[8]

The joint note was discussed and agreed upon by
the cabinet on January 6 and presented to the khedive
on January 8, 1882. But its effect upon the Egyptian
situation was the reverse of what had been anticipated.
Malet reported that it weakened the power of the khedive and united all parties against Britain and France.
The British government issued explanations in attempts
to make clear that its intention was not to weaken the
Egyptian government or to further the interests of the
foreign powers; but it achieved nothing beyond causing
misgivings in Paris where Gambetta expressed fear that
to give the Notables control over the budget would prove
very dangerous.[9] By the middle of January, 1882, he
urged joint, armed intervention by France and Britain.
Gladstone agreed to a telegram to Lyons, drafted by

[8] Original MS., Granville Papers.
[9] Earl of Cromer, *Modern Egypt* (New York, 1908), I, 236-253.

Granville January 12, wherein the British government voiced its aversion to intervention "either by ourselves or by others," and said that the experiment of the Chamber was viewed favorably and "that we wish to maintain the connection of Egypt with Turkey."[10] In a memorandum of January 16, Lord Tenterden, the permanent under-secretary in the foreign office, and C. Rivers Wilson analyzed the dangers connected with intervention in Egypt by England and France or by France alone or by England alone or by Turkey. All suggestions were rejected in favor of a plan to appoint a commission similar to the commission of inquiry of 1878 and the liquidation commission of 1880 in which England and France each had a double vote. The purpose of the new commission should be to inquire into the system of justice for the natives, the establishment of "a legislative authority," the definition of the powers of the Notables, and the "maintenance and limitation of the army or gendarmerie." This commission "might sit at Alexandria and be supported by the presence of A. An Anglo-French Squadron. B. An International Squadron."[11]

By this time the figure of Bismarck began to loom on the horizon. Freed from several of his fears by the conclusion of the agreement among the three emperors,

[10] Original MS., Gladstone Papers.
[11] Granville Papers. This memorandum seems to have supplied the basis for Granville's dispatch to Lyons, January 30, 1882. Cromer, *Modern Egypt*, I, 245-246.

June, 1881, he was ready to fish in the disturbed Egyptian waters. On October 11, 1881, Dufferin reported from Constantinople that he had had confirmation of rumors of German and possibly Russian plans for interference in Egypt; and on February 2, 1882, Bismarck struck through the issuance of identical notes by Germany, Austria, Russia, and Italy to the sultan wherein they claimed that no change could take place in the Egyptian arrangement without negotiations between the powers and the suzerain. The moment was well chosen. Gambetta, who throughout had opposed the idea of international action in Egypt, had resigned January 31, and his successor, Freycinet, was averse to an energetic policy in Egypt; and the sultan, who was angry with France because of Tunis and with England because of her attitude to the boundary disputes and to the Armenian question, now eagerly seized on the opportunity to embarrass the western powers.[12]

Gladstone's views of the Egyptian imbroglio were expressed in a series of letters to Granville. On January 17, Gladstone wrote: "I see Malet, No. 18, says he gave the President of the Notables no encouragement as to a compromise, & perhaps the matter was not ripe for it. But if they admit in good faith the international engagements, as a preliminary, might not a compromise

[12] The sultan placed Gladstone and Gambetta in the same class; both were hateful to him. Dufferin to Granville, January 31, 1882. Original MS., Granville Papers.

then be considered? Might not Rivers Wilson be asked to show us the figures how far they admit of one?

"Think of Bismarck & the Turk fighting the battle of representative and popular principles against us!

"Should you be very averse to extending the Anglo-French concert in Egypt to an European concert?"

January 19, 1882. "(1) I differ from nothing in your letters to Lyons on Egypt. (2) I quite agree with the French that we cannot compound the question with the Notables on the mere basis of time: on the other hand until I see Rivers Wilson's figures I hesitate to adopt the absolute proposition that no control over any part of the Revenue can be given them.

"(3) The notion of bringing in the other Powers is agreeable to me and may avert serious danger; it is also good in view of that Panama business from the other side of the world, which looms large, and may become awkward. But I quite agree in your view that this concert would not be applicable to the executive part of this business, requiring as it does sharp consideration from day to day: while there might be great advantage in having Europe pledged as to the general basis, were it only to prevent the Turk from intriguing.

"(4) When you and Rivers Wilson quite understand one another, I should think his seeing Gambetta would be good."

January 21, 1882. "Lyons has stated the case against general concert in Egypt very well. My bias is in favor of it; but bias should not govern; & I fully admit that we cannot have it (1) without positive & sufficient cause (2) without a limited and well defined purpose in view (3) without a confident hope, or at the least a better hope than any other mode offers, of attaining it.

"I am a little disappointed at not finding in Gambetta any sign that he counts popular principles for anything in the matter. But then we must remember that thro' the struggle on the Eastern question his paper went strongly against us."

January 31, 1882. "I cannot but be struck by the total absence from Gambetta's memorandum on the Notables of any indications of the spirit of a true Liberal.

"That however is not the question before us,—& probably we have now to deal with his successors.

"As I understand the matter we might adjourn, if we cannot get rid of, the differences between us.

"1. As to Controul and internationally sanctioned law we withhold it bodily from the Notables.

"2. We also withhold the taxing power.

"3. We differ with Gambetta as to certain functions which (I apprehend) *it is not for us to give or to withhold* but as to which *if* the Egyptian authorities are disposed to give them we think it is not for us to object.

"This seems not a bad ground to stand upon."[13]

As already indicated, Gambetta resigned on January 31, 1882, and was after a few days succeeded as prime

[13] Copies, letter books, XIX, 179, 181-184, 193, Gladstone Papers.

minister by M. de Freycinet. During the two months and a half when Gambetta had been in power, he had been the author of the joint note about which Gladstone had such qualms and he had opposed both the internationalization of the Egyptian question and an invitation to Turkey to assist in setting the house of Egypt in order. But the policy which he had initiated, and which Britain had accepted with misgivings, caused the Egyptian nationalists to throw their support to the military party, now led by Arabi Pasha, who became minister of war on February 5. Freycinet refused both to lead and to follow English suggestions with reference to Egypt. He leaned on Bismarck, who was anxious to keep Gambetta out; but, while on the one hand Freycinet objected to Turkish intervention in Egypt, on the other he fell in with the suggestion of Tissot, the French ambassador to Constantinople, to support the plan of the sultan for deposing Tewfik and replacing him with Halim Pasha. Thus, after France had led Britain into a morass in Egypt, she flitted away not knowing whither to turn.

The British government proved incapable of framing a policy of its own. The prevailing sentiment in the cabinet was unwillingness to become too deeply embroiled in Egypt—annexation which would have cut the Gordian Knot clear through was impossible; otherwise the leading members of the government seem to have agreed only on disagreeing. Nor did the experts prove of much assistance; C. Vivian, C. Rivers Wilson, Malet, and Baring often disagreed. The strange and picturesque figure of Wilfred Scawen Blunt also appeared on the scene. When unable to see either Gladstone or Granville, he wrote long letters about Egypt to Edward Hamilton, Gladstone's private secretary, who forwarded them to Granville's private secretary, Sir Thomas Sanderson. But the foreign office would not listen to Blunt, considered by its staff as being absolutely unreliable; and in May, 1882, even Hamilton agreed that his friend Wilfrid was a monomaniac on the Egyptian question. Gladstone, however, treated Blunt with unfailing though ill-requited courtesy. Throughout the winter and spring of the year 1882, Britain strove to secure French support for Turkish intervention in Egypt. Baring, now in India, wrote to his cousin, Lord Northbrook, who passed the letter on to Granville: "The *Turk* is the natural man to employ as policeman. He wd. do an infinite amount of harm to Egypt in many ways, but as a choice of evils I think the Turkish solution is the best."[14] Vivian thought it was right to ask Turkey to send troops.[15] Granville

[14] Baring's long and frequent letters to Lord Northbrook were sent to Granville and copies of several of them are preserved among the Granville Papers.

[15] C. Vivian, the later Lord Vivian, had served as British consul-general in Egypt, 1875-79, and was afterwards British minister to Berne and to Copenhagen. Salisbury considered him too pro-Egyptian; see notes by Tenterden and Salisbury, June 23, 1879, Tenterden Papers, F. O. 363:5. Vivian sent to Granville from Berne, May 31, 1880, a long memorandum entitled "Narrative of the Affairs of Egypt between October 1876 & June 1879," the tone of which was

forwarded to Paris the suggestion made by Tenterden and Wilson on January 16, 1882, to send a new commission to Egypt. But nothing worked. Toward the end of May, Freycinet agreed in principle to Turkish intervention, but refused to let it be known lest he be put out of office by the Chamber.

Gladstone was perplexed. He wrote to Granville, April 5, 1882:

"On the three points of the Egyptian case.

"a. Substitution of a new Khedive [i.e., Halim for Tewfik].[16] I entirely agree with you. It has not been shown either that Halim will do or that Tewfik will not.

"b. As to the Experts [i.e., new commissioners]. If you cannot send them, I would urge on your present agents the absolute necessity of taking out of the mouth of the Egyptians all just or plausible cause of complaint on the ground that foreigners are unnecessarily quartered on the Egyptian people.

"c. I think there is more in Freycinet's view on letting in the Sultan's wedge than on the other points. The Sultan is intensely false and fraudulent and tries to work everything against us." On April 6, Gladstone com-

---

very friendly to the Egyptians. On March 1, 1882, Vivian wrote from Copenhagen expressing approval of proposal to secure support of the powers for whatever should be done in Egypt, and on May 15 he indorsed forcible intervention and the plan to ask Turkey to supply troops. Original MSS., Granville Papers.

[16] This change was urged by the sultan and supported by France.

plained of the paucity of information, other than telegraphic, from Egypt. "I seem to depend chiefly on the
newspapers." Shortly afterwards it was suggested that
three generals, an English, a French, and a Turkish,
should be sent to Egypt for the purpose of bringing the
Egyptian army and its officers back to reason. Gladstone
thought (April 23) "such a plan . . . might be licked
into shape, if sensible and conciliatory men were
chosen."[17] But he was not convinced of the need for it.

In May, 1882, Egypt was torn with bitter factional
strife. The political element in the nationalist movement
sought to free itself from the control of the army officers; and the British consul-general, Sir Edward Malet,
strove vainly to remove leading officers including Arabi
from Egypt. The month of June found Arabi in control at Cairo. Meanwhile the khedive had asked for a
Turkish commissioner; and Gladstone believed Malet
had acted wisely in withdrawing his opposition to the
granting of this request, "and surely," Gladstone wrote,
"the French colleague ought to have gone at least as
far." Gladstone observed further: "The French resistance to Turkish action has probably been the cause of
all the mischief by causing the Sultan, with his usual
falseness, to egg on the Khedive's ministry underhand
. . . if Freycinet lags behind he will find himself in
self-wrought isolation."[18] By the end of May the joint

---

[17] Copies, letter books, XIX, 228-229, 232, 250, Gladstone Papers.
[18] Gladstone to Granville, May 28, 1882. *Ibid.*

squadron had reached Alexandria. The British admiral asked for more ships and Granville telegraphed to Gladstone in the afternoon, May 29, that he had informed the French "that we propose to agree, and at the same time inform the Powers, and ask the Turks to send a man of war." Gladstone replied the same evening: "I suppose we have no alternative but to persevere and urge decisively Turkish action with France or even without her if needful."[19]

A Turkish commissioner arrived in Egypt, and while he held conferences at Cairo and while British and French warships rode at anchor off Alexandria riots broke out in that city on June 11; much property was destroyed; many Christians, including about fifty Europeans, were killed; and the British consul, Sir Charles Cookson, was severely wounded. In the meantime plans had been completed for a conference of ambassadors at Constantinople to discuss the Egyptian problem. But despite the impetus which the riots at Alexandria had given to the demands for forcible intervention in Egypt with or without France, Gladstone clung to the idea that a strengthening of the khedival government and the removal of some of the worst Egyptian grievances might obviate the need for further action. Writing to Granville on June 17, he said that he approved of certain plans concerning the power to be allocated to or withheld from the Notables. "But," he continued, "if

[19] Granville Papers.

you are writing on the subject of the attributions to be
assigned to that body, do not the questions I mentioned
to you, 1. of exclusive taxation and 2. of sinecures for
foreigners seem to call for simultaneous or early notice?
I do not mean that they ought to be handed over to the
Notables but that they should be suggested to the Powers, or to the proper parties for review. It would seem
possible in the present state of things, when the Four
Powers [i.e., Germany, Austria, Russia, and Italy] have
got their fingers respectively in the pie, & when they
find that France & England have been feathering the
nests of their people in Egypt, that the Four Powers may
be ready enough to start criticism of this kind, and there
may be just ground for it, we might stand all the better
for having anticipated it."[20] When Malet continued his
efforts to prevent Arabi from becoming prime minister
of Egypt, Gladstone noted on the back of a long deciphered telegram, addressing the note to Granville:
"Might not the attitude of your agent at the moment
be . . . direct communication with the *de facto* men."[21]
But he refused to accede to the French plan for ignoring
the khedive and negotiating directly with Arabi. On
June 25, Granville and Gladstone decided to negative
the sultan's proposal for separate British action in Egypt;

[20] Copy, letter books, XIX, 303-304, Gladstone Papers. Lord Northbrook in a letter to Granville, February 24, 1882, urged the reduction in the number of foreigners employed in Egypt. Original MS.,
Granville Papers.
[21] Granville Papers.

two days later Gladstone said that there could be no separate action while the conference was at work; and on July 1 he wrote: "We [apparently meaning the cabinet] agree, I suppose, that *we* can take no definite course in regard to the 'Egyptian question' until the conference to which we have referred it, has either dealt or refused to deal with it."[22]

But events in Egypt and pressure at home soon compelled the cabinet to act. The disorders in Egypt continued after June 11, the khedive was powerless, and Arabi Pasha was unwilling or unable to control the forces that had been let loose. To the methodical mind of Chamberlain, president of the board of trade, this situation was intolerable, and he became an eager advocate of quick and decisive British action in Egypt.[23] The admiral commanding the British fleet at Alexandria, Sir Beauchamp Seymour, had early in June discovered that efforts were made to erect new fortifications at Alexandria which might endanger his ships. Upon orders from the sultan this work was discontinued for a while,

[22] "We are agreed also," he continued, "without doubt, in thinking that we ought not to give any countenance to the French idea of negotiating with Arabi apart from the Khedive. . . . If neither Sultan, nor conference, nor France will act—& if the Khedive, really or ostensibly, settles his affair with Arabi—& if we have no difficulty in dealing separately with the question of reparation—are we then, on our own sole account, to undertake a military intervention to put Arabi down? But this question has not yet, as it seems to me, arrived." Copy, letter books, XIX, 317, Gladstone Papers.

[23] J. L. Garvin, *The Life of Joseph Chamberlain* (London, 1932), I, 446-448.

but resumed toward the close of June. He then asked
for and received, on July 3, authority to prevent further constructions; and in case that a request to this
effect was refused, he might "destroy the earthworks
and silence the batteries if they opened fire." Two days
earlier Gladstone had speculated in a letter to Granville on the possibility that Britain might be expected to
put down Arabi, but he came to the conclusion that this
question had not yet arrived. On July 4 he wrote to
Granville with reference to a proposal to be presented
to the cabinet the next day: "I have thought it right to
give pretty broad and clear notice that I can be no party
to the adoption of the measure which I understand will
be suggested to us." The nature of the measure is not
clear, but not improbably it was that of military action
in Egypt, to which Gladstone consented on July 5. On
the same day Granville asked Northbrook: "What will
Admiral [Seymour] do about the guns which have been
put up [at Alexandria] since our order was sent?"
Northbrook replied: "He has no orders to do anything.
If we want to bring on a fight we can instruct B. Seymour to require the guns to be dismantled. My advisers
do not think they will do much harm where they are."[24]

When the French served notice that they would not
associate themselves with the English "in stopping by
force the erection of batteries or the placing of guns
at Alexandria," Gladstone admitted that they "have

[24] Original MS., Granville Papers.

acted (from their point of view) in the right." He did not see that the British government could improve matters by arguing with them. It was suggested that Britain might secure aid from Italy, but Gladstone remarked: "It would not I conceive be wise to ask them anything; but it seems a fine opportunity for them [i.e., the Italians]."[25] On Sunday, July 9, it was reported that more guns were being mounted at Alexandria, and then the general order to the admiral went into force. Should he ask for the surrender of the forts? Gladstone was troubled. At 9 p.m. he wrote to Granville: "The matter is one of much complication about 'surrender' *because* of the territorial question involved—so at least it seems to me. But on the other hand I had already before your messenger came said this to myself: 'If he [the admiral] is authorised to blow them [the forts] to pieces, may he not think it is as well to give the Egyptians the option of *placing them in his hands*.' "[26] The following morning Admiral Seymour demanded surrender within twenty-four hours of the forts that commanded the harbor, and threatened bombardment in case of refusal. The Egyptians refused, and the bombardment, followed by the burning of Alexandria and serious disorders in the city,

[25] Gladstone to Granville, July 7, 1882. Copy, letter books, XIX, 321, Gladstone Papers.
[26] Earlier in the day Gladstone had written: "The admiral's telegram read but I am at a loss to understand the meaning of the word surrendered. What title can we have to demand the surrender of any forts? and this without instructions? I suppose it may be a conjectural word." Original MSS., Granville Papers.

took place on July 11, 1882. The act was defended by
Gladstone in the house of commons July 12, and in
lengthy letters to John Bright. The house supported
him; but Bright's Quaker conscience would not allow
him to continue as member of the government. His resignation removed a formidable obstacle to further British
interference in Egypt.

That such interference was necessary soon became
abundantly evident. When the Egyptian troops withdrew from Alexandria, the city was pillaged and burned
and the British had to land a force from their ships to
prevent further destruction of life and property. This
left them in control of the principal port of Egypt; outside it Arabi had reduced the khedive's authority to a
shadow and made paramount his own. During the summer of 1882 the telegraph wires were kept busy between
the capitals of the powers transmitting proposals and
suggestions concerning Egypt. Efforts to induce the
sultan to act either on his own authority or as manda-
tory for Europe proved unavailing; the concert as a
whole refused to take action; and Britain sought vainly
to obtain the co-operation of France or Italy. Reluc-
tantly Britain sent an army to Egypt under the command
of Sir Garnet Wolseley, and Arabi Pasha was easily
defeated at Tel-el-Kebir on September 13 and captured
shortly afterwards. By this victory Britain was the *de
facto* ruler of Egypt; but how to regularize this control
while maintaining the khedival government with all its

international restrictions, what to do with Arabi, how to square themselves with France, Turkey, and the other powers supplied problems a-plenty for Gladstone and his colleagues. Most of these problems were not congenial to the prime minister; he worked hard to make the solutions conform, as far as possible, with his general principles concerning foreign policy; and not infrequently he viewed with misgiving the plans agreed upon.

By degrees Gladstone became reconciled to the idea of British intervention in Egypt. Writing to Granville July 22, 1882, Gladstone said: "I do not think I can march quite at the pace you propose." He favored that before "sole" action was undertaken every possibility for securing collective or joint action must be explored. But if these failed "we should," he wrote, "not be deterred by any apprehensions as to the magnitude of the enterprise, or the amount of the force required, if the way be clear in point of principle."[27] He still hoped to march with France and was anxious to bring Italy in; but he was bitterly opposed to a continuance or renewal of the French *entente* in Egypt as established by the Salisbury-Waddington agreement of September, 1879. In September, 1882, Gladstone felt strongly that his hands were tied and that he was unable to explain the policy his government had followed with reference to France and Egypt because of Salisbury's secret agreement. "Of all the outrages he committed," Gladstone

[27] Copy, letter books, XIX, 340, Gladstone Papers.

wrote to Granville, September 3, 1883, "even including the *fibs*, I am inclined to believe his three secret treaties, two of them still unpublished, are the most outrageous. . . . I am not aware of having ever during my half a century heard of such a thing as a secret treaty, except the three—I believe—made by Salisbury in his two years: if indeed he was not just about a fourth in the matter of Herat, when he was put out. It is my opinion that, in justice to Parliament and the country, means ought to be found for making such proceedings impossible and I am inclined to consider whether it may not be right, without going into the particulars, to allude to his system as a system and to denounce it. Such is the wrong done by it to Parliament and the country."[28]

After the battle of Tel-el-Kebir it had become evident that the Anglo-French *entente* belonged to the past. "There is nothing more clear I think in the Egyptian question," Gladstone wrote on September 29, "than that the *dual action* must be abolished." If France demurred, Gladstone believed the abolition could be based on the grounds of the failure of the dual control and "That it has de facto disappeared together with the revo-

[28] Copy, letter books, XIX, 377, Gladstone Papers. He had discussed this topic in letters to Granville, July 26 and August 25, 1882. Original MSS., Granville Papers. Granville instituted a search in the matter of secret treaties before the time of Salisbury and found that they were more numerous than Gladstone had supposed, although he thought only two, "Aberdeen's with Portugal, 1842 & Malmsbury's of 1852" were "not related to occupations & wars." Gladstone to Granville, September 8, 1882. Copy, Gladstone Papers.

lution and anarchy (which it helped to bring about)." Later he admitted, however, that the latter point might be made largely for the sake of argument. "I am far from thinking," he said on October 3, "the controul has *entirely* failed. But it seems to me that in the face of France we are entitled to say it has failed, and for this reason. It afforded Arabi the pretext, & in the face of the world the justifying reason, on which he founded his movement, disturbed Europe, & cost us our lives & our millions. This being so the parties to the controul did not act jointly in upholding it, and in meeting the consequences it had entailed. Therefore I think we are in a condition not to go before France with a request, which would involve us in much risk, but in the most delicate manner to convey to them our full belief that they with us will see it cannot be maintained."[29] In a later letter Gladstone elaborated on the point that "the Controul (with which I associate the Secret Treaty agreement) brought us into the war. The Secret Agreement of itself prevented our taking a narrower part than France, and the Controul seemed to put upon us a moral compulsion to advise the Khedive in his difficulties. Having thus advised, and the advice having been taken, we could not abandon him in his difficulties but had to carry him through, *ergo* to make war."[30] Although France did not prove so accommodating in the

[29] Copy, letter books, XX, 26, Gladstone Papers.
[30] Gladstone to Granville, December 21, 1882. Copy, *ibid.*, 112-113.

matter of withdrawal from "the controul" as Gladstone
had anticipated, he and his colleagues remained firm in
their conviction that Britain should go it alone in Egypt;
and the dual control ended officially with Lord Granville's circular note to the powers, January 3, 1883.[31]

In the winter of 1882 Gladstone had favored internationalization of the Egyptian question; but Bismarck
showed no interest in this, and the experience with the
Constantinople conference seems to have convinced
Gladstone that international action was impracticable.
"I hope," Gladstone wrote to Granville, September 7,
1882, "you will not agree to any words [in the protocol
of the conference] which make us dependent upon all
and each of the Powers for our eventual settlement in
Egypt. Is not the following a possible combination: that
Russia and perhaps Austria should sell Egyptian interests to the Sultan against some boon to themselves? Each
has selfish aims to prosecute, and neither can be supposed
to care much for Egyptian liberties."[32] In a later memorandum on Egypt, Gladstone took it for granted that
the military settlement of Egypt should "remain in the
hands of England as a consequence of the war and to
avoid the inconvenience and delays of a reference to the
Powers." He admitted that the powers might partici-
pate in the political settlement, but he thought Britain
should take the initiative and provide the basis for an

[31] Cromer, *Modern Egypt*, I, 340-341.
[32] Copy, letter books, XIX, 382, Gladstone Papers.

arrangement. Gladstone had in the earlier stages of the Egyptian discussions advocated using Turkey and the suzerain powers held by the sultan; but the experiences with Turkey in the summer of 1882 and the British military intervention caused Gladstone to define the sovereignty of the sultan as limited to "(a) the continuance of the tribute [and] (b) the homage of the Khedive." The right to demand military aid from Egypt "must go to the ground when Egypt will not, in the proper sense, possess an army." Gladstone thought that the power of the sultan to make and unmake khedives was lost since he had proved "unable or unwilling to maintain them."[33] But Gladstone objected to independence for Egypt. The reasons were stated in a letter to Granville of October 17, 1882. "Besides the argument of the Debt," Gladstone wrote, "I am averse to establishing Egyptian Independence on account of the general fabric of the Ottoman Empire, about which I for one have been steadily conservative, I think like you, not from love of it but from dread of the evils of a general scramble for the spoils."[34]

Gladstone rejected a British protectorate over Egypt, "which I incline to think would be worse than annexation." He considered the position of Britain to be "somewhat analogous to that held by Russia in Bulgaria—the result of past services to the country." British statesmen

[33] Appendix II.
[34] Copy, Gladstone Papers.

should, he thought, be guarded in their "utterances about Egypt & though we may have to listen, yet shall for ourselves eschew discussion on the particulars of the coming settlement."[35] The settlement which Gladstone favored was outlined in a memorandum of September 15, 1882. On the military side it should consist of the disbandment of the rebel force with banishment of its officers as a dangerous class, the organization of a military force and police for the maintenance of order and to provide security for the khedival throne, and the speedy withdrawal of foreign troops. The cost of the military operations "now concluded" should not constitute a charge on Egypt, but a force was to be kept until the khedival army had been created, and during the occupation it might be paid for by Egypt. "Such force ought if possible not to exceed two, or from two to three, thousand men." Concerning the local political institutions the plan embodied: 1. Confirmation of the privileges accorded Egypt in the past and such others as might prove necessary for a stable settlement. 2. Neutralization of Egypt. 3. "Subject to all due provisions for the fulfillment of international engagements, it is presumed that England will make a firm stand for the reasonable development of self-governing institutions in Egypt."[36] The last topic Gladstone declared especially important. "We have now," he wrote to Granville, September 16, 1882,

[35] Gladstone to Granville, October 17, 1882. *Ibid.*
[36] Appendix II.

"reached a point at which to some extent the choice lies between *more* intervention and less—, and the question is fairly raised whether [we] are to try to prepare Egypt for a self-governing future. I believe our choice has been made." This choice he explained on October 3. "We have concluded that the safest basis [for the future] is to be found in freedom and self-development, as far as may be, for Egypt."

But the settlement which Gladstone wished to make for Egypt could not, he thought, be planned by a military man. He therefore proposed immediately after Tel-el-Kebir that a civilian should be sent out for that purpose. After various names had been mentioned and rejected, the choice fell on Lord Dufferin, the British ambassador at Constantinople. He was given a free hand. "With the confidence we repose in Dufferin," Gladstone wrote, "I should be inclined to give him much latitude, and let him, knowing our views, make the best settlement he can."[37] When Dufferin's report reached London, January, 1883, Gladstone was leaving for Cannes. He desired a complete holiday, but on account of his great interest in the development of local institutions in

[37] Gladstone to Granville, November 19, 1882. Copy, letter books, XX, 74, Gladstone Papers. "Our ideas," wrote Granville to Dufferin, November 23, 1882, "are not cut and dried about those liberal institutions which we desire to develop—we do not wish to put people unfitted for it [sic] in a position to do harm.—But the Conservatives are ready to join the Radicals in attacking us [if] we neglect our pledges—& we are inclined to think that the fear of those who dread the mischief the notables may do is exaggerated." Copy, Granville Papers.

Egypt, a concise summary of the report was forwarded
to him. However, his comments on it were brief and
chiefly confined to a suggestion that the method of elec-
tions to the legislative council might be simplified.

In the autumn of 1882 the trial of Arabi Pasha created much interest. Gladstone considered him a villain,
but he believed that Britain should abstain from inter-
fering with his trial. Later, when reports of keel-haul-
ing and other methods of ill-treating prisoners reached
England, Gladstone urged vigilance on the part of the
British representatives in Egypt. Dufferin reported from
Egypt, December 12, 1882, that "Arabi and his con-
federates seem to be a very poor set of creatures from
all I can hear . . . colonels were prompted by low and
selfish motives." Although Gladstone at one time believed that Arabi deserved to be hung, he was satisfied
with the sentence of banishment, without being much
worried as to where Arabi went so long as he left Egypt.

No sooner had Dufferin reached Egypt than he asked
for a speedy reduction of the army of occupation and
its staff. Egypt was appalled at its cost. Recommendations and advice to the same effect came afterwards
from Baring, who arrived in Egypt as agent of the
British government in September, 1883, and from Sir
Garnet Wolseley and Sir Evelyn Wood. This was in
accord with Gladstone's own view; and he suffered much
abuse because the greater part of the British army had
been withdrawn when the Sudan situation became seri-

ous, the withdrawal of the troops being interpreted as indicative of a desire to abandon Egypt. But an examination of the documents reveals that the financial motive suggested by Dufferin was uppermost in the mind of Gladstone. The riots in Alexandria on June 11, and the looting and burning of the city on and after July 11, 1882, caused Egypt to be confronted with large claims for indemnities. The maintenance of the British army of occupation constituted another heavy drain upon a budget which had been balanced only with great difficulty when the native army and its officers were ill-paid or not paid at all. By the Law of Liquidation more than one-half of the revenue had been pledged for the debt, and the unpledged revenue suffered greatly on account of the stagnation in trade. Thereupon Britain, as receiver for the bankrupt client, Egypt, faced a combination of the powers which had no regard for the welfare of Egypt but simply sought to derive all possible advantages from the embarrassments of Britain.[38]

The years 1883 and 1884 were transitional years in Egypt, years wherein various experiments were tried in administration and when the British government attempted to keep hands off. But the experience of these years compelled Britain to assume a more direct though still veiled control over Egyptian affairs and to seek modifications in the rights and immunities enjoyed by

[38] Lord Milner, *England in Egypt.* Eleventh edition (London, 1904), 54, 80.

foreigners and in the Law of Liquidation. However, no changes could be made without negotiations with the powers, thereby giving each of them a chance to squeeze Britain. The era of a more active British supervision of Egyptian affairs dawned with the return to Egypt of Sir Evelyn Baring, later Lord Cromer, as British agent. But the matter of finance presented greater difficulties due to the peculiar status of the country.

During the year 1883 the Egyptian government refused to relinquish its precarious hold on the Sudan where a religious leader, styled the Mahdi, had raised the standard of revolt and was sweeping everything before him. In normal years when the Sudan was tolerably well governed, it constituted a drain upon the Egyptian exchequer amounting to about £100,000 annually.[39] In 1883 it cost more, and a reconquest of the Sudan by Egypt was financially impossible; hence Baring and the British government insisted that Egypt must abandon the Sudan. In Egypt the reforms in army, police, and administration, under the direction of Sir Evelyn Wood, Valentine Baker, and, for a limited period, Clifford Lloyd, necessitated the services of highly paid British officials. Trade failed to revive, and the revenues, except those that had been assigned by the Law of Liquidation to the bondholders, proved entirely inadequate for the current needs. At the opening of the year 1884 the finances of Egypt presented curious contradictions.

[39] Bernard M. Allen, *Gordon and the Sudan* (London, 1931), 137.

Large surpluses were being accumulated from the assigned revenues, and considerable sums were set aside
as a sinking fund for debts paying an interest of four
per cent, when even larger deficits were piling up on
current accounts and a loan had to be negotiated to
cover these and to pay the Alexandrian indemnities.
But such a loan could be contracted only with the consent of the powers and of Turkey, and it would be
impossible to arrange for it without important changes
in the Law of Liquidation. British financial experts
studied and reported on the situation. They recommended among other things reduction in the interest on
the funded debt from four to three and a half or three
per cent, the suspension of or a great reduction in the
sum set aside for the sinking fund, a British guarantee
of a new loan for Egypt, and either reduction in the
interest paid by Egypt to Britain on the Suez Canal debt
or another rather complicated arrangement whereby
Britain might grant credit to Egypt in anticipation of
large earnings from Suez Canal dividends which would
become available in 1894 and run until 1968.[40] But the

[40] Memoranda on Egyptian finance by Alonzo Money and Edgar
Vincent, printed for the foreign office, April 8, 1884, Granville
Papers. The question of reducing the interest on the Suez Canal
debt had been discussed in December, 1883. On December 28, 1883,
Northbrook wrote to Granville: "I do not see how we shall be able
to avoid some financial sacrifice by remission or reduction of the
annual payment for the Suez Canal shares or otherwise—especially
if the interest of the bondholders is reduced." Original MS., Granville
Papers.

latter alternative had such a speculative foundation that it did not command serious attention.

The plan to reduce the interest on Egyptian bonds aroused apprehension in France and neither this nor the reduction of the sinking fund could be accomplished without international sanction. Sole British guarantee of an Egyptian loan meant international recognition of the paramountcy of Britain's position in Egypt and was therefore objectionable to France; and the suggestion to reduce the amount of money payable to Britain without a corresponding sacrifice by the bondholders met with much opposition in England. Chamberlain led this opposition in the cabinet; it might be pointed out that the Egyptian bondholders who collected four per cent had bought the bonds under par, while Britain had paid in full the sum on which she charged an interest of five per cent. In the summer and autumn of 1884, when the question came before the British government, the fate of the third reform bill hung in the balance. To agree to special British sacrifices in Egypt over and above those already made in connection with the restoration of order might have ruined the chances of extending the franchise to the agricultural laborers. This then, in brief, is the background against which we shall try to depict Gladstone's policy in regard to Egypt, 1883 and 1884. The problem of the Sudan will be left for separate treatment.

Too optimistically Gladstone had assumed in September, 1882, that all would "agree that the exemptions from taxation now enjoyed by foreigners as such ought not to continue." A year later he urged a speedy reduction in the number of European civil servants in Egypt and again suggested the taxation of foreigners; both measures would, he thought, help the finances and the popularity of the khedive. On December 9, 1884, Gladstone wrote to Granville: "It is only just now that I have learned the grossness of the inequality between taxation of the rich in Egypt & that of the poor . . . it is quite monstrous. It really would seem as if the imposition of a fair share of taxation on the rich now so unjustly favored wd. serve the Bondholders & everybody else. When I acquiesced . . . in Northbrook's recom[n] not to touch the land settlement, I had not an idea of the grossness of the case. I dare say we could not *standing alone* bring about this change; but it is a common interest of all the Powers."[41] But unfortunately the powers were more interested in preserving the immunity of taxation enjoyed by their own subjects than in an equitable distribution of taxes in Egypt. The two questions were insolubly linked, as Northbrook assured Gladstone, December 12, 1884. Nevertheless, Gladstone remained firm on the point that "we must not oppress the people of Egypt."

But how to prevent this and to secure the other point to which Gladstone gave much prominence, namely, not to allow the powers through Egypt to "lay an intoler-

[41] Copy, letter books, XXI, 290-291.

able burden on the neck of England," proved a task of
immense difficulty. In the summer of 1884 a conference
at London wrestled with the Egyptian financial question. Its failure was almost a foregone conclusion. Britain
insisted on reducing the interest of the unified debt by
one-half of one per cent. France, as always in the Egyptian discussions, acted as the agent of the bondholders
and refused to agree to such a reduction. The pound of
flesh must be collected. That she and others of the Egyptian creditors should fifty years hence be in the position of a defaulting debtor could, of course, not be foreseen. Bismarck was now at the zenith of his power;
Austria and Italy were his allies, Russia was bound by
a special agreement; in France, Gambetta was dead,
Boulangerism had not yet raised its head, Bismarck had
Ferry in tow. The German chancellor was playing a
game of high politics in which the fellaheen of Egypt
counted for naught. Into the Egyptian financial discussions England came with hands not clean, but those of
the other powers were positively foul. In the summer
of 1884 they won "a resounding victory" by defeating
the English suggestions for an Egyptian settlement; and
to curb further the British influence over Egyptian finances a plan was presented to have a German and a
Russian representative added to the debt commission,[42]
the members of which had little to do except kick their

---

[42] The commission consisted of representatives of Austria, Britain,
France, and Italy.

heels at Cairo. But each drew a salary of about £3,000 per annum—thus there was also the possibility of morsels for a deserving German and a Russian from the Egyptian carrion.

In September, 1884, Lord Northbrook went to Egypt. He traveled by way of Paris and Vienna and became convinced that neither France nor Austria would agree to a reduction of the interest on the Egyptian bonds. At Vienna Kalnoky blandly told the British ambassador, Sir A. Paget, that the powers were not "responsible for the present state of things in Egypt, and the deplorable condition of its finances, and they therefore did not see why their subjects were to be mulct [sic] out of their property in the shape of a reduction in the interest on their coupons."[43] Before Northbrook left England he had a conference with Gladstone. They were, Gladstone reported to Granville, agreed as to Egypt. Gladstone expressed himself as impressed with "the trumpery difficulties of the Egyptian question." "I will not say," he wrote, "of the failure of the conference because I think Bismarck wished it to fail." He was still sanguine about France. The French proposal which "recognized the principle that the Law of Liquidation was to be altered, the surpluses to be appropriated, and, if the Egyptian revenues finally were adjudged insufficient for the purposes of Govt. the dividend might be touched," afforded

[43] Paget to Granville, August 10, 1884. Printed dispatch, Granville Papers.

a basis for negotiations. Gladstone thought a bridge might be built between the British and the French plans by a proposal "that any unpaid portions of this half per cent [reduction proposed by Britain], or the whole of it, if unpaid, should be a charge upon any future surpluses of Egyptian revenue."[44] But the French unfortunately refused to admit the existence of or the need for a deficit. They thought higher land taxes might be imposed—apply the kourbash more vigorously on the back of the fellaheen and the money would be forthcoming. A suggestion by Gladstone that Britain might turn the difficulties of France in Madagascar and in China to account for the benefit of Egypt was apparently found inexpedient. Northbrook studied the Egyptian situation, recommended reforms, and presented a financial plan wherein the bondholders escaped but Britain had to take a reduction of one and a half per cent in the interest on the Suez Canal debt. On these points Lord Northbrook had made up his mind shortly after his arrival in Egypt. It may be well to give his own arguments when advocating a reduction in the interest collected by Britain. "We paid," he wrote in a memorandum of November 14, 1884, " £4,000,000 for these [i.e., Suez Canal] shares when they were at £22. The Egyptian Government paid us 5 per cent. upon the purchase money, while we borrowed it at 3 per cent. The value of the shares has gone up to £76. If the

[44] Gladstone to Granville, August 28, 1884. Copy, Gladstone Papers.

transaction is completed according to the present arrangement, the British tax-payer will make a profit in 1894 of no less than 11½ millions. Under these circumstances, I think not only that no reasonable person can object to my having included a deduction of 1½ per cent. from the interest paid to us by the Egyptian Government among the deductions of the sinking funds, but also that I have been somewhat shabby in not advising Her Majesty's Government to remit the whole, instead of converting the residue into a larger annuity, for if the claim for interest was given up, the British tax-payer would still realize a profit on the transaction in 1894 of about 9 millions."[45] A point of importance in Lord Northbrook's final report was the suggestion that Britain should guarantee an Egyptian loan of eight and a half million pounds. The total effect of his plan would, he frankly admitted, "undoubtedly be to substitute the financial control of England for the international control which was proposed at the Conference." When this report came before the cabinet the peers supported it and the commoners opposed it. Meanwhile the Egyptian government at the advice but apparently against the

[45] Printed paper, Gladstone Papers. On September 14 Northbrook had written to Granville that he was ready to propose that England should grant Egypt credit for about 5 million pounds and reduce the interest on the Suez Canal debt from 5 to 3 per cent. Original MS., Granville Papers. On July 1, 1894, when the British government gained full possession of the Suez Canal shares they had a market value of nearly £24,000,000 and they yielded an income of £670,000 per annum. J. L. Garvin, *The Life of Joseph Chamberlain* (London, 1934), III, 176.

better judgment of Northbrook had diverted surpluses in the *Caisse de la Dette* to meet current expenses of the government.[46] The foreign powers protested; not even Italy, whose aid Northbrook suggested should be bought by an offer of Massowa on the Red Sea, supported Britain. And in the late autumn of 1884 the protestants secured judgment against the Egyptian government in the mixed tribunals.

In order to make clear the attitude of Gladstone toward the financial scheme presented by Northbrook, we must retrace our steps for a moment, and all the while keep in mind that almost up till Christmas, 1884, the fate of the reform bill was uncertain. When Northbrook left England, he and Gladstone appear to have been "agreed as to Egypt"; but the prime minister did not have the advantage of discussing the question at Paris and Vienna as Northbrook did. When "probing" letters from Northbrook began to arrive, Gladstone observed that the plan seemed to be that the Egyptian bondholders should be paid with English money, "and this in my opinion will not work."

"I greatly doubt," he wrote on another occasion, "whether Parliament would or should assume new responsibilities for Egyptian finance and as an equivalent full financial control." He feared the latter would prove

[46] On September 23, 1884, Northbrook wrote that he thought it better to make payment now than to attempt to drive a bargain. Original MS., Granville Papers.

"a certain though possibly circuitous path towards annexation." Gladstone did not want "to knuckle down" to Kalnoky on the matter of the reduction of interest, and underestimated the power for mischief wielded by Bismarck. "I think," he wrote, September 19, 1884, "we are all too much afraid of Bismarck. He will never be really associated in feeling with this Govt., until it ceases to be, what it is, the main obstacle to the accomplishment of his schemes in the Balkan Peninsula. Such is my opinion. Something between a surmise and a conviction."[47]

Gladstone kept an open mind on the question of using the prospective profit from the Suez Canal shares as a means for relieving the financial difficulties of Egypt. Already in March, 1884, when a financial report of Sir Edgar Vincent was before the cabinet, Gladstone had considered the possibility of using the accrued value of the Suez Canal shares as a means for making financial adjustments in Egypt. When this topic was again brought forward by Northbrook, he discussed it seriously in conferences with Childers, then chancellor of the exchequer. Childers was, of course, deeply interested in Northbrook's proposals concerning Egypt, and he and Gladstone ultimately framed the plan submitted to the powers November 24, 1884. "I have," Gladstone informed Granville, November 14, "again been into the

---

[47] Gladstone to Granville. Copy, letter books, XXI, Gladstone Papers.

depths of the Egyptian question with Childers, and I
think we have hammered out something that will hold
water certainly to the extent of warranting us in going
before the Powers, and perhaps as a permanent basis.

"It is to offer towards making up the full Dividend
for the Bondholders should there be a deficit a direct
money boon out of the accruing profits on our Suez
Canal shares from the date when we begin to receive
Dividend.

"The form would be to constitute any unpaid portion of the Dividend a charge upon our Suez Canal Dividends after they had paid us five per cent interest. It
might be a charge with a limit, i.e., for a part of the
deficit, or it might [be] . . . for the whole deficit."[48]

This point is, however, missing from the memorandum
concerning the Egyptian debt settlement which Granville sent to the British representatives in the capitals of
the great powers on November 24. The plan was, in the
main, prepared by Childers. It differed in many important respects from that suggested by Northbrook, the
most important being that Northbrook had recommended a 1½ per cent reduction in the interest on the
Suez Canal debt and none on the interest collected by
the bondholders, whereas Childers' plan provided for a
one-half of one per cent reduction in interest on both

[48] Copy, Gladstone Papers. Writing to Granville, October 17, 1884,
Gladstone said that Britain might hold the door open to relieve
Egyptian finances on the basis of prospective value of Suez Canal
shares. Original MS., Granville Papers.

the unified debt and the Suez Canal debt. Childers retained the suggestion of a guaranteed loan but reduced the amount from 8½ to 5 million pounds. Both plans advocated the taxation of foreigners.[49] The powers delayed replying to the proposals contained in Granville's memorandum until January, 1885. In the meantime the lord chancellor had expressed the opinion that Britain was responsible for the sum sequestrated from the *Caisse de la Dette* by the Egyptian government, and Bismarck had shown his fangs in the Anglo-German colonial disputes. Advance information from Italy encouraged Granville to expect support from that quarter, but it soon became evident that France would be the bellwether and that the other powers would follow her lead.

Gladstone discussed the various aspects of the Egyptian situation in letters to Granville. On December 7, 1884, he wrote: "I wd. give Bismarck every satisfaction about his Colonial matters, and I am ashamed of the panic about Germany in South Africa; but about Egypt we ought not to be kept dangling in the air as is now the case. If Bismarck be unapproachable might not Lyons speak seriously to Ferry on the risks of delay and the impossibility of averting serious consequences if it be protracted?" Gladstone considered whether "the more slack Powers" might not be stimulated "by referring to

[49] *P.P.*, *1884-1885*, LXXXVIII, c.-4337, pp. 20-21. Northbrook objected strongly to Childers' plan in a memorandum of November 20, 1884. Granville Papers.

the possibility of comm^n with Turkey." And before the
mind of Granville flitted the possibility of hinting to
France that Britain might "Tunisify Egypt," but he
checked himself with the thought, "That is a threat we
cannot make."

Finally on January 17, 1885, the French counter-
proposals were presented to Granville. They agreed
with the English on several points including that of the
taxation of foreigners; but France was not satisfied that
Egypt was really unable to carry on under the existing
plan, and suggested a commission of inquiry. She proposed, further, that instead of a reduction of one-half of
one per cent in the interest, a tax of five per cent might
be levied on the coupons, and that the new Egyptian
loan should be increased to 9 million pounds and guaranteed by all the powers. The French plan had the support
of the powers. Gladstone, who had feared that the idea
of international control in Egypt might be revived, was
pleased because the French no longer deemed the coupons inviolable. He was not so disappointed with the
French plan as were some of his colleagues; and he was,
as already stated, ready to accommodate Germany in the
matter of colonies. Nevertheless, it took more than six
weeks and a frank though ill-mannered hint from Bismarck linking Egyptian finance with German colonization, before the British government agreed to a compromise. Gladstone apparently wished to concede the
French request for a commission of inquiry but was out-

voted in the cabinet. Under the final agreement of March 18, 1885, such an inquiry might be undertaken after two years, the sinking fund on the debt was suspended, the coupons and the foreigners could be taxed as proposed by France, and the new loan of 9 million pounds would be guaranteed by the powers. The door was thus kept ajar for a possible international interference with the finances of Egypt.[50]

With the establishment of the British military occupation and the abolition of dual control the question was asked, not unnaturally, how long will Britain remain in Egypt? It was a question which France asked with embarrassing frequency during the next twenty years. Gladstone was opposed to a protectorate and to annexation, but the restoration of law and order and the development of liberal institutions in Egypt had become an obligation which Gladstone felt must be honorably fulfilled. His innate caution warned him against setting a date for the evacuation, but, on the other hand, he was anxious that Britain's stay should be short. Discussing a letter from Ponsonby which embodied the queen's views on the evacuation of Egypt, Gladstone wrote: "To disclaim annexation is of little use, if indefinite occupation is intended and desired—if for instance we are to remain where & while there are 'friendlies' to be supported. At the bottom of the whole affair lies an opinion that the

[50] *P. P.*, *1884-1885*, LXXXVIII, c.-4337, pp. 20-21; Milner, *England in Egypt*, 185-190.

extended military occupation of Egypt is a good for us
(1) as securing high military establishments, (2) as promoting 'prestige.' But I am one of those who look upon
it as a certain weakness, a possible discredit & even
danger."[51]

When discussing Egypt in the closet or on the platform, Gladstone remained true to his views concerning
the dangers lurking in an over-extension of the empire,
to his ideals that people should be trained for self-government, and to his principles regarding the observance
of international obligations. He kept the interest of the
Egyptians before his mind; he was willing to make reasonable concessions to the other powers in order to secure a settlement in Egypt; his intuition warned him of

[51] Gladstone to Granville, January 10, 1885. Copy, letter books,
XXI, 321, Gladstone Papers. On January 6, Gladstone had written to
Granville: "I am disposed to admit that the conduct of the Powers
(except Italy), active only in thwarting, & absolutely useless in
helping the execution of a task, which we undertook with their
approval & greatly for their advantage, has given to this country
(whether to this ministry or not) rights & claims beyond what, if
enjoying their cooperation, it might have been entitled to: rights
& claims growing out of the necessity of the case." Copy, Gladstone
Papers.
The plan to neutralize Egypt appealed strongly to Gladstone. It
was dropped in 1884 because of the controversies over finance; but
in the spring of 1885, Gladstone discussed it informally with Waddington and on June 3 Gladstone wrote to Granville: "Probably
there is no hope at all from the Sultan as to the neutralisation or
anything else. But I had the idea that if the French went keenly
into it they might join us in pressing the Sultan. The matter seems
perhaps less urgent now that the Financial Convention is safe, and
we may get to know what Bismarck the 'overlord' of France thinks
of it." Copy, letter books, XXII, 47, Gladstone Papers.

dangers connected with many measures and policies; but he felt too keenly his lack of first-hand information, he was too much occupied with domestic issues, and he perhaps regarded himself too much as "a vanishing quantity" to urge positive action, exert the influence, and supply the leadership necessary for a quick and satisfactory solution of a very knotty problem.

Chapter VIII

THE SUDAN AND GORDON

THE Egypt which lay at the feet of Britain in September, 1882, claimed a vast dependency to the south, the Egyptian Sudan. Bounded on the east by the Red Sea and the mountains of Abyssinia and stretching southward to the great African lakes, the region covered more than a million square miles, and contained a medley of races and peoples—Negro, negroid, and Arab with varying degrees of intermixtures. In the south the natives worshiped many gods and practiced weird rites, but in the north the religion of Mohammed prevailed. It was a land of vast distances only partially knit together by the Nile and its tributaries, of deserts and of jungles, of burning sand and of pestilential swamps. From the point of view of the area as a whole, the population was scant and the climate deadly for Europeans.

The Egyptian conquest of this region had begun about the middle of the nineteenth century when Mehemet

Ali held sway in Egypt, and under the Khedive Ismail the dependency had reached its greatest extent. As Europeans and Levantines had bled the Egyptians, so Egyptians, Levantines, and Arabs had combined to plunder the Sudanese. Except for the brief period, 1877-79, when General Charles Gordon resided at Khartoum as governor-general of the Sudan, the unhappy people had been exposed to the rapacity of unscrupulous merchants, the brutality of the slave hunters and slave dealers, and the greed, corruption, and inefficiency of the servants of the Egyptian government. The Sudanese hated their Egyptian masters and only lack of union and of leadership had prevented them from putting officials, garrisons, and foreign residents generally to the sword. But almost simultaneously with the nationalistic and military upheaval in Egypt a Mahdi, or guide, appeared in the Sudan in the person of Mohammed Ahmed, the son of a Dongolese boat builder, who had won renown as a holy man and who soon gained a tremendous following in the Sudan. The old religious leaders and the native chiefs offered some resistance, but the multitude hailed with delight the new prophet who seemed capable of inspiring Mohammedans with great religious and martial fervor. Undaunted by early setbacks, the Mahdi and his military adviser, Abdullahi, the Khalifa, swept everything before them when in 1882 they assumed the offensive against the Egyptian rule. In January, 1883, El Obeid, the capital of Kordofan, was captured; and in Novem-

ber an Egyptian army numbering about 10,000 ill-trained
and ill-equipped men led by Hicks Pasha, a retired English officer in the Indian service, was annihilated. The
Mahdist leader in eastern Sudan was Osman Digna, a
former slave dealer. Everywhere the hated foreigners
were driven out or compelled to acknowledge the spir-
itual and political leadership of the Mahdi. The upheaval
was both political and religious, and the representatives
of the Egyptian government were driven out or killed.
Egypt at its best as it was under Mehemet Ali could
hardly have withstood the uprising, and Egypt under
Tewfik was bankrupt, without an army, and buffeted
about by the powers.

The British troops had no sooner occupied Cairo, in
the autumn of 1882, than Sir Edward Malet directed
the attention of his superiors at home to the confused
reports from the Sudan. Some discussion took place, and
Malet declared in a telegram to Granville, November
16, 1882: "Unnecessary to send three officers to Soudan.
Propose to send Lieut. Col. Stewart & an Italian Messe-
daglia who was governor of Darfur under Gordon."
Gladstone noted on the back of the decipher: "This is
a trumpery change, but I should have thought eminently
Egyptian—we disclaim all Soudan business?" To this
Granville replied: "We disclaim to have any responsibility for military operations in the Soudan, but the
mission of these officers to obtain information was asked
for by Malet & [illeg.], in order that they might have

information, and not by the Egyptian Gov. Our War
Office approved. I should have thought it was for the
War Office possibly or for the F.[oreign] O.[ffice] to
pay." Gladstone noted: "I am quite satisfied."[1] Thus the
Sudan began to cast its fateful shadow over the work of
Gladstone and his ministry.

About this time Lord Dufferin, the British ambassador to Constantinople, arrived in Egypt to study and
report on the situation. During his stay there Colonel
Hicks appeared on the scene. Dufferin thought Hicks to
be a good man but carefully avoided contact with him,
and Dufferin refused in any way to identify himself
with the Sudan business. Malet, on the other hand, was
not so discreet, and he seems to have gone beyond what
was desired by the home authorities in acting as the
channel for communications between Hicks and the
Egyptian government. Faithful to the Gladstonian policy
of avoiding meddling in the affairs of Egypt, more than
was absolutely necessary, the British government abstained from giving any advice concerning the Sudan.
During 1883 the khedive recalled Abd-el-Kader, the
energetic governor-general of the Sudan, and sent Hicks
Pasha on a foolhardy campaign against the Mahdi. When
the news of his defeat reached London, plans concerning
the Sudan sprang up like mushrooms. Baring proposed
Turkish troops with English officers and Northbrook
suggested using Indian troops in the Sudan. The latter

[1] Original MSS., Granville Papers.

suggestion ultimately won support from the queen. But any employment of British troops, whether from India or from home, under the British flag implied British responsibility for the Sudan, and the use of British officers for Turkish soldiers might give rise to difficulties equally serious. With the death of Hicks Pasha, English blood had been shed in the Sudan, and this altered the situation in the eyes of many Englishmen.

Gladstone was startled by the proposal of Northbrook to use Indian troops. "It seems to indicate," Gladstone wrote, "a great movement of his mind since the last Cabinet." And with reference to the plan itself, Gladstone observed: "There may be risk from moral contagion in Egypt (emanating from the Sudan), & the duty to keep English force there till that danger has overblown may be clear but our engaging in warfare to recover the Soudan is quite another matter, esp. now that it seems so clear that Egypt has not strength enough to hold it."[2] On this point Gladstone and Baring agreed, and in a dispatch of December 3, 1883, the latter said: "I venture to express a hope that H. M. Government will adhere steadfastly to the policy of non-interference in the affairs of the Soudan." However, the government of Egypt was unable to decide on a policy concerning the Sudan; it put itself in the hands of the British government, and at the same time offered the opinion that

[2] Gladstone to Granville, November 29, 1883. Copy, letter books, XXI, 5, Gladstone Papers.

the sultan as suzerain should be asked to aid in restoring order in the Sudan. Baring mentioned as an alternative the withdrawal of Egyptian forces south of Wadi Halfa.

Baring's telegrams and suggestions were forwarded to Gladstone at Hawarden. He was, however, handicapped by lack of a detailed knowledge of the geography of the country and of the conditions, both military and otherwise, between Wadi Halfa and Khartoum. The idea that Turkish troops might be used, to which Baring seemed to lean, appeared to Gladstone worthy of consideration; "We are perhaps," wrote Gladstone on December 12, 1883, "exposed to as much danger now from that wretch the Sultan, who has nothing at stake, as we should be if he had troops in Nubia while we should hold the key to the sea-route. I think also there is force in Baring's plea that we cannot well forbid Cherif [the prime minister of Egypt] to apply to the Turk while we refuse him aid ourselves."[3]

On the following day Granville sent a telegram to Baring the draft of which had been seen and altered by Gladstone, who had suggested Assuan as the southern boundary for Egypt. On this point Granville compromised so that the telegram recommended abandonment of the territory "south of Assuan, or, at least, of Wadi Halfa."[4] The telegram vetoed the proposal to use

[3] *Ibid.*, 26.

[4] Granville to Gladstone, December 14, 1883. Original MS., Gladstone Papers; Allen, *Gordon and the Sudan*, 204.

British or Indian troops in the Sudan, but did not object to an application to the sultan for aid, and it expressed disapproval of a plan for Zebehr, an ex-slave dealer, to be employed by the Egyptian government. At the time Gladstone did not know who Zebehr was, and Granville had to identify him in a letter of December 14, 1883. Shortly afterwards it occurred to Gladstone that something might be done by means of negotiations to obtain peace in the Sudan. "Is it wholly impossible," he wrote, December 18, "that the Mahdi, who has no quarrel with us (unless as Xians) might be disposed to accept us as mediator? I speak very doubtfully for we know neither his disposition nor his powers, & even if there be a chance in the right direction the question rises how to break the ice & make the first communication"[5]—the idea of sending someone as harbinger of peace to the Sudan had begun to occupy the mind of Gladstone.

In order to secure an intelligent discussion of the Egyptian-Sudanese complications it was suggested that Baring should be asked to come home, but this was opposed by Granville on the ground that Baring's "absence from Cairo might be dangerous, and his coming here will give rise to all sorts of rumours here, and abroad." The government continued to grope its way through the maze of Egyptian difficulties, and in a lengthy letter

[5] Copy, letter books, XXI, 31, Gladstone Papers.

of December 24, 1883, Gladstone offered the following suggestions with reference to the Sudan:

> "1. Not to press at once for abandonment.
> "2. Not to oppose calling on the Turks, nor make wry faces about it.
> "3. To ask the Egyptians to begin by assuming Turk will pay, & if compelled to recede from that ground to be bound only for certain terms within certain *times*, for certain amount of force, & on no account to undertake indefinite pecuniary obligations.
> "4. Egypt should also press the anti-slave trade policy on the Sultan.
> "5. And fix geographical limits of the intervention.
> "6. Also stipulate for withdrawal when pacification is accomplished (but probably stoppage of pay is the only sort of security worth having)."[6]

There is, however, an air of unreality about this discussion of the use of Turkish troops in the Sudan and who should pay for them; Cromer claims that the Egyptians did not much want to call in the Turk, and both Egypt and Turkey were bankrupt. More practical was the discussion of the abandonment of the Sudan, on which Baring and the British government insisted, but to which the government of Egypt objected on political grounds. The divergence of views led to the resig-

[6] Copy, *ibid.*

nation of the ministry of Cherif Pasha on January 7, 1884. This decided the issue; the Sudan must be abandoned, but how and by whom were the beleaguered garrisons to be extricated?

On the day of Cherif's resignation Gladstone wrote, from Hawarden, to Lord Granville:

"I return the Wilson [i.e., Sir C. W. Wilson] paper on the Soudan and I am much struck with what he says (besides Suakim) on

(1) Zebehr or Zebir
(2) Abyssinia
(3) Sending some to Khartoum for authentic information—if it cannot be had more quickly without the measure.
(4) The advantage of Assuan as a point for military resistance.

"It seems a little strange that we never hear anything of the sectarian rivalry & mutual hatred of Sunnite & Shiite as entering into this question at all."

.   .   .   .

["P.S.] I am not sorry to see the Porte disposed to send troops, France notwithstanding; for I care *more* that we keep out of the Soudan than who goes in."[7] But the Porte in the end refused to send troops, Egypt was powerless, and the British government, as well as every-

---

[7] Copy, letter books, XXI, 50, *ibid.*

body else, remained in the dark about the actual situation in the Sudan. At this stage we must introduce the hero of the Sudanese tragedy, General Charles Gordon, our special object being, of course, to show the part played by Gladstone in the tragedy, or perhaps we may call it the apotheosis, of General Gordon.

Gordon had the fortune, or misfortune, of firing the imagination of the English people by his exploits in suppressing the Taiping rebellion in China, 1862-64. His character and achievements appealed strongly to the sentimentally minded Englishmen of the Victorian era. Like Sir Henry Havelock and other heroes of the age, Gordon was a good Christian, quiet and unassuming in social intercourse, yet wonderfully cool, brave, and daring in an emergency. As governor of the Equatorial Sudan, 1874-76, and governor-general of the Sudan, 1877-79, he had won great renown as administrator and ruler of the dusky millions of that great province. He was the idol of the God-fearing and slavery-hating Englishmen as well as of the ultra patriots who rejoiced in the alleged super-man qualities of one of their own race. He and his work had been exploited by the newspapers, and he was adored by W. T. Stead, a humanitarian and the leading "stunt" journalist in the England of the eighties.

Since Gordon was supposedly the greatest living English authority on the Sudan, it is not surprising that Lord Dufferin mentioned him, November 18, 1882, as the most suitable agent to gather information and report on the state of the province; but at this time Col. Stewart was chosen. When the news of the disaster which had befallen Hicks Pasha reached England earnest souls naturally thought of Gordon as the right man for any mission to that region. Suggestions to this effect reached Granville, who passed them on to Gladstone with the remarks: "Do you see any objection to using Gordon in some way? He has an immense name in Egypt—he is popular at home. He is a strong but very sensible opponent of slavery. He has a small bee in his bonnet. If you do not object I could consult Baring by telegraph."[8]

Gladstone's reply was unenthusiastic and non-committal. "I can quite understand," he wrote, "that there might be advantages in the employment of Gordon—but for what? & by whom?"[9] Granville considered the reply satisfactory, and on December 1, 1883, he proposed Gordon to Baring, who refused to accept him.

Sponsors for the employment of Gordon soon appeared in many quarters. Sir Evelyn Wood, commander-in-chief of the Egyptian army, writing to the queen on December 11, 1883, called her attention to a book on *Col. Gordon in Central Africa, 1874-79*, by G. Birkbeck Hill, and proceeded: "Sir Evelyn has never met Gordon; but after allowing for his peculiar views about religion,

[8] Granville to Gladstone, November 27, 1883. Original MS., *ibid.*
[9] Gladstone to Granville, November 29, 1883. Copy, letter books, XXI, 5, Gladstone Papers.

Sir Evelyn believes his account of Egyptian-caused-misery in the Soudan is accurate, and that he is the only man who could do anything up there at this moment without a good army."[10] Lord Wolseley, the victor of Tel-el-Kebir and a lifelong friend of Gordon, agreed with Wood that Gordon was *the* man for the Sudan. Sir Samuel Baker, who had won fame as explorer and governor of the Sudan, used *The Times* in urging the appointment of Gordon as high commissioner of the Sudan; and on January 9, 1884, Stead rallied demos through a stirring appeal in the *Pall Mall Gazette*, in support of the ever growing demand for sending Gordon to the Sudan.[11] Meanwhile Gladstone had, as we have seen, been pondering the possibility of dispatching a messenger of peace to the Sudan or of employing someone who could inform the government of the actual state of affairs in that region; and Baring had expressed the opinion that if the British government insisted upon the abandonment of the Sudan "an English officer of high authority" should be sent to Khartoum to effect the withdrawal of the garrisons and arrange "for the future government of the country."[12] Since the government continued to adhere to the policy of withdrawal, the contingency anticipated by Baring had arisen, and on January 10, 1884, the queen seconded Baring's re-

[10] *Letters of Queen Victoria*, 2nd series, III, 457-458.
[11] Allen, *Gordon and the Sudan*, 211-218.
[12] *Ibid.*, 206.

quest for an English officer.[13] Furthermore, parliament
would convene early in February—the parliament which
was scheduled to pass the reform bill—and discussions
about the Sudan might create an awkward situation for
the government. Experts on Egypt, members of parliament, and a powerful section of the press had chosen
Gordon as the man for the Sudan. There seemed nothing for the government to do but to heed a request so
well sponsored and so powerfully supported.

How Granville and Gladstone viewed the proposal
to send Gordon is revealed in their letters. Granville on
January 14, 1884, called attention to the popular clamor
concerning Gordon, noted that his name had been suggested twice to Baring and rejected by him, that the
reason for the refusal may have been purely personal,
and that Wolseley would have a conference with Gordon on the following day "and will ask him as a friend,
what are his views." And then Granville makes the re-
vealing statement: "If he [i.e., Gordon] says that he
cannot go to Egypt, or that he cannot go without a
considerable force, such as he mentions in rather a
foolish letter in the Times of today, we shall be on
velvet."[14] But if he said that he believed that by his per-

[13] "The Queen regrets to perceive that Sir Evelyn Baring's repeated
requests for an answer on the employment of English officers are not
noticed." *Letters of Queen Victoria*, 2nd series, III, 469. That evening Granville inquired from Baring if Gordon or Sir Charles Wilson could be of any use. Allen, *Gordon and the Sudan*, 217.

[14] Original MS., Gladstone Papers. For some mysterious reason this
sentence is not quoted by Morley, *Gladstone*, III, 149-150.

sonal influence he could arrange for the safe evacuation of Khartoum, Granville suggested "little pressure" on Baring. Gladstone replied by telegraph, January 15, that he agreed with Granville's statements concerning Gordon.[15] On the same day Granville sent to his chief the result of Wolseley's interview with Gordon and declared it "not very satisfactory"[16]—no impossible condition had been presented. Gordon had declared that if he were in authority "he would send himself out direct to Suakim without going to Cairo" and offered a sketch of the terms upon which he was willing to go. Some of these were later incorporated in his instructions, and Gordon's notes included the following points: "1. To proceed to Suakim & report on the Military situation & return. Under Baring for orders & to send through him letters &c under flying seal.

.   .   .   .   .

"7. I understand H. M. G. only wish me to report & in no way bound to me." But at the interview Gordon

[15] Gladstone jotted on Granville's letter: "Your letter of yesty. on G[ordon] I agree throughout." Original MS., Gladstone Papers. The telegram is found among the Granville Papers.

[16] Copy, Granville Papers. The message reads: "I send you the result, not very satisfactory, of the interview at the War Office. Wolseley did not mention us in his conversation with Gordon. I have sent the enclosed telegram to Baring." The report was written by Lord Hartington, the secretary of state for war. See below, note 17. The statement, "Wolseley did not mention us," which must mean the government, contradicts the account later given by Wolseley. Allen, *Gordon and the Sudan*, 221.

refused to intimate what his recommendations might be after he reached Egypt and the Sudan. He would have to see the "state of affairs on the spot."[17] After this interview, obviously satisfactory to the advocates of sending Gordon to the Sudan, arrangements were made concerning his status in the British army, and he went to Brussels to be released from an agreement with the king of the Belgians to go to the Congo. This was effected without a hitch, and Gordon returned to London early on January 18.

In the two days that had elapsed since Gordon's meeting with Wolseley many things had happened. On the 15th Hartington reported to Gladstone on Wolseley's interview with Gordon and enclosed Gordon's notes, and on that day Granville officially proposed Gordon to Baring; on the following day Gladstone recorded his opinion of Granville's plan to send Gordon. Gladstone did not object; but he believed that the government must be very careful in framing Gordon's instructions, they must guard against the possibility that he might involve Britain in heavy responsibility, and not allow him to be the judge of what should be done and who should do it.[18] On the same day Baring renewed his request for a British officer to conduct the retreat from Khartoum,

[17] Hartington to Gladstone, January 15, 1884. Original MS.. Gladstone Papers. This report is misdated January 18 in Holland, *Life of the Duke of Devonshire*, I, 418, and the misdating has caused Dr. Allen a good deal of trouble, *Gordon and the Sudan*, 233-234.

[18] Morley, *Gladstone*, III, 150.

and in a private message to Granville he expressed the belief that "Gordon would be the best man if he will pledge himself to carry out the policy of withdrawal from Sudan as soon as possible. . . . He must also fully understand that he must take his instructions from the British representative in Egypt and report to him." This was communicated to Gladstone who replied: "Baring's cypher sixteenth. I had come to same conclusion that G[ordon] should be instructed by and report to him."[19]

With matters thus arranged Gordon was recalled from Brussels and had his fateful interview with Granville, Hartington, Northbrook, and Sir Charles W. Dilke at the war office, January 18, 1884. The accounts given of this interview by Gordon differ from those given by the ministers, the reason being perhaps that each reported what he considered the essential points, and their judgments on those did not agree. The ministers' accounts stressed the topics which went into Gordon's instructions, namely, that he was sent to report on the conditions in the Sudan, which, incidentally, was the only sort of mission the British government could authorize inasmuch as it exercised no authority in the region or over the garrisons found there. Gordon, as a man of action, fastened on what may have been chance remarks of the ministers but what seemed to him essential. The instructions to Gordon drawn up by Granville followed in several particulars Gordon's own notes

[19] Granville Papers.

written three days previously. He was to report on the situation in the Sudan and to perform such other duties as might be intrusted to him by Baring.[20] The text of the instructions were sent in cipher to Gladstone, who was then at Hawarden, at 3 o'clock p.m., January 18, but his approval did not reach London until the following day. Simultaneously with the sending of the above-mentioned telegram to Gladstone, Granville wrote to him as follows:

"Northbrook, Hartington, Dilke & I took a good deal of responsibility on ourselves, but I think we have acted within the limits of your views. *He Gordon perfectly understands that he is to consider the evacuation as a final decision & that his only mission is to see how it can be best carried out.*[21] He likes Baring and is glad to be under his orders. His views are optimistic. He does not believe in the Mahdi, the fanaticism of the Arabs or in the probability of massacre. He was very pleasing & childlike in his manner."[22]

[20] Allen, *Gordon and the Sudan*, 231-232; Morley, *Gladstone*, III, 554-555. Gordon had suggested in his notes that he should be "under Baring for orders"; the instructions ran: "You will be under the instructions of Her Majesty's agent and consul-general at Cairo. . . . You will consider yourself authorised and instructed to perform such other duties as the Egyptian government may desire to entrust to you, and as may be communicated to you by Sir E. Baring." Dr. Allen claims that the last sentence changed completely the character of the Gordon mission. *Gordon and the Sudan*, 230-232.

[21] Italics are my own. This sentence contains the essence of the controversy over Gordon's instructions.

[22] Original of letter and deciphered telegram are found among the Gladstone Papers. Gladstone's reply to the telegram read: "Your

The action of the four ministers was discussed at a cabinet meeting, January 22, 1884, and Gladstone jotted down the following: "Gordon's mission—a mission to report. Instructions to him read placing him under Baring. His suggested proclamations read. Baring authorized to settle the terms & put them in operation."[23] From these proceedings and the accounts thereof arose long and bitter discussions, not yet quieted down, concerning what took place at the war office on January 18, the nature and character of Gordon's instructions, whether they were violated by him, and the responsibility of Gladstone for these transactions. Some reference to these controversies will be made later; but before we proceed further we shall put on record an interesting letter from Gordon to Lord Northbrook, dated Brindisi, 20 Jan. 1884.

"My dear Lord Northbrook

"I would like to mention how I look upon the question of the Soudan. I think that any reconquest unless under the guarantee of a future better government would have been unjust. Consequently I would never wish the reconquest, however easy it might be, unless with the guarantee of future good Governt.

---

cipher telegram I see no reason to doubt you have done right." This was written in the evening of January 18, but the telegraph station at Chester could not be roused so that it was not sent until the following morning. Morley, *Gladstone*, III, 151 note 2.

[23] Notes taken at meeting of the cabinet. Original MS., Gladstone Papers.

"I never contemplated with pleasure the deeds of our Army in Egypt, for up to nearly now those deeds only brought back the old oppression without any guarantee for the better government of Egypt. It is wonderful that the wretched, despised Soudan has forced our hand, and that we are now really going to benefit the people of Egypt.

"The Government decision to evacuate the Soudan is based therefore on the impossibility without inordinate efforts, of securing a good future Govt. and I think it is a good decision.

"It is no use resurrectioning questions of whether we acted right in letting Hicks go up, and of allowing the Cairo Funds to be spent on the Expedition, but I am glad that this did happen, for nothing short of the Soudan explosion appears to have awakened us to our position in Lower Egypt.

"As for slave trade, as long as Tewfik keeps slaves I do not believe him, and no doubt there will be a merry trade to Egypt now. It, the slave trade, can only be stopped from the Congo.

"I apprehend no difficulty with the evacuation vis-à-vis the Soudan but I fear great distress to the Egyptian employees who want to go to Egypt and for that and the removal of the troops I ought to have £100,-000 available for the purpose, and Egypt will supply this.

"Col. Stewart is a capital fellow and knows the Soudan well.

Believe me

My dear Lord Northbrook

Yours sincerely

(Sig.) C. E. Gordon."[24]

This letter was read by Northbrook's colleagues, and Gordon's full agreement with the government's views concerning evacuation and the avoidance of responsibility for the future government of the Sudan could not but please the ministers. They were, however, contrary to ideas attributed to him by London newspapers shortly before he accepted the commission to the Sudan, and at a later date the government had cause to complain that he had abandoned them for views that were diametrically opposite to those held by the leading members of the cabinet.[25]

[24] Copy, MS., Granville Papers. For text of a memorandum written by Gordon on January 22, see Allen, *Gordon and the Sudan*, 230. Lord Northbrook read his letters from Gordon to the queen, who considered his attempt "a very daring one." *Letters of Queen Victoria*, 2nd series, III, 474.

[25] A further testimony as to how the ministers looked upon the nature of Gordon's mission is found in a private letter from Granville to Dufferin, January 23, 1884. "He [Gordon] went under the promise to act entirely upon our policy and not upon his own rather inaccurately reported by a Pall Mall interviewer. If it is a complete fiasco, we shall look ridiculous, but we shall not be much worse off than we are now—I rather believe in a success. It is not altogether bad for us that there has been such a panic, and with absurdly exaggerated descriptions of the situation. But there is no doubt that there is a general lust for annexations." Copy, MS., Granville Papers. See also Cromer, *Modern Egypt*, I, 389-391.

The appointment of Gordon was hailed with joy by a large section of the press and by public opinion generally. Humanitarians and jingoes united in approving this act by the government, which now enjoyed a moment of considerable popularity. Even Baring joined in the chorus. Although he considered Gordon "half cracked" and had some vague misgivings, Baring was charmed by the honesty and simplicity of Gordon's character, and wrote: "I am very glad he came, for I believe he is the best man we could send."[26]

At Baring's request, Gordon came to Cairo instead of going to the Red Sea and attempting to reach Khartoum by the Suakim-Berber route. At Cairo, Gordon made his peace with the khedive; met Zebehr, the slave dealer, whose son he had had executed; and became immensely impressed by his old enemy. From the government of Egypt Gordon received a formal appointment as governor-general of the Sudan with authority to conduct the evacuation of the Sudan, to restore the petty chiefs to their former independence, and to make this decision known to the people of the Sudan—which was done, perhaps prematurely and unwisely at Berber, on February 13, 1884. Five days later Gordon reached Khartoum and was hailed as savior by the inhabitants.

During the month that elapsed between Gordon's departure from London and his arrival at Khartoum im-

[26] Baring to Granville, "Private," January 28, 1884. Original MS., Granville Papers. For misgivings then entertained by Baring, see quotation in *Modern Egypt*, I, 433.

portant events transpired in eastern Sudan. The local
Mahdist leader, Osman Digna, had threatened the Egyptian garrisons at Tokar, Sinkat, and Suakim. To relieve
them an Egyptian force under an Englishman, General
Valentine Baker, was sent to Suakim, but this army, if
so it may be called, was destroyed on February 5, 1884.
Sinkat and Tokar were now in great danger. English
gunboats under Admiral Hewett were at Suakim and
the British government relied on them to protect this
port. But an intense agitation arose in favor of more
active British intervention in eastern Sudan. The queen,
the humanitarians, and the jingoes urged it so persistently
that the government gave way and dispatched a British
force to Suakim, too late, however, to save the garrisons at Tokar and Sinkat. This force, under General
Graham, defeated the Mahdists on February 29 and
March 13, and it was proposed that the little army
should move westward to Berber. But the Mahdist forces
had proved stronger than Gordon and the government
had anticipated. The two hundred and fifty miles from
Suakim to Berber was a waterless desert through which
communications could be kept open only by use of a
comparatively strong army. On March 12 telegraphic
connections with Khartoum were severed and the place
was soon put in a state of siege by the Mahdists.

Whether the military operations conducted by General Graham in eastern Sudan materially affected Gordon's negotiations for a peaceful evacuation of Khar-

toum is doubtful. They did, however, involve Britain in hostilities and marked a departure from Gladstone's policy of peace, and he had agreed to them with the greatest reluctance. If a military force at Suakim would facilitate the work of Gordon, Gladstone would consent to it; otherwise not. When Admiral Hewett recommended raids on the Arabs, Gladstone wrote: "I cannot get over the sickening effect produced upon me by Hewett's . . . proposal of a vengeance raid upon men who are fighting to deliver their country from the stranger." The phrase applied by Gladstone to the Sudanese, that they were a people "rightly struggling to be free," was not a mere rhetorical flourish. But in the end Gladstone consented to the Graham expedition as he had, with misgivings, consented to the appointment of Gordon, and as he, against his better judgment, agreed to the cabinet's refusal to allow Zebehr to go to Khartoum. Gladstone suffered from a severe attack of influenza during the greater part of the winter of 1884, and as a result he was absent from several important meetings of the cabinet and could not press his views on parliament.

After the appointment of Gordon, Gladstone favored giving him a considerable amount of independence. When a report reached London that Gordon wished to seek a personal interview with the Mahdi and that Baring had vetoed the plan, Gladstone remarked: "I should not like to assume the responsibility of *ordering* a man like Gordon not [to] do what he deems essential. But Baring on the spot has better means of judgment both about the Mahdi personally and otherwise. And if he is not satisfied with urging Gordon to consider well so serious a step, and deems it essential to lay a prohibition upon the person to whose discretion we are entrusting so much, I would not refuse to support him in it."[27] Mention has been made of Gordon's meeting with Zebehr in Cairo. At that time Gordon wished to take him along to the Sudan, but Baring feared that the slave dealer, who hated Gordon bitterly, might kill him on the way and therefore refused the request. Later, however, after Gordon had reached Khartoum, he renewed his attempt to obtain the service of Zebehr and declared his firm conviction that Zebehr was the proper and only fit man to put in charge of the government after Gordon had left Khartoum. Now Baring joined his prayer with that of Gordon and asked that the home government should grant it. About the employment of Zebehr, Glad-

[27] Gladstone to Granville, February 6, 1884. Copy, MS., Gladstone Papers. Baring to Granville, February 4, complained of Gordon's "wild letters," he should be forbidden to go to the Mahdi and should not be supported by men and money as *The Times* had advocated. Original MS., Granville Papers. When Granville sent the Gordon plan to visit the Mahdi to Gladstone, he wrote, "It is more like the Arabian Nights than real life. Shall I telegraph to Baring 'your message to Gordon is approved, no further order is required'?" Original MS., Gladstone Papers. Childers, the chancellor of the exchequer, hinted that the government should limit the authority of Baring over Gordon, who might throw up his commission if hampered too much. Childers to Granville, February 7, 1884. Original MS., Granville Papers.

stone said, February 11, 1884: "What curious papers about Zebeir. Even here I wd. be governed by his [Gordon's] aye or no. For us, at the present moment, the whole question will be, I think, Gordon or no Gordon."[28] As a possible means of solving the problem of who should succeed Gordon, Gladstone threw out the suggestion that since Britain had no legal authority to appoint a ruler for the Sudan the Khedive might nominate to the sultan the proper person for this post "and in case of hesitation arrange with the man provisionally & leave him to make good his ground." Another plan promulgated by Gladstone was that a fixed time should be set for Gordon's appointment "with liberty as to the persons he should employ to co-operate with him & serve under him—of course this would mean Zebeir." But the humanitarians who had been so powerful in sending Gordon to the Sudan now proved equally influential in blocking the execution of his plans for the country— the English conscience would not allow the appointment of an old slave dealer as a ruler of the Sudan. Their success on this point the humanitarians owed in part at least to the influenza which laid Gladstone low. When the cabinet met on March 11, 1884, to decide on Gordon's request for Zebehr, Granville reported from Gladstone's bedchamber that the prime minister

[28] Gladstone to Granville. Copy, letter books, XXI, 76, Gladstone Papers. Gladstone was unable to attend the meeting of the cabinet on that day.

"thinks it very likely that we cannot make the House swallow Zebehr, but he thinks he could." Ministers laughed and refused without a dissenting vote to let Gordon have Zebehr.[29] Gladstone, however, continued to wish the government could employ Zebehr in some way. Writing to Granville May 14, 1884, Gladstone said: "Consider what more can be done in the use of money to get at Gordon (is it possible that even Zebehr might be used for this?)."

On the question of Zebehr, Gladstone followed an old practice of his, which was to allow the man on the spot considerable latitude in the choice of means for the accomplishment of his work. But when this man altered the nature and purpose of his mission and by his acts compromised the government, the situation became, of course, different. Now this is precisely what Gladstone thought Gordon did, and this lies at the root of misunderstandings and controversies which distressed friends and admirers of both. It will be remembered that when Granville proposed Gordon for the Sudan, Gladstone was anxious that Gordon should not be the judge of what should be done by the British government and who should do it. The government should be left free to decide upon methods and policies. We have also seen that when Gordon accepted the appointment to the Sudan he, honestly of course, told the ministers that in his judg-

[29] Allen, *Gordon and the Sudan*, 303.

ment the Mahdi was not a serious menace, and Gordon fully concurred in the policy of abandoning the Sudan and leaving the people to their fate. Later, however, he arrived at the conclusion that Egypt should retain a suzerainty over at least portions of the Sudan, that he and those who had sent him were in honor bound to set up a stable government at Khartoum, and that it was necessary "to smash the Mahdi." Not all of his proposals reached London, and it appears that some of Gordon's explanations either did not reach the government or arrived too late to make clear his suggestions. While telegraphic communications were open Gordon kept the wires burning with the plans and ideas he sent to Cairo. Baring was bewildered by them, and ministers in Downing Street to whom the Sudan was but one of many issues, and not a big one as it seemed, became utterly confused. Gladstone complained, February 27: "It is as much as my poor head can do to take in and properly dispose of the Franchise Bill which I am to introduce tomorrow. But with reference to this extraordinary proclamation of Gordon's about English troops . . . I presume you [i. e., Granville] will say something to Baring leaving him a descretion probably as to what he shall say or do upon it. Gordon assumes a license of language to which we can hardly make ourselves parties."[30] The last sentence contains a censure which ulti-

[30] Gladstone to Granville, February 27, 1884. Copy, letter books, XXI, 88, Gladstone Papers.

mately grew into a charge of willful insubordination when Gordon appeared to have thrown his instructions to the winds.

On February 9, 1884, Gladstone commented on a memorandum by Gordon concerning the nature of his mission. Gladstone wrote: "The 'irrevocable decision' of which he speaks is, it will be found, not a decision under no conceivable circumstances to employ a soldier in the Soudan, but the decision 'to evacuate the territory' and 'not to incur the very onerous duty of securing to the peoples of the Soudan a just future government.' "[31] Gladstone was willing to send troops from Suakim to Berber to aid Gordon, but the troops should not remain there. During April and May, Gladstone urged that information should be collected concerning the various routes to the Sudan; he was much impressed with General Stephenson's arguments in favor of the Suakim-Berber route; but when a railroad was proposed he perceived "the most formidable difficulties of a moral & political kind. . . . It is I think very doubtful whether, from a practical point of view, the 'turning of the first sod' of a Soudan Railway will not be the Substitution for an Egyptian there of an English domination over the whole or a part, more immaterial, more costly, more destructive, & altogether without foundation in public right. It would be an immense advantage that the ex-

[31] Copy, MS., *ibid.*

pedition (shd. one be needed) should be one occupying little time, & leaving no trace behind it."[32]

But even a relatively small desert expedition as projected by Stephenson foreshadowed an alarming cost in
"English treasure and life."[33] Indeed, Kitchener spoke
in May, 1884, of the need for a British army of 20,000
men to achieve the objects of Gordon.[34] Summer came
and with it the high Nile when a river expedition could
have been most successfully undertaken, but by then
new complications arrived. Humanitarians and jingoes
called for a Sudan expedition which might mean that
Britain would have to remain in the Sudan—at least it
might be so interpreted by the powers—and thereby
seriously interfere with the success of the Egyptian financial conference at work in London from June 28
until August 2, 1884. While there seemed to be a possibility that France would agree to a change in the Law
of Liquidation, the chances of success could not be

[32] Gladstone to Northbrook, May 28, 1884. Copy, letter books, XXI,
132-133, *ibid.*

[33] Gladstone to Hartington, May 16, 1884. *Ibid.*, 127. In this letter
Gladstone suggested that the war office should prepare estimates of
costs of a Nile and a desert expedition and secure medical reports
on the degree of risks to life that might be encountered. In letters
to Childers, Dilke, and Northbrook, May 30, June 2, and June 4,
Gladstone discussed the possibility of an expedition; on June 8, he
inquired from Childers whether £300,000 could be used for an
expedition in the Sudan without disturbing financial plans or creating
a call for new taxation. "In a month more we ought to hear per
Zebehr from Gordon: & one would say any preparation now
ordered ought at any rate to be limited to what would fill that
month." *Ibid.*, 141.

[34] Sir George Arthur, *Life of Kitchener* (New York, 1920), I, 65.

jeopardized by a forward move in the Sudan. To those who object to thus balancing ducats against life the answer is obvious: considering the strength of the forces of the Mahdi and the effects of the climate, the loss of English lives would probably have exceeded in number the lives saved by such a move—of course charges of pusillanimity in such matters are always made by persons who run no risks. Nor was the need for a Sudan expedition, with its possibly very serious consequences, so clear in the summer of 1884 as it seems in retrospect. Sir Edwin Egerton, acting consul general at Cairo, informed Granville, July 14, "The Khedive tells me it is nonsense to talk of bringing away Egyptian garrisons." The soldiers were local people with local attachments. And on July 27 he wrote: "We think here the news from Gordon satisfactory, & that it is clear the Mahdi is not very prosperous."[35] A few days earlier Sir Henry Gordon told Gladstone that in his opinion his brother was safe at Khartoum and that he could go southward any day he pleased. "An English expedition to Khartoum would not convey what Gordon wants and would simply have to remain there." The question of Britain going to Khartoum to stay seemed to be the real issue.[36]

But by the end of July military men in England

---

[35] Original MSS., Granville Papers.
[36] Gladstone to Granville, July 22, 1884. Copy, letter books, XXI, 171, Gladstone Papers.

computed that Gordon's ammunition must be nearing ex-
haustion; and Wolseley who, by working through Hartington, had been responsible for the expedition to Suakim now utilized the same channel in bringing pressure
to bear on the government. Lords Hartington and Selborne had long favored a Sudan expedition and they
now threatened resignation if it was not sent. Gladstone
admitted that this created "a very formidable state of
things, at a moment when we have already on our hands
a domestic crisis of the first class likely to last for
months, & a foreign crisis of the first class, morally certain however to be decided or developed in a few
days." To the sending of a brigade to Dongola he objected strenuously, and he did not feel certain "that the
evidence as to Gordon's position requires or justifies, in
itself, military preparations for the contingency of a
military expedition." He believed, however, that there
were other preparations "which are matters simply of
asst., & do not involve necessary consequences in point
of policy. To these I have never offered an insuperable
objection, & the adoption of them might be, at the
worst, a smaller evil than the evils with which we are
threatened in other forms."[37] But by this time all members of the cabinet, save Gladstone, had become convinced of the need for an expedition; parliament voted
money; and Lord Wolseley, the chief advocate of the
Nile route, was put in command.

[37] Gladstone to Granville, August 1, 1884. Copy, MS., *ibid.*

Six weeks after the government had decided to send an expedition to the Sudan, Baring received messages allegedly from Gordon in which he spoke about a vast campaign with 200,000 Turkish troops and made other wild statements.[38] The dispatch from Baring which contained this information reached Gladstone in Scotland, and he immediately wrote to Granville: "The Gordon telegram in Baring's 588 beats anything I have ever seen. I called him at the outset inspired and mad, but the madness is now uppermost."[39] Gladstone and Granville, independently of each other, arrived at the conclusion that Gordon must be put under Wolseley; and instructions to this effect were sent by Granville to Baring on September 20.[40] Gladstone now felt con-

[38] *P.P.*, *1884-1885*, LXXXVIII, c.-4203, p. 95.

[39] Copy, MS., Gladstone Papers. A postscript to the letter reads: "No 587 arrived. Only seems to show profound discrepancy of ideas, & to raise more seriously the question whether to inform him categorically that if he cannot act on our policy he must cease to act in our name."

[40] On September 19 Granville telegraphed to Gladstone: "How would it do to place Gordon under Wolseley's command and ask Egyptian Government to do the same." Decipher, Gladstone Papers. Gladstone answered that he had already made same suggestion in a letter. MSS., Granville Papers. In discussing this episode Dr. Allen assumes that Gladstone acted on information supplied by the *Dundee Advertiser* instead of on reports officially made by Baring who forwarded messages from Gordon. See *Gordon and the Sudan*, 350-351.

Writing to Granville, September 20, Gladstone said: "Reflecting on Gordon's wild telegram I think our message in May is hardly sufficient for the present circs.

"I paraphrase him thus——

"'Send troops to Khartoum, that may hold it while I go all over

vinced that Gordon was acting contrary to his instructions and must be removed as speedily as possible. Not
a day must be lost in getting him out "or else unship-
ping him"; Wolseley must act swiftly. The prime minister's ire had been aroused and he was eager to bring
"to issue the question of his future conduct & position."[41]
But Wolseley was careful and methodical in his preparation. Swift movements such as those undertaken by
Roberts in Afghanistan were necessary but they were
beyond the ability of the man sent to relieve Gordon.
Moreover, ill fortune continued to dog the steps of the
government's Sudan venture. Col. Stewart, sent by Gordon in September to bring authentic information to the
outside world, was trapped and killed by Bedouins. Gordon held out at Khartoum with marvelous skill and
bravery, but the relieving force lost precious days in apparent inactivity and its vanguard reached Khartoum

---

the Soudan to fetch out (or otherwise) the Egyptian garrisons.
This is contrary I know to yr. policy, but probably you have
altered it in deference to me. Let me know whether this is so.'

"Ought he not be informed at the earliest moment that no troops
will be sent to Khartoum for any such purpose?" In a second letter
to Granville on the same day, Gladstone wrote: "I believe you are
probably right in your retrospective regret about Gordon's recall,
but the truth is that we have on hand an impossible task, & scarcely
even have sufficient knowledge to base our judgment on." Copies,
letter books, XXI, 220-221, Gladstone Papers. Northbrook, then in
Egypt, wrote to Granville, September 22, that he was glad Gordon
was to be put under Wolseley.

[41] Gladstone to Granville, September 24 and 25, 1884. Copies,
letter books, XXI, 224, 226, Gladstone Papers.

two days after the place had been stormed by the Mahdists and its heroic defender killed.[42]

The storm now broke over the head of the prime minister. Men like Stead and Wolseley on whom rested the chief responsibility for the tragedy eagerly joined the hue and cry. Gladstone faced the attack with fortitude. For a moment he bowed to the inevitable and sanctioned military operations against the Mahdi; but no sooner had this decision been taken than Russia appeared to threaten the gates to India. Although the queen, Wolseley, and the jingoes generally continued eager to shed rivers of blood to avenge the death of a man for whom death had no terror, Gladstone prevailed in his decision to recall the army from the Sudan. In view of the international situation his argument was unanswerable: "While we remain for war in the Soudan all the world can bully us, and they have come to know it."[43]

During the winter of 1884-85 various projects for the Sudan were discussed—the Italians were to be let in and there sate their thirst for colonies, or the Sudan might be turned over to Turkey and Britain should aid in the pacification of the country. In the end noth-

[42] Gordon was killed at dawn, January 26, 1885. Allen, *Gordon and the Sudan*, 432; John Buchan, *Gordon at Khartoum* (London, 1934), 156-158.

[43] Gladstone to Granville, April 19, 1885. Original MS., Granville Papers.

ing was done.[44] The people of the Sudan were left as "God has placed them," to quote Gordon's famous phrase. Indeed, the majority of its inhabitants speedily succumbed under the vile and bloodthirsty régime of the Khalifa.

The mission and the death of Gordon caused bitter controversies which have not yet subsided. Political partisanship, conflicting ideas of values, and various theories concerning duties and obligations, right and wrong, justice and humanity have supplied premises for conclusions and arguments in their support. At the outset, Gladstone, Gordon, Baring, and almost everyone in authority agreed that the Sudan should be abandoned and that Britain had no special obligations toward the people who were seemingly eager to join the standard of the Mahdi. Mention has often been made of Gordon's alleged mental aberrations: whatever they were, they do not seem to have impaired his skill and his judgment in military matters. On the other hand, it seems certain that his political judgment was defective, and the question arises as to why this had escaped the notice of Wolseley who had known Gordon for years. We lack means for solving this riddle. But it was Wolseley who "sold" the idea of employing Gordon to some of the ministers; and Stead, who had not met Gordon until

[44] A lengthy memorandum in which he proposed to hand the Sudan over to Turkey was prepared by Lord Northbrook in March, 1885. Original MS., Granville Papers.

January 8, 1884, created a tremendous popular enthusiasm for sending him to the Sudan at a time when Granville had begun to have misgivings about Gordon's fitness. Stead, no doubt, acted in good faith, but he acted on a snap judgment; he showed good journalistic instinct and he was in the happy position of wielding power without responsibility. Gladstone, who had never met Gordon, relied upon the recommendations of those who supposedly knew both Gordon and the Sudan, and upon the advice of Granville.

Debates have raged over the character of the instructions to Gordon and whether he violated them. Without resurrecting old ghosts, it may be well to call to mind that Gordon's conception of the nature of his mission changed. After he had reached Khartoum he arrived at the conclusion that the people of the Sudan could not be left as God had made them. His duty as he saw it was to stay with them, protect them, and not leave until they had been provided with a good government. These sentiments do him honor. He could have escaped but refused to do so. He died at his post, conscious of having honestly performed his duty, certain of the reward promised to those who are faithful unto death. But admiration for his sense of duty and of honor, for his constancy and his skill, for his heroism in life and in death should not blind us to the fact that the various proposals of Gordon which reached London, in the eyes of the ministers amounted to this, that Britain was in duty bound to smash the Mahdi and provide a government for the Sudan. In the winter and early spring of 1884, Gladstone was willing to employ British troops for the purpose of aiding in the evacuation of the Sudan, but he was unalterably opposed to the plan that Britain should undertake a campaign against the Mahdi and be responsible for the government of the country. The people of the Sudan had joined the Mahdi; he apparently invested Khartoum with an army of 200,000 men, not well equipped, of course, but animated with the warlike spirit of Islam; and the climate of the region was known to be deadly to Europeans. The cost in men and money of the campaign of 1898 supplies us with no dependable basis for computing what the cost might have been in 1884, inasmuch as medical science had advanced and technical equipment had improved greatly between the two dates. Furthermore, in 1884 the Mahdist movement was young, and the Mahdi was still with his people. If, as Kitchener seems to have thought, a British force of 20,000 men would have been required, it was absolutely certain that a very large percentage of them would never have returned; that the campaign would have complicated the situation in Egypt; and that the international position of England would have become similar to that of France in the sixties with her army in Mexico. Simply to be rescued was not what Gordon wanted, and it would by no means have settled the issue. These aspects of the Sudanese policy advocated by Gordon and his supporters weighed heavily with the prime minister. He had to scan a wider horizon than that visible from the roof of the palace at Khartoum; he saw breakers and storm clouds not visible to those who had lightly decided that Gordon was the man for the Sudan and who now with no greater sense of responsibility urged that Britain should sacrifice thousands of lives in an effort to give the people of the Sudan what they most likely did not want—British rule. It was easier for Gordon to decide and choose than it was for Gladstone. Both honestly did their duty as they saw it. The tragedy that followed the failure to undertake at an early date a campaign in the Sudan is known; the greater tragedy to which such a campaign might have been a cause and a prelude cannot be estimated.

Chapter IX

FROM the close of 1885 until the end of his official career, Gladstone was absorbed with the Irish question. His brief terms in office, 1886 and 1892-94, were devoted in the main to this all-absorbing topic. "It is . . . very desirable," Gladstone informed Rosebery, April 28, 1886, "while we have this big Irish business on hand, that no other important issue of disturbing character should be raised. Many tactical lessons are to be learned from Peel's conduct, and I recollect that in 1846, with the repeal of the Corn Law in view, he went very great lengths indeed, perhaps even too great, in order to avoid side issues."[1]

But there were questions pending which could not be sidetracked while the parties in England wrangled over Ireland; and Rosebery, the third Whig earl to hold the seals of the foreign office under Gladstone, was a

[1] Copy, MS., Gladstone Papers.

new broom that swept, perhaps not cleaner, but at least
more vigorously than its predecessor. In the spring of
1885, Rosebery had paid an unofficial visit to Bismarck,
and they had agreed upon a certain line of proceedings
concerning Zanzibar.[2] This affair was not yet settled
when Rosebery entered the foreign office in February,
1886. Bismarck grumbled and threatened. Rosebery
wished to be friendly to Germany, but at the same
time he gave "Hatzfeldt a strong hint that they must
take at Berlin of this style of communication which is
apt to savour distinctly of menace." It was a language
which Bismarck understood. He had respect for the
new British foreign secretary, and the rise of Boulanger
in France made it impossible to keep her in his pocket.
These factors contributed to improved Anglo-German
relations; and Bismarck showed a tendency to support
Britain in a Greek controversy, an attitude which pleased
Gladstone, who advocated accommodating Germany
"when at all practicable."[3]

France continued to be irritated about Egypt and
sought to hamper Britain's work there in nearly every
way. Moreover, the French activities in the South Pacific kept the Australasians in a state of apprehension.
Here, too, Rosebery used firm and even strong language. Such language might, he thought, have a whole-

---

[2] Rosebery to Gladstone, May 30, 1885. Original MS., Gladstone
Papers.
[3] Gladstone to Rosebery, April 28, 1886. Copy, *ibid.*

some effect upon France, and it would please the colonies "whose views as to language," Rosebery wrote, "are primitive and spicy."[4] During Gladstone's fourth ministry Anglo-French relations were strained over Egypt and over Siam. In the former case Gladstone agreed to arrangements for keeping a larger British force available for Egypt, but he was more inclined than was Rosebery to recognize the priority of French interests in Egypt over those of any other power except Britain. "It seems to me," Gladstone told Harcourt, July 19, 1893, "that *if* we gave the same sort of priority to France as we gave under the 1880-5 [sic], she would not be difficult to manage. We have in this matter something to give, and a vantage ground in giving it." He hoped that by doing so matters could be more easily arranged both with the other powers and with the sultan. In the Anglo-French dispute involving Siam, Gladstone apparently left Rosebery unfettered, and the latter's plan for a joint guarantee of Siam by Britain, France, and Germany won unstinted praise from the prime minister.[5]

In the summer of 1886 Russia announced that Batoum on the Black Sea was no longer to be a free port. Rose-

[4] Rosebery to Gladstone, July 12, 1886. Original MS., *ibid*.
[5] "The plan of a joint guarantee seems to me excellent, but I am not sure what may be your idea in naming Germany, unless it be to stick a pin into the side of the French by showing this formidable figure on the horizon." Gladstone to Rosebery, September 11, 1893. Copy, letter books, XXIII, 247, Gladstone Papers.

bery judged this to be a violation of the Treaty of Berlin, making it clear at the same time that Britain considered the question largely from the point of view of the maintenance of the sanctity of treaties. Gladstone's ideas on the Batoum dispute were expressed in a letter to Rosebery of July 4, 1886. "Your news," he wrote, "is certainly bad, and as regards the faith-keeping disposition of Russia extremely bad. And evidently the step you have taken is the proper one, nor, upon reading the marked parts of the protocols, can I see that you said too much of it to Staal,[6] while I am extremely glad you told him that it concerned all the signatory Powers.

"It is a noteworthy fact, if you are right in supposing it to be a fact, that Russia has squared the Powers. On the occasion of the fleets article, Austria was by no means squared, and held I think language which implied that if we chose to resent the breach of Treaty she wd. march abreast of us, but we should I think have found her a wretched ally in such a case.

"As the breach of faith is evident, there remains the question how far in international Law, by precedent or otherwise, is an act of this kind equivalent to a breach of one of the articles of the Treaty [of Berlin] to which the Protocol belong [sic.]"[7]

While out of office, 1886-92, Gladstone found time

[6] M. de Staal, the Russian ambassador in London.
[7] Copy, letter books, XXII, 214, Gladstone Papers.

to study the position of Italy and he arrived at the conclusion that she had committed a serious error by joining the triple alliance. In January, 1889, he proposed to air these views, but Rosebery expostulated. "Now is this necessary?" he asked in a letter to Gladstone of January 15, 1889. Rosebery called attention to Gladstone's advice, 1886, not to raise new issues while the home rule question called for settlement, and to the effects of Gladstone's utterances concerning Austria in 1880. If Gladstone made a statement against the Italian-Germanic alliance, the powers of the triple alliance would be antagonized and he might thereby add to the divisions and dissensions within the Liberal party.[8] The letter was strongly worded and the advice was accepted in a generous spirit; but it did not prevent Gladstone from writing anonymously in the *Contemporary Review*, October, 1889, on Italy and the triple alliance. In this article Gladstone also discussed the rumors concerning Salisbury's Mediterranean agreements of 1887. They squared with what Gladstone knew about Salisbury's liking for secret treaties; and he discussed with much insight the nature of moral obligations assumed without any formal treaty. Needless to say, Rosebery's scrapping of the Mediterranean agreements by ignoring their existence met with Gladstone's approval. In general, Gladstone, 1892-94, observed the pledge given before the

[8] Original MS., *ibid.*

election of 1892 not to reverse or seriously alter the foreign policy of Salisbury.

Toward the end of Gladstone's life his interest was directed toward the affairs of the Scandinavian peninsula. Unlike the peninsula in southeastern Europe, Scandinavia occupies but little space in the diplomatic history of Modern Europe, thereby perhaps offering a striking proof to the truth of the old saying, "Happy is the country whose annals are few." While the countries of the Balkans strove hard to be freed from the Turkish bondage, disturbed themselves and others by massacres and uprisings, and were used as pawns by the great powers, those of Scandinavia were left to work out their own destinies, largely unhampered by advice and guidance from the great European statesmen. But in the eighties and nineties events in Norway and issues affecting the relations between that country and Sweden drew the attention of Gladstone to Scandinavia. He showed his sympathies clearly in the constitutional struggles, and he used his influence to dampen the chauvinistic spirit which in 1892-94 threatened to gain the upper hand in Sweden and almost precipitated an armed conflict between her and Norway.

With the beginning of the eighties the Norwegian radicals under the leadership of Johan Sverdrup gained control over the Storthing and attempted to make the legislature the controlling influence in the government. In three successive Storthings after three successive elec-

tions an amendment to the constitution which compelled
the attendance of ministers at the meetings of the Storthing had passed, only to be vetoed by the king. The
radicals then claimed that this measure had become
law despite the vetoes. The contest therefore became
one over the royal veto power as well as over responsible
government. The king maintained that the destruction
of his veto power over constitutional amendments might
throw the government of the country into confusion
and seriously impair the union between Norway and
Sweden. The radicals, however, insisted upon their
point; and after they had succeeded in impeaching the
Conservative Selmer ministry, the king ultimately submitted to the establishment of parliamentary government in Norway. Shortly afterwards a similar change
took place in Sweden, with the result that the Swedish
foreign minister, who conducted the foreign affairs for
both kingdoms, became subject to the control of a
Swedish parliamentary majority instead of, as heretofore, to the king. The Norwegians asserted that this destroyed the equality of the two kingdoms as stipulated
in the Act of Union; and in the nineties the Norwegian
party of the left began to demand a separate consular
service, thus raising the issue which led to the severance
of the union between the two countries in 1905.

In the constitutional struggle between King Oscar II
and the Norwegian radicals in the eighties and when
the issue of separate consular service was raised ten years

later, the British ministers to Stockholm, Sir Horace Rumbold and Sir Frank Lascelles, and the British consul-general at Christiania (now Oslo), Mr. Tom Michell, adopted throughout the conservative, Swedish, and royal point of view. They contended that Norway was not ready for responsible government and that this measure as well as the separate consuls for Norway would seriously weaken the Scandinavian union which Britain should strive to maintain since it was a barrier to a possible Russian acquisition of an ice-free port in northern Norway.[9] In the early eighties Joseph Chamberlain visited Stockholm. Sir Horace Rumbold reported that Chamberlain showed much interest in the issues connected with the union between Norway and Sweden; he may have drawn therefrom certain lessons or deductions concerning the impossibility of home rule for Ireland.[10] Gladstone visited Norway in September, 1883, and in August, 1885. His impressions of Norwegian politics were received from the British consul at Bergen, whose accounts differed radically from those of Michell at Christiania. Gladstone read several of the dispatches from Rumbold dealing with the conflicts of those years; but Gladstone's sympathies were with Sverdrup and his

[9] See Public Record Office MSS., Sweden, F.O. 73:473, 478, 486, 487, 489; private letters from Sir Horace Rumbold, Granville Papers; and dispatches and memoranda printed for the foreign office in 1893, Gladstone Papers.

[10] Rumbold to Granville, September 27, 1882. Original MS., Granville Papers; Sir Horace Rumbold, *Further Recollections of a Diplomatist* (London, 1903), 291-293.

party, who strove to establish responsible government; and although Gladstone strongly favored the maintenance of the Norwegian-Swedish union, he believed that Sweden must recognize the constitutional equality of the two kingdoms and, above all, abstain from attempts to enforce by arms her interpretation of the character of the union.

In commenting on a dispatch from Michell dealing with certain commercial disputes between Norway and Sweden and the nature of the Norwegian democracy, Gladstone observed, May 18, 1886: "What he says there is absolutely in contradiction to all I saw & heard in Norway (where my movements were all in the democratic part & almost all whom I saw were democrats) & to all that was told me by our consul at Bergen. I wish Mr. Michell would give me the evidence on which he founds himself in that paragraph."[11]

When Michell submitted his evidence in the form of an anonymous statement by a Norwegian, Gladstone remarked that the author "appears, from that memo. to be one of the few Norwegians that take the side opposed to the plain meaning of the Constitution in late struggle between the large majority of the nation & the King of Sweden. If time permitted me I should probe into this subject myself by correspondence with some of those whom I saw in Norway; where all the evidence

[11] Gladstone to Rosebery. Copy, letter books, XXII, 177-178, Gladstone Papers.

I received was in a direction entirely opposed to Mr. Michell's views. The song he [Michell] incloses is certainly a serious piece of evidence: but the utter jejuneness of Mr. Michell's reply & his personal avoidance of the whole case after the demand made upon him leaves the subject of his despatch in a condition totally unsatisfactory."[12]

When in the early nineties the conflict over separate consular service arose, the British foreign office showed some interest. Dispatches from Sir F. Plunkett and T. Michell, a French translation of the Act of Union between Norway and Sweden, and other documents were printed for the cabinet in March, 1893. Shortly afterwards Gladstone wrote to the foreign secretary, Lord Rosebery: "I cannot help wishing we could use 'good offices' . . . between Sweden and Norway. So far as I yet know, Norway has a strict *right* but is making a bad use of it." And again: "I have read Plunkett's letter with much distress but it is comforting to observe that there seems to be sense in the Swedish Foreign Minister. Though the *juridical* question between Sweden & Norway seems to me pretty plain, I shd. much like to know what is thought of it *in that light* in the F[oreign] O[ffice], & whether there is any and what grounds for asserting that Norway is bound otherwise than by Constitutional documents."[13]

[12] Gladstone to Bryce, June 4, 1886. *Ibid.*, 206.

[13] Gladstone to Rosebery, March 30 and April 25, 1893. *Ibid.*,

Sir Edward Hertslet of the foreign office then prepared a memorandum on Norwegian-Swedish disputes
and relations which Gladstone described as "extremely
interesting, but in the last paragraph inadequate, if *as I
imagine* Sweden became distinctly a party to the Declaration that Norway was a free and independent
State."[14] When the reports of the intentions of the Swedish government grew alarming, Gladstone requested that
"Plunkett . . . be informed that when he hears from
the Prime Minister of Sweden words distinctly or probably pointing to the military coercion of Norway, he
sh.d. drop some friendly expression to the effect that he
thought his Govt. would earnestly desire that anything
of such a tendency would be very carefully considered
in its juridical as well as its political aspect."[15] Gladstone in another letter desired Rosebery to express to
Plunkett "in the strongest terms our desire for the maintenance of the union between Sweden & Norway and
of our belief that the only safe course for the attain-

XXIII, 152, 166. With reference to Gladstone's idea about "good
offices" Rosebery wrote, April 4, 1893: "As to intervention or mediation between Sweden and Norway, I would make three remarks.
I dislike, firstly, anything like intervention unasked in so delicate
a matter. Secondly, the bystander who interposes between two quar-
relsome parties usually gets cuffed by both. But, thirdly, if you were
asked, I can imagine, from your peculiar position, that your personal
mediation might have an excellent effect; much better than ours as
a Government." Original MS., *ibid*.
[14] Gladstone to Rosebery, April 28, 1893. Copy, letter books, XXIII,
167, *ibid*.
[15] Gladstone to Rosebery, May 10, 1893. *Ibid*., 173.

ment of that object lies in the strict observance of the law by the Sovereign. Different parts of the King's communication as reported seem to me not to hang consistently together." And on June 4, 1893, he again wrote to Rosebery: "I am afraid that peace in Scandinavia is in danger from folly on both sides & I cannot forget that sometime back the King was totally defeated by the Norwegians in a strictly Constitutional manner and in a case where his contention was totally unwarrantable; and it makes me therefore uneasy when I see from the despatches that he continues comfortably to believe in his own infallibility and pays Plunkett the compliment of asking him to acknowledge it. He seems very little impressed with the value of the word legality."[16]

Rosebery then urged Plunkett to point out to the government of Sweden "how suicidal would be a civil [sic] war between Sweden and Norway."[17] The war scare blew over. But Gladstone did not cease to present his view of the Scandinavian situation. When Canon MacColl in August, 1893, argued on the royal side of the dispute, Gladstone asked him not to make up his mind until he had "read the fundamental pact between the two countries. It is contained in the constitution and in a preliminary international document. It describes Norway as an independent nation, and this pact Norway does not ask to break."[18]

[16] Gladstone to Rosebery, June 4, 1893. *Ibid.*, 187-188.
[17] Rosebery to Gladstone, June 9, 1893. Original MS., *ibid.*
[18] Copy, letter books, XXIII, 232, *ibid.*

The Scandinavian disputes touched so few British interests that the prime minister seems to have stood practically alone in considering them worthy of attention.
It was otherwise with issues related to the expansion
of the British empire and its defense against foreign foes;
but on these topics Gladstone cherished ideas considered
antediluvian before he retired from public life. In a sharp
tussle with Rosebery over Uganda, Gladstone had to
bow to the younger man who represented the spirit of
the age, and on the issue of increased naval appropriations Gladstone staked his continuance in office, but lost
and retired rather than surrender to his colleagues.

A British company and British missionaries had gone
into Uganda in the eighties. The company was financially unable to carry through the task of governing and
exploiting this region, but a British foothold had been
secured, and in 1892 the question arose whether the
British government should continue the work begun by
private enterprise. At first Rosebery thought that the
outgoing government had decided to withdraw from
Uganda, but he later arrived at the conclusion that Britain would have stayed there if Salisbury had remained
in office. Soon old and well-worn arguments in favor
of imperial expansion were repeated in numerous private
letters from Rosebery to his chief: commitments had
been made which Britain must honor; there must be
continuity of policy; humanity and Christian duty required Britain to stay; withdrawal meant either a return
to savagery on the part of the natives or their being sub-

jected to exploitation by powers more unscrupulous than Britain.

Gladstone, true to his old ideals, objected to the assumption of new burdens by Britain; he claimed Salisbury had decided to withdraw, that no obligations had been contracted, and that to stay would involve the British government in war with the natives. Writing to Rosebery, September 23, 1892, Gladstone declared: "It appears clear to me that any interposition on our part to interfere with the evacuation would saddle us with the entire responsibility of the case, which now belongs to the Co., with *some* share for the late Govt." And in another letter of the same date he alluded to his position as the head of the government and the responsibility he carried for its decisions.[19] The inference was obvious; the foreign secretary should obey his chief. To Asquith, who seemed inclined to agree with Rosebery and had proposed a compromise, Gladstone wrote: "Some ten years ago we sent Gordon on a mission which he and we alike declared to be essentially one of peace; but to a country some hundreds of miles off, not under our control. The difference now is that we should *begin* with military measures." Harcourt and Kimberley agreed with Gladstone, but Rosebery stood his ground. He admitted that the prime minister had a general responsibility for the act of every branch of the government, but the minister in charge had special responsibilities,

[19] Copies, MSS., Gladstone Papers.

and if policies were adopted in opposition to him "the burden of the last is heavy if not intolerable." The prophecies of evil to follow withdrawal, had, in the judgment of Rosebery, "their root in the facts and the common sense of the case." The issue before the government, he declared, was not now "the expediency of an East African Empire" or "the question of assisting the East African Company" or maintaining "a sphere of influence" or the "intentions of the late Government" or "whether it is wise to interfere in Uganda at all. But whether in view of the fact that a company has been allowed so to interfere, with a royal charter granted by the Executive for that purpose, we are content to face the consequences of leaving the territory, the inhabitants, and the missionaries, to a fate which we cannot doubt."[20]

[20] Rosebery to Gladstone, September 22, 25, and 29, 1892. Original MSS., *ibid.* The tension between the prime minister and the foreign secretary was very great. Gladstone wrote, September 25: "It is with pain, though with no hesitation, that I meet your wish in summoning this Cabinet [to discuss Uganda]. I could not until the last abandon my hope that you might forbear to press the suggestion. You are in no way responsible for my reluctance to part company with that hope. It was my weakness.

"It is the *first* time, during a Cabinet experience of 22 or 23 years, that I have known the Foreign Minister and the Prime Minister to go before a Cabinet on a present question with divergent views. It is the union of these two authorities by which foreign policy is ordinarily worked in Cabinet; not that I have the smallest fear that this incidental miscarriage of ours will occur again." Copy, MS., *ibid.* Rosebery replied on September 26 that he was conscious of self-reproach when differing with Gladstone and he wished they could agree, but he felt the government was bound by previous commitments and must act accordingly. Original MS., *ibid.* On

As a compromise it was suggested that Uganda might be attached to the dominions of the sultan of Zanzibar. Gladstone thought this "a good idea & well worth examination." "A native Govt.," he wrote October 21, 1892, "is far more likely to succeed than we are; and if cause can be shown for giving money, that is a definite matter, does not entail the impracticable, and need not load us with indeterminate responsibilities." The suggestion found favor with Harcourt and also, to some extent, with Rosebery himself.[21] But France appeared on the scene; and Waddington, the French ambassador, made claims in behalf of France and tried to convince members of the British government of the justice of the French claims. Rosebery became irritated with the methods employed by Waddington and suggested that Gladstone might convey to Waddington "a gentle reminder

---

September 30, Rosebery wrote that he realized that in dealing with the Uganda question the previous experiences in the Sudan "bulk largely in your mind and his [i.e., Harcourt's]. But do they not principally teach that the policy was unfortunate because it was a compromise policy of a sharply divided Cabinet? And is not history likely to repeat itself now? In this matter I am content to bow to your unrivalled political experience, and I fully acknowledge how considerable was the concession made by you yesterday [to postpone decision]. But I cannot sail under false colours, and I should be wanting in manliness and candour if I allowed any false impression as to the spirit in which I accept it and as to the future complications that I foresee." *Ibid.* For the Harcourt-Rosebery controversy over Uganda, see A. G. Gardiner, *The Life of Sir William Harcourt* (New York, 1923), II, 187-198.

[21] Copy, letter books, XXIII, 59, Gladstone Papers. This proposal had been explained in a letter from Rosebery to Gladstone, October 20, 1892. Original MS., *ibid.*

that the most convenient course is to treat foreign policy through the Foreign Office."[22] However, the French pretensions worked in favor of Rosebery's policy, and the upshot of many debates and more correspondence was that Uganda became a British protectorate on June 19, 1894.[23]

At the beginning of the Gladstone-Rosebery controversy over Uganda, the majority seems to have been on the side of the prime minister; but in the dispute between him and Lord Spencer over the proposed increases in the naval estimates for 1894 his cause appears to have been hopeless from the start. On the continent the powers were, in the early nineties, building up military establishments; the competition for overseas possessions and overseas commerce grew keener each

[22] "With regard to Waddington. I have no personal feeling against him. But I am obliged from regard to my office to nip this style of diplomacy in the bud. He has asked for an interview with Kimberley. So you see he is extending his operations. He will soon be sapping the Colonial office and possibly besieging the Admiralty." Rosebery to Gladstone, November 7, 1892. Original MS., *ibid*. The question of Egypt as well as Uganda had been discussed in this manner by Waddington.

[23] Gardiner, *Harcourt*, II, 312. When Balfour and Chamberlain asked questions about Uganda in the house of commons on February 3, 1893, Gladstone and Harcourt answered evasively. This apparently irritated Rosebery, who, writing to Gladstone on February 4, expressed surprise at the apparent difficulties in the way of giving assurances concerning Uganda. Portal had been sent to make provisions for "the administration of Uganda pending the consideration of his report, it was certainly not in the contemplation of the Cabinet that he should go as a mere reporter to take down something in writing and hurry away bag and baggage to the coast, leaving the population to its fate." Original MS., Gladstone Papers.

year; Britain had no allies, and her empire and her sea power were regarded with envy; and the thesis that sea power had decided the great wars of the past was fast gaining in popularity and pointed an obvious moral. Under these circumstances, British public opinion moved steadily in the direction of demanding a naval strength so overwhelming that no power or combination of powers would dare to challenge it. With an eye to what seemed to be the needs of the future as well as to the rising popular clamor, the lords of the admiralty, with Lord Spencer as their spokesman in the cabinet, proposed increased naval appropriations. Gladstone objected, but found to his dismay that he stood alone. After a protracted but futile struggle, he retired—a leader rejected by his host. The issue was one closely associated with foreign affairs and foreign policy. It was so regarded by Gladstone, and it is, therefore, proper and fitting to present his views, at the close of his long official life, on armaments and the outlook for international relations.

Writing to Lord Acton, February 9, 1894, Gladstone said: "Whether it be true that everyone of my best friends is against me I do not know. I admit that I am without support. But the world of today is not the world in which I was bred and trained and have principally lived. It is a world which I have had much difficulty in keeping on terms with and those difficulties increase and are not wholly confined to this matter. I will not draw comparisons. I take the *worst* at the worst and say that if the whole generation be against me, even that is far better than that I should with my eyes open (to say nothing of this country) do anything (according to my measure) to accelerate, exasperate, widen, or prematurely take or verge towards taking a part in the controversies of blood which we all fear and seem to see are hanging over Europe."[24]

Thus the Grand Old Man left the field, defeated in an effort to prevent measures which in his judgment would lead to war. Gladstone retired from public life, but, as in 1876, he emerged once more to address his countrymen on an issue that concerned humanity. Even before the Liberals were overthrown in the election of 1895 ominous signs presaged bloody deeds by the Turks in Armenia. In April of that year, Gladstone completed a memorandum, begun in 1894, in which he endeavored to show that in the Dulcigno episode of 1880, the Turks submitted when confronted with evidence that Britain, even single-handed, was prepared to use force. This lesson could, he thought, be applied to the situation in Armenia. "Should," he wrote, "the necessity for coercive pressure upon Turkey, the only kind of pressure

[24] Copy, letter books, XXIII, 370, *ibid*. To Mundella, the president of the board of trade, Gladstone wrote, February 17, 1894: "Reflection day by day continually blackens my opinion of it [the proposed increase in the naval estimates]. But perhaps I am like the recalcitrant juryman who complained that he was associated with 11 of the most obstinate, impracticable, incomprehensible fellows on the face of the earth." *Ibid.*, 375.

available in certain cases, arise with respect to Armenia it may seem that the question of concert will not cause now the trouble which it gave us in 1880: since Germany and Austria have already executed their renunciations, and it is to be supposed that Italy would be very ready to concur."[25] But nothing resulted from his effort.

The Liberals went out, and the Conservatives under Salisbury came in. In the valleys and on the mountain slopes of Armenia were enacted scenes so ghastly that those staged in Bulgaria in the summer of 1876 paled in comparison. Salisbury seemed inclined to act; but the powers held back, and Britain could not, it was deemed, go it alone. At Liverpool, September 24, 1896, Gladstone sounded the tocsin and tried to rouse his countrymen and the Christian nations to embrace the cause of humanity and save an ancient people. He regretted the weight of his eighty-six years. "Had I the years of 1876 upon me, gladly would I start another campaign, even if as long as that."[26] But his appeal went unheeded by those who sat in the seat of the mighty.

The spring of 1898 came. The din of war and rumors of war filled the air. In the United States the war fever had spread from the Atlantic to the Pacific and the great republic was massing its forces for the destruction of the last remnants of the ancient Spanish empire; in the valley of the Nile, Kitchener was moving south-

[25] Original MS., Gladstone Papers.
[26] Morley, *Gladstone*, III, 521-522.

ward to overthrow the Khalifa and avenge Gordon; in South Africa the stage was being set for a life-and-death struggle between Britons and Boers; the great powers were plotting against China; the naval yards of England and Germany teemed with activity, preparing for *der Tag*; and triumphantly Joseph Chamberlain, the erstwhile radical, could have proclaimed, "We are all imperialists now." Faintly the echoes from the great world now reached the Welsh foothills amid which nestles Hawarden Castle, the home of Gladstone. His own as well as the other nations had forsaken his ideals. It mattered little to him now. The long-expected summons had come. The statesman and crusader went to his rest. The sovereign whom he had served so long and so loyally begrudged him the last tributes; the great ones of the land paid homage to the fallen leader and proceeded to guide Britain away from the roads he had advised them to tread; but millions of common folk of many nations sincerely mourned the passing of Gladstone, who, they believed, had striven to lead mankind onward to liberty and to peace.

Appendix I

MEMORANDUM BY GLADSTONE, NOV., 1870

ALSACE & GERMAN LORRAINE[1]

Copy.

Private and Confidential

It is admitted that Germany has received, in the infliction of the present war an injury from France about the magnitude of which there can be no doubt.

It is known that France is willing to grant to Germany a pecuniary compensation, & that Germany in her present mood not only declines to accept such a compensation as a sufficient atonement for the wrong done, but insists upon the annexation of territory.

In general terms the demand of Germany is compensation for the past, & security for the future: nor can any objection be taken in limine [sic] to such a claim. But it should be observed that there are certain conditions attaching to the course of human affairs by which demands of this kind are practically limited, & neither between individuals nor between nations does it commonly happen that when a wrong has been inflicted, either the compensation obtained for the past or the security taken for the future is complete.

[1] Granville Papers, Public Record Office.

The arguments which have been used for the severance of Alsace & (part) of Lorraine from France, and for their annexation to Germany are as follows

1. That the French, had the fortune of war been in their favour, would have appropriated territory now German without resistance or objection from the Neutral Powers.

That the population of the Provinces is German by blood & language, that Europe not having assisted Germany in the attainment of the results of the war, has no right to prevent her from profiting by the fruit of labours & sacrifices altogether her own.

4. That the German people unanimously demand these provinces.[2]

5. That they are necessary in a strategical point of view for the future defensibility of the German frontier.

6. That as France cannot be expected to be friendly or pacific in time to come, the Germans must seek their security in the reduction of her power.

7. That European wars, in which one of the parties gets the upper hand, commonly close with severance & annexation of territory.

8. That as the Germans are not an aggressive people, France will incur no risk from their possessing the strongly fortified places of Metz & Strasbourg.

Finally it is well to remark that one argument, most summary & drastic in its character, has not been employed to justify this annexation—that is the supposed right of the Conqueror to do what he will with the territory as with the other possessions of the conquered.

It is felt that in our day this argument of naked force

[2] Reasons 2 and 3 are not numbered.

Answer 1   does not command, but repel the mind & conscience of Europe.

It is probably true that France if successful would have proceeded, or endeavoured, to annex territory.

It is most improbable however that she could have annexed the Rhenish Provinces without complaint or resistance.

When she annexed the small acquisitions of Savoy & Nice in 1860, even *they* all but produced a quarrel with England.

Yet they were ostensibly willing to become French.

Is it likely that England would have been silent had France annexed much larger countries, inhabited by palpably unwilling populations?

Even if silent she would have been radically & thoroughly estranged.

2. In a question of disannexation, it is not blood & language but will, conviction, & attachment which are to be principally regarded.

See Lord Palmerston's Life. Vol. I, p. 224, with reference to a war between Russia & Turkey

Quite independently of participation in a conflict to which she is indebted for nothing but uneasiness, interruption of industry & no inconsiderable amount of military charge entailed on Neutral States, Europe has an unquestionable title to object to any arrangements which tend to lower the principles & throw back the usages of international conduct, or to endanger the peace of the future: if the proposed annexation be liable to either of these objections—

4. The desire of the German people cannot be so declared as to be beyond dispute because the expression of opinion is not altogether free.

But this unanimity, if it existed, tho' an important element in the case, cannot of itself absolutely decide the question either of right or prudence.

5. This has never been proved or even argued, but simply asserted.

Venetia, with magnificent fortresses, was not found a security to Austria in 1866—The aversion of the people was a standing cause of danger. Austria is safe towards Italy with her present unprotected (or less protected) frontier: & would have been safer in 1866 with an attached people, & with no fortresses at all in Italy.

Several alternative methods of proceeding have been proposed though not by Authority, among them are these—

(a) That Alsace & German Lorraine should be erected into a Neutral State under European guarantee.

France & Germany would then be separated by a line of neutral States from the Alps to the North Sea.

(b) That Alsace & Lorraine should continue to be under the dominion of France but that all fortresses in them should be demolished, & that France should not be entitled to keep in them any military force beyond their local proportion of her standing army unless & until they are invaded by a Foreign Power.

German occupation to continue until the demolition is completed & the indemnity paid.

There may be serious objections to these, or to any mode of settlement founded upon the admission of the German claim to something in the nature of territorial security; but such objection can hardly be taken on the ground that they would give Germany less security than the possession of a disaffected territory which would be a perpetual focus of machination for an enemy.

Germany would by either of these arrangements have a tract which would be neutralised for military purposes, interposed between her & France, & this tract would be supplied at the cost of France.

6. If the security of Germany is to be found in the weakening ie. the permanent weakening of France, then France, to attain such an end must be weakened considerably—But Alsace & German Lorraine are taken to represent only about 1/25 of her population—A deduction of four per cent in men & territory leaving ninety six per cent behind, is much more likely to exasperate, & to drive into violent courses than to deter from such courses—

7. This is untrue. France herself affords the proof—she has been worsted in several wars of the 18th & 19th centuries, especially in the war of the succession, & in the final issue of the Revolutionary war.

At the close of the war of succession it was the feeling of Spain not the strength of France that kept Philip V on the throne.

In 1709 & 1710 when France was at the last extremity, the surrender of Alsace was at length tendered—But Alsace though possessed by France was hardly at that time to be considered as *French* both because the rights conveyed by the Treaty of Munster were only limited & qualified rights, not those of full Sovreignty, & because these rights themselves had never ceased to be in contest especially until the peace of Ryswick.

But the very small turn of the tide in favour of France

before the peace was enough to secure to her the continued possession of Alsace at the close of the war.

Perhaps the decision of Europe in 1815 is itself the strongest precedent against the allegation—for not only was France at that time worsted, but she was exhausted: & further as all Europe was against her, there was a power of enforcing new arrangements against her, such as Germany single handed certainly does not possess. It was the weight of England & Russia the two most powerful enemies of France, whom alone she had failed to conquer at any period of the war, that prevailed against the German demand—No one can doubt that this decision was agreeable to the sense of Europe, which may be thought to have had a stronger case against the France of 1815 than Germany has against the France of 1870.

8. No people whatever can assert for itself that absolute exemption from National passion & frailty, which this argument assumes: & it is difficult to suppose that it can have much currency even in Germany. It is needless therefore to discuss the point historically—

Further as it is admitted by the highest German Authorities that Alsace & German Lorraine are French in feeling, it may surely be contended that to tear them from France, & to chain them to Germany would be not a security but a danger to Germany herself, from the fixed sentiment of the population.

This is a sentiment on which Germany cannot claim an exclusive right of judgment; for whatever endangers the peace between France & Germany, endangers, as we now see & feel, the peace of Europe. Europe therefore has a

right to an opinion about it—There is another form of
danger to that Country arising out of the proposed arrangement which ought also to be borne in mind—the aggrandisement of Germany by consolidation from within her own
territories, is not a matter of which other countries are entitled to take any hostile cognisance. But so soon as Germany begins the work of aggrandisement by the annexation
of territory taken from a neighbour she steps out of her
own bounds & comes upon a ground where every country
is entitled to challenge & discuss the title, & is competent by
the general rules of public right if it shall think fit, to consider whether the aggrandisement thus acquired in the shape
of territory which had belonged to another power ought or
ought not to be curtailed—It was on this principle of resistance to territorial aggrandisement not actual but simply
apprehended that the great Powers of Europe in 1853
sought to abridge the rights & power of Russia.

But over & above the question of danger to Germany this
violent severance & annexation of an unwilling population
would be a measure of a nature entirely retrogressive with
reference to the public practice of Europe—After the peace
of 1815, various populations were attached for the first time
to various countries without any assurance of their favoura-
ble inclination to the connection.

But in none of these cases were they known to be averse,
& in none of them were the annexed populations severed
from another State to which they were known to be attached—In those instances, when at a later period, the population showed their aversion to what had been done, it has
eventually been undone: & in other cases of a different class

Venetia
Rhenish
Provinces
Belgium

where dynasties or Governments were set up by European authority against the National feeling, they have one & all been overturned—The result has been the gradual growth of a Conviction, by no means associated with mere democratic leanings, that the Treaty of Vienna (due no doubt to the extraordinary condition of Europe at the time) should not be repeated, & that, in questions of annexation at least, much regard ought to be had to the known inclination of the people.

Consequently, for more than half a Century, there cannot be said, among many territorial changes to have been one, in which a population has been unwillingly severed from one country & annexed to another—If the Schleswig annexation has been (thus far) pushed beyond what was due, this is a question of exactitude in drawing a line, rather than an admitted variation from the rule, since there is (I presume) no doubt that by far the greater part of the Schleswig Holstein population have in becoming German, found the fulfilment of their own desire.

On the other hand the Protectorate of the Ionian Islands was relinquished by Her Majesty & those Islands were annexed to Greece, in deference to the popular wish, expressed by the legislative assembly. This example indeed goes far beyond what is necessary for the present purpose: it was a voluntary surrender of established & lawful right, whereas the present argument is intended only to deprecate the violent invasion of such right from without.

In the case of Savoy & Nice the transfer of allegiance was effected with the consent of the government & by the vote of the population.

In the case of the separate Italian States generally it was by similar votes that they attached themselves to the Italian Kingdom.

Reference might also be made to the manner in which the people of the Danubian Principalities have consulted under the auspices of the great Powers of Europe, with respect to the political arrangements to be adopted in those Provinces—These acts may be said to form a series—They are no longer mere isolated precedents; They go near to constitute one of those European usages, which when sufficiently ascertained become the basis of public international law, & they appear moreover to be founded on natural equity, at least to this extent, that whatever be the right, or want of right, to disturb established relations, at least it is equitable not to break them up & effect a transfer of a whole population from one Nationality to another in defiance of the attachments & desires which they entertain. The violence done in the case of Alsace & Lorraine would indeed be extraordinary. For there the proposal is that the people of those districts should become not only the friends of their enemies, but the enemies of their friends, & this at a time when the greatest political authority of Germany declares that the present war must very speedily be followed by another between the same belligerents, & when the laws which regulate the military organisation of Germany would make the mass of the able bodied population of these provinces in whatever rank of life soldiers, or liable to become soldiers against the very armies in which they have now been serving.

But on the other hand it must be admitted that Germany exercising the self command & prudence necessary for the abandonment of this extreme claim would raise herself thereby to a remarkable height of moral dignity, & would acquire a claim to the lasting gratitude of Europe.

THE SETTLEMENT OF EGYPT[1]

PRELIMINARY PAPER

15: Sept: 1882

Preliminary Paper

When armed resistance in Egypt has altogether ceased, the settlement of the country will have to be considered at once, and it will have to be

1. *Military*

2. *Political*

Of these the first is of necessity immediate; the second though requiring prompt treatment will be subsequent.

There is also the great question of the Suez Canal.

I. *Military* Settlement

In regard to the military settlement of Egypt, among its heads will be

1. The total disbandment of the rebel force—trial of criminals—disposal (by banishment?) of officers or others now constituting a dangerous class.

[1] Granville Papers, Public Record Office.

2. The organisation of a force under the Khedive to maintain order and to secure his throne.

This force to be

a. Military—as far as is requisite to defend the territory especially in the direction of the Soudan, and the person of the Khedive. This force should be fixed at a minimum.

b. Police for the maintenance of order.

It will have to be considered from what source other than indigenous the military force can be supplied:—especially with reference to Mahometans or others from India.

3. The withdrawal of the foreign occupation as early as possible. This will be regulated exclusively, and from point to point, by the consideration of security for life and property.

No charge will be imposed upon Egypt in respect of the military operations now concluded. But it will have to be considered whether, in respect of such force as may have to remain, while the new force for the Khedive is in preparation, Egypt should bear the charge or a portion of it. Also after the country is so to speak handed over, a small British force may be retained, at the desire of the Khedive and at the cost of Egypt, until the new state of things shall have been adequately considered.

Such force ought if possible not to exceed two, or from two to three, thousand men.

4. As in the political settlement of the country, its neutralization will be provided for, so also the seaward fortifications of Egypt should be dismantled and destroyed.

Would it be right however to allow certain defensive works at the entrance and issue of the Canal?

5. Provision has already been made for the due trial of offenders especially those accused of *crime* (other than rebellion) and against the use of barbarous methods of punishment.

6. It is assumed that the military settlement of Egypt will naturally, as to the first three heads, remain in the hands of England as a consequence of the war and to avoid the inconvenience and delays of a reference to the Powers, in a case where Society has not only been disturbed by war but disorganised through the total overthrow of civil authority by the very instrument appointed to maintain it.

II. *Political Settlement*

In regard to the *political* settlement of Egypt, the following heads will have to be considered

1. The Sovereignty.
2. The local institutions.
3. The Canal.
4. The international engagements.

Here, & especially as to the two last, the agency of the Powers will properly come in. But it seems needful, at least in regard to the two first that England should have a well defined basis on which to proceed, in the use of the initiative which will naturally fall to her and otherwise; and that all the preliminary steps she may have to take before the Powers are in action should be taken in view of this basis.

I. *The Sovereignty*

The Sovereignty of the Sultan has wholly failed to fulfil its purposes, and the re-establishment of orderly Government against lawlessness and anarchy has been left to foreign intervention.

The commision of Dervish Pasha produced no result for good while it gave time for organizing the rebel power.

When its failure was obvious, and when the Powers desired the armed interference of the Sultan as Sovereign it could not be had.

The movements of the Sultan towards armed interference have been subsequent to the decision of England and to her proceeding to act upon that decision, and have taken no effect.

Finally, the work has been accomplished not by the Proclamation of the Sultan but by the victory at Tel-el-kebir.

The former basis of the Sultan's power in Egypt has therefore failed both *de jure* and *de facto*.

The Sultan may justly claim

a) The continuance of the tribute.

b) The homage of the Khedive.

c) But the title to demand the aid of Egyptian forces must go to the ground when Egypt will not, in the proper sense, possess an army.

d) So will the title of the Sultan to appoint local sovereigns whom he is unable or unwilling to maintain.

Would it not be well if the Committee hereinafter mentioned were, besides the question of the Canal, to examine into the conditions of the Balkan and Rouman Suzerainties, in order to clear the question as to

1. Any further rights which it may be desirable to reserve to the Sultan.

2. A law of succession to the local throne in case the present law should be deemed insufficient.

3. The conduct of the foreign relations of Egypt.

II. *The Local Institutions*

1./ It appears absolutely necessary that the privileges heretofore accorded to Egypt by firman, and all that may be found requisite for the future well being and order of that country in the course of the impending arrangements, should be made irrevocable as between Turkey and Egypt.

2./ And further that the Egyptian territory should be neutralized.

3./ Subject to all due provisions for the fulfilment of international engagements, it is presumed that England will make a firm stand for the reasonable development of self governing institutions in Egypt.

These if successful would form the best security against any attempts of the Sultan to re-establish the former state of things. Would it not be well if this part of the subject were treated promptly with the Khedive, whose authority is presumed to be adequate for the purpose; and on whom the consideration of the matter seems almost to be forced in connection with the recent organic law?

Little sympathy could be expected from the Powers in promoting the development of securities for liberty; while in England they will be demanded, and will be hailed with satisfaction.

4./ All it is assumed will agree that the exemptions from taxation now enjoyed by foreigners as such ought not to continue.

III. *The Control*

Under this head I would suggest that the Khedive should signify in a formal manner his intention to use the aid of foreign officers with a view to the maintenance of Egyptian credit and the faithful discharge of obligations.

But that the tenure of office by these functionaries should no longer be dependent on the consent of the respective Governments.

The subject of international obligations would it is presumed be matter for consideration of the Powers.

There remains still for consideration the question of the Suez Canal under the two main heads of

1./ The recent conduct and the powers of the Company in the face of the Khedive—this branch of the subject has been far advanced by the valuable memorandum of the Lord Chancellor.

It now appears that the rights of the Khedive may have to be enlarged, and in any case will have to be backed by executory provisions which at present seem to be wanting.

2./ There is also the great question whether for the general interest and for our own the Canal should be neutralised.

It is proposed that a preliminary examination of the whole subject of the Canal should be undertaken, to aid the Cabinet in forming its conclusions, by a Committee composed of representatives of

The Foreign Office

The Law
The Naval and Military Departments, with
the addition of individuals whose aid may
be desirable.

under the presidency of a Cabinet Minister.

This division of the subject, though it calls for early
treatment, seems to be less urgent than those which have
been previously sketched.

(initialled) W. E. G.   Sep: 15. 1882

BIBLIOGRAPHY

I. Sources

A. Manuscripts

At the British Museum
 Gladstone Papers
 Layard Papers
At the Public Record Office
 Foreign Office Papers
 Granville Papers
 Tenterden Papers

B. Printed

1. Articles and Pamphlets by Gladstone. *Gleanings of Past Years*. 7 vols. New York, 1886.

 "England's Mission," in the *Nineteenth Century*, September, 1878.

 "Aggression in Egypt and Freedom in the East," in the *Nineteenth Century*, August, 1877.

 "Kin beyond Sea," in the *North American Review*, September, 1878.

 The Bulgarian Horrors and the Question of the East. London, 1876.

 Lessons in Massacre. London, 1877.

"Liberty in the East and West," in the *Nineteenth Century*, June, 1878.

"Greece and the Treaty of Berlin," in the *Nineteenth Century*, June, 1878.

"The Friends and Foes of Russia," in the *Nineteenth Century*, January, 1879.

"The Hellenic Factor in the Eastern Problem," in the *Contemporary Review*, November, 1876.

"The Paths of Honour and of Shame," in the *Nineteenth Century*, March, 1878.

"Germany, France and England," in the *Edinburgh Review*, October, 1870.

"The Peace to Come," in the *Nineteenth Century*, February, 1878.

"The Triple Alliance and Italy's Place in It," in the *Contemporary Review*, October, 1889.

2. Speeches by Gladstone.

For speeches in parliament, see *Parliamentary Debates*, cited as *Hansard*, 3rd series, 1833-1891; 4th series, 1891-1894.

Political Speeches in Scotland. Rev. ed., 2 vols. Edinburgh, 1880.

Speeches of—1888-1891. Ed. by A. W. Hutton and H. J. Cohen. London, 1902.

Gladstone's Speeches. Ed. by A. T. Bassett. London, 1916.

3. Other Collections of Diaries, Letters, and Speeches.

Bright, John. *The Diaries of*. Ed. by R. A. J. Walling. New York, 1931.

Bright, John. *The Public Letters of*. Ed. by H. J. Leech. London, 1885.

Cobden, Richard. *Speeches on Questions of Public Policy*. Ed. by John Bright and J. E. Thorold Rogers. London, 1880.

Disraeli, Benjamin, Earl of Beaconsfield. *Letters to Lady Chesterfield and Lady Bradford*. Ed. by the Marquis of Zetland, 2 vols. New York, 1929.

Gladstone, Mary. *Her Diaries and Letters*. Ed. by Lucy Masterman. New York, 1930.

Guedalla, Philip. *The Queen and Mr. Gladstone*. 2 vols. London, 1933.

Queen Victoria. *Letters of*. Ed. by G. E. Buckle. 2nd series, 3 vols. London, 1926-28; 3rd series Vols. I and II. London, 1930-31.

West, Sir Algernon. *Private Diaries of*. Ed. by Horace G. Hutchinson. London, 1922.

4. Official Documents.

British and Foreign State Papers. Ed. by Sir Edward Hertslet.

British Parliamentary Papers. Cited as P. P.

Die Grosse Politik der Europaischen Kabinette. Ed. by Johannes Lepsius, Albrecht Mendelssohn Bartholdy, and Friedrick Thimme. Berlin, 1922-1927.

Pribram, Alfred F. *The Secret Treaties of Austria-Hungary*. Cambridge, 1920.

5. Newspapers.

The Times.

6. Autobiographies, Biographies, Memoirs, and Recollections containing much source material.

Allen, Bernard M. *Gordon and the Sudan*. London, 1931.

Argyll, Duke of. *Passages from the Past*. 2 vols. London, 1908.

Arthur, Sir George. *Life of Kitchener*. 3 vols. New York, 1920.

Barclay, Sir Thomas. *Thirty Years: Anglo-French Reminiscences*. London, 1914.

Cecil, Lady Gwendolen. *Life of Robert Marquis of Salisbury*. Vols. I and II. London, 1921.

Childers, Spencer. *Life of Hugh C. E. Childers*. 2 vols. London, 1901.

Crewe, the Marquess of. *Lord Rosebery*. New York, 1931.

Edwards, H. S. *Sir William White*. London, 1902.

Elliot, Arthur D. *Life of Goschen*. 2 vols. London, 1911.

Gardiner, A. G. *The Life of Sir William Harcourt*. 2 vols. New York, 1923.

Garvin, J. L. *The Life of Joseph Chamberlain*. Vols. I and III. London, 1932, 1934.

Gladstone, Viscount. *After Thirty Years*. London, 1928.

Gwynn, Stephen, and Tuckwell, Gertrude M. *The Life of the Rt. Hon. Sir Charles W. Dilke*. 2 vols. London, 1917.

Holland, Bernard. *The Life of Spencer Compton, Eighth Duke of Devonshire*. 2 vols. London, 1911.

Lyall, Alfred. *The Life of the Marquis of Dufferin and Ava*. 2 vols. London, 1905.

Mallet, Bernard. *Thomas George Earl of Northbrook*. London, 1908.

Maxwell, Sir Herbert. *The Life of Fourth Earl of Clarendon*. 2 vols. London, 1913.

Monypenny, W. F., and Buckle, G. E. *The Life of Benjamin Disraeli*. 6 vols. New York, 1910-20.

Morley, John. *The Life of William Ewart Gladstone*. New edition, 3 vols. in 2. New York, 1911.

Morley, Lord. *Recollections*. 2 vols. New York, 1917.

Newton, Lord. *Lord Lyons*. 2 vols. London, 1913.

Rendel, Lord. *The Personal Papers of*. London, 1931.

Rumbold, Sir Horace. *Further Recollections of a Diplomatist*. London, 1903.

Selborne, Earl of. *Memorials 1865-1895*. 2 vols. London, 1898.

Watson, Sir Charles M. *The Life of Major-General Sir Charles W. Wilson*. London, 1909.

Wemyss, Mrs. Rosslyn. *Memoirs and Letters of the Right Hon. Sir Robert Morier*. London, 1911.

Whyte, Frederic. *The Life of W. T. Stead*. 2 vols. New York, 1926.

Wilson, Sir C. Rivers. *Chapters from My Official Life*. Ed. by Everilda MacAlister. New York, 1916.

II. SECONDARY

A. Books.

Bowen, W. D. *The Story of "The Times."* London, 1931.

Buchan, John. *Gordon at Khartoum*. London, 1934.

The Cambridge History of the British Empire. Ed. by J. Holland Rose, A. P. Newton and E. A. Benians. Vol. VII. Cambridge, 1933.

Cromer, Earl of. *Modern Egypt*. 2 vols. New York, 1908.

de Kiewiet, C. W. *British Colonial Policy and the South African Republics.* London, 1929.

Flournoy, F. R. *Parliament and War.* London, 1927.

Headlam-Morley, Sir James. *Studies in Diplomatic History.* London, 1930.

Hearnshaw, F. J. C. (Editor). *The Political Principles of Some Notable Prime Ministers of the 19th Century.* London, 1926.

Hirst, F. W. *Gladstone as Financier and Economist.* London, 1931.

Knaplund, Paul. *Gladstone and Britain's Imperial Policy.* London, 1927.

Langer, William L. *European Alliances and Alignments 1871-1890.* New York, 1931.

Lovell, R. I. *The Struggle for South Africa 1875-1899.* New York, 1934.

Marriott, Sir John A. R. *Queen Victoria and Her Ministers.* New York, 1934.

Masterman, Sylvia. *The Origins of International Rivalry in Samoa.* London, 1934.

Milner, Viscount. *England in Egypt.* Eleventh edition. London, 1904.

Ponsonby, Arthur. *Democracy and Diplomacy.* London, 1915.

Pribram, Alfred F. *England and the International Policy of the European Great Powers 1871-1914.* Oxford, 1931.

Raymond, Dora Neill. *British Policy and Opinion During the Franco-Prussian War.* New York, 1921.

Schuman, Frederick L. *War and Diplomacy in the French Republic*. New York, 1931.

Spender, J. A. *Fifty Years of Europe*. New York, 1933.

B. Special Articles.

Headlam-Morley, Sir James. "Treaties of Guarantee," in *The Cambridge Historical Journal*, II, 151-170.

Langer, William L. "The European Powers and the French Occupation of Tunis," in *The American Historical Review*, October, 1925, and January, 1926, XXXI, 55-78, 251-265.

Satow, Sir Ernest. "Peacemaking Old and New," in *The Cambridge Historical Journal*, I, 23-60.

Seton-Watson, R. W. "The Rôle of Bosnia in International Politics (1875-1914)," in *Proceedings of the British Academy*. London, 1933, pp. 335-368.

Temperley, Harold. "Lord Acton on the Origins of the War of 1870, with some Unpublished Letters from the British and Viennese Archives," in *The Cambridge Historical Journal*, II, 68-82.

Temperley, Harold. "The Bulgarian and Other Atrocities, 1875-78, in the Light of Historical Criticism," in *Proceedings of the British Academy 1931*. London, 1933, pp. 105-130.

Temperley, Harold. "The Treaty of Paris of 1856 and Its Execution," in *The Journal of Modern History*, September and December, 1932, IV, 387-414, 523-543.

INDEX

Abd-el-Kader, 214

Aberdeen, Lord, 3-5, 8, 13, 15, 83, 102, 187 *note* 28

Aborigines Protection Society, 99

Acton, Lord, 266

Adriatic, the, naval demonstration in, 140-142

Afghanistan, 69, 87, 119

Africa, 127; East, 93, 96-97, 120, 124; Portuguese, 88-90; South, 40, 84-85, 88-91, 95, 99, 124, 129, 206; Western, 92, 97

Alabama question, the, 16, 38, 41-42

Alexander of Battenberg, Prince, 150-151

Alexandria, 180-186

Alexandrian indemnities, 196

Allen, Dr. Bernard, 225 *note* 17, 227 *note* 20, 242 *note* 40

Alsace-Lorraine, 13, 54, 59-61, 270-279

Ampthill, Lord. *See* Russell, Lord Odo.

Anglo-French alliance, 13; *entente*, 128, 187-189; relations, 251; treaty of 1862, 93

Anglo-German colonial disputes and Egypt, 206

Anglo-Russian relations, 81

Anglo-Turkish relations, 133-137

Arabi Pasha, 15, 176, 179-185, 188, 193

Argyll, Duke of, 57

Armaments, dangers of, 44; limitation of, 11, 12

Armenia, 12, 16, 36, 152-155, 159-160, 267-268

Asquith, H. H., home secretary, 1892-5, 262

Assab Bay, 121

Australasia, 24, 98-116

Austria-Hungary, 43-44, 50, 76, 85, 128, 141, 199; and the Balkans, 79-81, 149-150, 157-158; and Egypt, 189

Austro-German alliance, 79

Baden, the grand duke of, 44

Bagdad railway, 157

Baker, Sir Samuel, 222

Baker, Valentine, 195, 236

Balfour, Arthur, 265 *note* 23

Balkans, the, 12, 82, 137-138

Baluchistan, 68, 87

Baring, Sir Evelyn, British agent and consul-general at Cairo, 121, 177, 195, 214-218, 221-223, 225-226, 231 and *note* 26, 234 and *note* 27, 237, 242, 251-252

Beaconsfield, Earl of. *See* Disraeli, Benjamin.

Belgian question, the, 50 *note* 15, 58

Berlin, conference of ambassadors at, 1880, 140, 144; Congress of, 12, 68, 82, 121, 138, 139, 144, 149; Treaty of, 68, 134, 145, 151 *note* 31, 252

Bernstorff, Count, 33

Bismarck, Herbert, 31, 125, 128-129

Bismarck, Prince Otto, 3, 11, 17, 24-25, 31, 35, 48, 52, 54-55, 58, 62-63, 67, 75, 77-80, 82, 85-86, 110, 113 and *note* 41, 114, 125-130, 141-144, 147-148, 153, 157,